Managing Challenging Behaviors in Schools

WHAT WORKS FOR SPECIAL-NEEDS LEARNERS

Karen R. Harris and Steve Graham
Editors

Strategy Instruction for Students with Learning Disabilities
Robert Reid and Torri Ortiz Lienemann

Teaching Mathematics to Middle School Students with Learning Difficulties
Marjorie Montague and Asha K. Jitendra, Editors

Teaching Word Recognition:
Effective Strategies for Students with Learning Difficulties
Rollanda E. O'Connor

Teaching Reading Comprehension to Students with Learning Difficulties
Janette K. Klingner, Sharon Vaughn, and Alison Boardman

Promoting Self-Determination in Students with Developmental Disabilities
Michael L. Wehmeyer with Martin Agran, Carolyn Hughes, James E. Martin, Dennis E. Mithaug, and Susan B. Palmer

Instructional Practices for Students with Behavioral Disorders:
Strategies for Reading, Writing, and Math
J. Ron Nelson, Gregory J. Benner, and Paul Mooney

Working with Families of Young Children with Special Needs
R. A. McWilliam, Editor

Promoting Executive Function in the Classroom
Lynn Meltzer

Managing Challenging Behaviors in Schools:
Research-Based Strategies That Work
Kathleen Lynne Lane, Holly Mariah Menzies, Allison L. Bruhn, and Mary Crnobori

Explicit Instruction: Effective and Efficient Teaching
Anita L. Archer and Charles A. Hughes

Managing Challenging Behaviors in Schools

Research-Based Strategies That Work

Kathleen Lynne Lane
Holly Mariah Menzies
Allison L. Bruhn
Mary Crnobori

THE GUILFORD PRESS
New York London

A Division of Guilford Publications, Inc.
370 Seventh Avenue, Suite 1200, New York, NY 10001
www.guilford.com

Printed in the United States of America

This book is printed on acid-free paper.

Last digit is print number: 9 8 7 6 5 4

Library of Congress Cataloging-in-Publication Data

Managing challenging behaviors in schools: research-based strategies that work / by Kathleen Lynne Lane … [et al.].
p. cm. — (What works for special-needs learners)
Includes bibliographical references and index.
ISBN 978-1-60623-951-3 (pbk.: alk. paper)
1. Problem children—Behavior modification. 2. School discipline. 3. Classroom management. 4. Communication in education. I. Lane, Kathleen L.
LB3013.M3255 2011
370.15′28—dc22

2010026574

To my family—Craig, Nathan, and Katie.
The greatest part of my life is our family,
those who have gone before me—Grandpa and Grandma Frank,
Grandpa and Nana Fanning—those still here,
and those who have yet come.

And to my dear friend and respected colleague Holly.
Words cannot express how thankful I am for your friendship
and how much I value you as a colleague.
Thank you for continuing to stretch my thinking and for believing in me.
The world is a better place with you in it.
—K. L. L.

To my family.
—H. M. M.

To Grandma and Grandpa Beard—you are my inspiration.

To Mrs. Raker, my eighth-grade teacher—
for teaching me to go above and beyond.

To Kathleen and Holly—for having the confidence in me
to provide such an awesome opportunity. Thank you!

To Mary—for sharing this crazy journey of motherhood
and the VU doc program with me.

To Michael, Loxton, and Bauer—for providing me smiles
to come home to. I love you!

To Mom, Dad, and Cari—for your unwavering love and support
and, of course, the frequent phone calls.
—A. L. B.

To David, Aiden, and Jonah; Mom and Dad; and Kathleen.
I am so lucky to have you all!
—M. C.

About the Authors

Kathleen Lynne Lane, PhD, is Associate Professor in the Department of Special Education at Peabody College and an Investigator in the John F. Kennedy Center for Research on Human Development at Vanderbilt University. Prior to entering academia, Dr. Lane served as a classroom teacher of general and special education students for 5 years and provided consultation, intervention, and staff development services to five school districts in Southern California for 2 years as a Program Specialist. Dr. Lane's research focuses on school-based interventions (academic and behavioral) with students at risk for emotional and behavioral disorders (EBD). She has designed, implemented, and evaluated multilevel prevention models in elementary, middle, and high school settings to prevent the development of EBD and respond to existing instances. Dr. Lane is the primary investigator (PI) of Project WRITE, a Goal Area 2 Grant funded through the Institute of Education Sciences. Project WRITE focuses on the impact of writing interventions for students at risk for EBD who are also poor writers. She was also the PI of an Office of Special Education Programs (OSEP)-directed project studying positive behavior support at the high school level and of an OSEP field-initiated project studying prevention of EBD at the elementary level. She has expertise in school-based intervention and statistical analysis, including multivariate analysis of longitudinal data sets. Dr. Lane is the coeditor of *Remedial and Special Education* and the associate editor of *Journal of Positive Behavior Interventions* and *Education and Treatment of Children*. She also serves on several editorial boards, including *Exceptional Children, The Journal of Special Education,* and *Journal of Emotional and Behavioral Disorders*. She has coauthored four books and published more than 100 refereed journal articles and book chapters.

Holly Mariah Menzies, PhD, is Associate Professor in the Charter College of Education at California State University, Los Angeles, and the program coordinator in mild–moderate disabilities in the Division of Special Education and Counseling.

She worked as both a general educator and special educator for over 10 years. Dr. Menzies has provided staff development in the areas of assessment, language arts, and schoolwide positive behavior supports (SWPBS). Her scholarly interests focus on inclusive education and school-based interventions. She serves on the editorial board of *Learning Disabilities Research & Practice.*

Allison L. Bruhn, MA, is in her third year of the doctoral program for special education at Vanderbilt University. She previously worked for 3 years as a middle school science teacher. At Vanderbilt, she coordinates professional development trainings for teachers, administrators, and behavior specialists on SWPBS, systematic screening, and behavior management strategies. Her research interests include functional assessment-based interventions, treatment integrity of SWPBS, and motivation.

Mary Crnobori, MEd, is in her third year of the doctoral program for special education at Vanderbilt University. She worked as a special education teacher for students with EBD and other disabilities for 5 years in both self-contained and inclusionary public school settings. In her current research at Vanderbilt, she assists schools in designing and implementing individualized positive behavior support plans with primary, secondary, and tertiary levels of support and coordinates professional development workshops and follow-up on-site support for educators. Her scholarly interests include positive behavior support, school-based interventions for students with and at risk for EBD, systematic screening, and issues surrounding diversity.

Acknowledgments

We begin by thanking Karen Harris and Steve Graham, Series Editors, for the invitation to write this book and Rochelle Serwator, Senior Editor at The Guilford Press, for seeing it through from conceptualization to the book you hold in your hands. We also thank Mich Yell for his support and expertise in ensuring the accuracy of the legal and legislative content related to functional assessment-based interventions.

This book represents a culmination of years of learning and mentoring—from those K–12 teachers who taught the four of us when we were children and youths; to our university professors who continued to shape our thinking; to our mentors (the graybeards) who stretch us beyond what we initially thought was possible; to the administrators, teachers, parents, and students on our projects who continue to provide determined efforts to learn how best to support all learners and their families; and to our dear friends and family who continue to support our learning and keep us grounded by reminding us of what is important.

Our goal in writing this book is to "pay it forward"—to support those who pursue the most noble and meaningful job of all: teaching.

To the teachers who read this book, please know how much we respect your efforts to provide a safe learning environment—intellectually and otherwise—for those you serve now and in the future. The greatest teachers are those who continue to learn, thereby improving their own skill sets that will influence many generations to come, including the three children—Loxton, Jonah, and Maisie—who came to be during the writing of this book. Welcome to the world, little ones! We hope you will be as inspired by your teachers as we have been by ours.

Finally, to the veteran children of academia—Lucia, Nathan, and Katie Scarlett—thank you for continuing to teach and support us; you have taught us that each year of parenting is better than the next. We love you and we are so proud of how you make the most of your educational experiences, with careful attention to supporting and respecting students who are exceptional in other ways.

Contents

PART I. PREVENTING BEHAVIOR PROBLEMS

PART II. RESPONDING TO PROBLEM BEHAVIORS

PART III. GETTING STARTED

Purchasers of this book can download and print copies of the reproducible figures from *www.guilford.com/lane2-forms.*

Managing Challenging Behaviors in Schools

PART I

PREVENTING BEHAVIOR PROBLEMS

CHAPTER 1

Preventing and Managing Learning and Behavior Problems

An Overview

Many teachers in the field of education begin this journey with the intent of teaching and maybe even inspiring students with meaningful, well-planned instruction. We would venture to say that few teachers enter the fields of general or special education to work with students with social and behavioral challenges. In our many years as classroom teachers, behavior specialists, and researchers, we have often heard teachers express frustration that they did not "sign up to deal with behavior problems." Yet, it is all too often the case that these problems must be handled.

A teacher's lack of confidence in his or her classroom management skills can be a major detriment to his or her ability to be an effective educator. Brouwers and Tomic (2000) found that teachers' self-efficacy for classroom management has a longitudinal effect on teacher "burnout." Teachers who do not view themselves as capable of managing a range of behaviors in the classroom are more likely to leave the field than teachers who feel confident and capable. Martin, Linfoot, and Stephenson (1999) found that teachers who had low confidence in their behavior management skills were more likely to refer students to other school personnel and less likely to use positively focused strategies. In fact, statistics show that more than 58% of first-year teachers wish they had had more practical training before beginning their first year of teaching. This number increases to 61% immediately following their first year (Harris, 1991). Even teachers who elect to work with students with and at risk for emotional and behavioral disorders (EBD) report difficulties in managing students' behavior efficiently (Walker, Ramsey, & Gresham, 2004).

These are teachers who have been trained to manage both externalizing (e.g., noncompliance, aggression) and internalizing (e.g., anxiety, depression) behaviors.

Consequently, it is important that teachers acquire the knowledge and confidence to use a range of strategies to (1) prevent problem behaviors from occurring in the first place and (2) respond effectively and efficiently to problems that do occur. In short, teachers must have an extensive repertoire of skills so they can deliver instruction in a manner that allows them to meet the academic, social, and behavioral needs of the increasingly diverse set of students they serve (Lane, 2007; Walker et al., 2004).

Ideally, teachers' knowledge of classroom management and individual student behavior supports should start with proactive strategies that are aligned with the school's primary prevention plan. It is much less effective to *begin* with reactive strategies, such as imposing consequences, without first addressing the fundamental components of proactive classroom management. These essentials include establishing a positive classroom climate; creating a physical room arrangement that facilitates instruction; providing clear, consistent reinforcement of behavioral expectations; determining the procedures and routines that smooth transitions and maximize instructional time; and managing paperwork efficiently (see Chapter 2, this volume). Poorly managed classrooms are characterized by teachers who wait for problems to occur and then attempt to respond to issues as they arise. This is unfortunate, as unstructured (or even unsafe) learning environments pose challenges to teachers and students alike in that they do not facilitate the overall goal of providing meaningful, rigorous learning experiences for all learners.

In this book, we provide preservice and inservice teachers, teacher educators, administrators, school psychologists, and behavior specialists with a continuum of strategies to prevent and respond to student behavior problems. The strategies are recommended for use in schools that subscribe to three-tiered models of prevention, although they can be implemented by classroom teachers working in schools that have not yet developed such models. The strategies begin with the least intensive supports (e.g., how to create well-managed classrooms) that take minimal resources (e.g., time, effort, or training) to implement and move to increasingly more intensive supports (e.g., functional assessment-based interventions; Umbreit, Ferro, Liaupsin, & Lane, 2007) for students who do not respond to less intensive interventions. In the beginning chapters, we provide information that is grounded in research (research based) as well as in our collective professional experiences (practice-based). In the later chapters, many of the strategies and procedures introduced (e.g., functional assessment-based interventions) are evidence-based practices that are supported by scientifically rigorous studies.

Because we recommend that these strategies be implemented in conjunction with three-tiered models of prevention, we begin by describing the full continuum of behavior support, which includes primary (Tier 1), secondary (Tier 2), and tertiary (Tier 3) levels of prevention. Then we focus on primary prevention, which is a comprehensive and systematic approach to supporting *all* students in a school. An additional benefit is that this approach is particularly beneficial for students with more challenging behaviors, including those at risk for EBD (Kauffman & Landrum, 2009; Lane, 2007). Next, we provide an introduction to the relation between teachers' and students' behavior, emphasizing how changes in teacher behavior can lead to changes in student behavior (Walker et al., 2004). Finally, we conclude by providing a preview of the content to be covered in each of the eight chapters in this book.

CONTINUUM OF BEHAVIOR SUPPORT

Ideally, school site teams would have a three-tiered model of prevention in place to prevent and respond to learning and behavioral challenges to meet the full range of students' academic, behavioral, and social needs (Lane, 2007; Lane, Kalberg, & Menzies, 2009). Many schools and districts across the country have developed such models that focus on the school as the agent for change (Horner & Sugai, 2000). Response to intervention (RTI; Gresham, 2002a; Sugai, Horner, & Gresham, 2002) and positive behavior support (Lewis & Sugai, 1999; Sugai & Horner, 2002) are two such models that use a systematic, data-driven approach to providing increasingly more intensive levels of support according to how students respond to the various levels. Some schools have developed comprehensive, integrated models that include academic, behavioral, and social components rather than addressing these components separately (see Lane, Kalberg, & Menzies, 2009). Although we strongly believe that schoolwide models offer the best support for all members of the school community, we realize that not all teachers, administrators, and support personnel (e.g., school psychologists, behavior specialists, and paraprofessionals) have the advantage of being in a school that uses such an approach. In such cases, this book is doubly important as it provides information about the benefits of implementing such a system. It also gives an overview of each of the components and how they work, which may be useful for those working at the school-site level, as well as for those individuals involved in professional development, teacher preparation, and research activities. In this section, we briefly describe each level of prevention.

Primary Prevention

Primary prevention plans serve as the basis of this model. The intent of primary prevention efforts is to prevent harm from occurring. All students in a school receive primary prevention efforts—such as an effective or validated literacy curriculum, violence prevention programs, and/or character education programs—just by virtue of attending school. These prevention efforts and programs should be backed by research that demonstrates their effectiveness so as to avoid such wasting precious resources as personnel time and money.

There is no need to screen for possible participation or to determine eligibility; all students participate. The goal here is to provide universal supports to prevent undesirable outcomes in academic, social, or behavioral domains (e.g., school failure or impaired social relationships; Lane, Robertson, & Graham-Bailey, 2006).

For approximately 80–90% of the student body, these efforts are likely to suffice (Gresham, Sugai, Horner, Quinn, & McInerney, 1998; Sugai & Horner, 2006). Schoolwide data such as curriculum-based measures, office discipline referrals, and behavioral screening data (systematic tools designed to measure students' behavioral performance patterns) are analyzed to determine which students might benefit from targeted supports such as secondary and tertiary prevention efforts, which are described next.

Secondary Prevention

Secondary prevention efforts are intended to address more serious behavior issues by reversing harm (e.g., identifying and supporting students who *might* be headed down an undesirable path; Walker & Severson, 2002). Namely, students who do not respond favorably to primary prevention efforts are offered secondary support programs to meet their specific acquisition (can't do), fluency (trouble doing), or performance (not motivated to do) deficits (Elliott & Gresham 2007). For example, students with limited reading fluency skills may receive small-group instruction in evidence-based interventions to address this skill (e.g., peer-assisted learning strategies; Fuchs, Fuchs, & Burish, 2000; Fuchs, Fuchs, Mathes, & Martinez, 2002; Fuchs, Fuchs, Mathes, & Simmons, 1997). Students who struggle with work completion or high levels of impulsivity may benefit from self-monitoring strategies (see Chapter 6, this volume; Mooney, Ryan, Uhing, Reid, & Epstein, 2005).

Approximately 10–15% of the overall student body may need such secondary prevention. Once these supports are in place, additional information (e.g., weekly oral reading fluency probes, percentage of assignments completed, or percentage of academic engagement) will need to be collected to determine how well the student is responding to this additional support. In cases in which students are not responding, or if students are exposed to more extensive risk factors (e.g., chaotic family environments, poverty, mental health issues; Reid & Patterson, 1991), then tertiary prevention efforts may be warranted.

Tertiary Prevention

Tertiary prevention is the most individualized, intensive level of support within a three-tiered model of prevention. The intent here is to intervene with students who exhibit the most challenging behaviors—again, in this case, to reduce harm. Functional assessment-based (Umbreit et al., 2007) and individualized reading (e.g., Clarke-Edmands, 2004; Lindamood & Lindamood, 1998; Lockavitch, 2000; Wilson, 2000) interventions are two such examples, both of which require an extensive time investment, as well as monitoring of the student's progress throughout the intervention. Given that this level is highly resource intensive in terms of time, personnel, and expertise, these interventions are reserved for students with complex, long-term, and resistant behavioral or academic issues (Kern & Manz, 2004).

Approximately 5–7% of the student body may need tertiary-level supports. Although many of these students may already receive special education services, some will be general education students who exhibit bullying behavior or chronic absenteeism, who are isolated from their peers, or who experience extreme family problems such as domestic violence. However, if a student does not respond to this most intensive level, then it may be necessary to refer him or her to a multidisciplinary team to determine whether special education services are warranted.

Summary

If comprehensive three-tiered models of intervention that include academic, behavioral, and social components can be designed with an appropriate balance between scientific rigor and feasibility, schools have the potential to meet the needs of all students—including the most difficult population for schools, those with and at risk for EBD (Lane, 2007; Walker et al., 1996; Walker & Severson, 2002). For all levels of support, it is important that certain core features be evaluated systematically so that one can draw accurate conclusions about how well these various levels of prevention are working. Specifically, it is important to monitor the extent to which such interventions are implemented as planned so that the school staff can be confident that the improvements they see are a result of the intervention (*treatment integrity*; Gresham, 1989). This is also important information when the intended results do not occur. Lack of sufficient implementation (also referred to as *low treatment integrity*) can be the cause of less powerful or nonexistent outcomes. Also, the participants' perceptions of the goals, procedures, and outcomes should be ascertained to be sure that the program is one that they can comfortably support (*social validity*; Wolf, 1978). Finally, the degree to which the new behaviors continue over time (*maintenance*) and in new environments or circumstances should be examined to determine how effective the intervention is (*generalization*; Lane & Beebe-Frankenberger, 2004). This type of information increases participants' involvement in a schoolwide model because it allows them to make informed decisions about the time and energy they are devoting to the system of supports.

THREE-TIERED MODELS OF PREVENTION: BENEFITS FOR STUDENTS WITH AND AT RISK FOR EBD

Primary prevention efforts are particularly beneficial for students with and at risk for EBD. This is especially encouraging given that prevalence estimates suggest that anywhere from 2 to 20% of the school age population has or is at risk for EBD but that fewer than 1% of students are eligible for special education services under the category of emotional disturbance (ED;Individuals with Disabilities Education Improvement Act [IDEA], 2004). This means that it is very important for general education teachers, administrators, and other school-site support staff members (e.g., behavior specialists) to be prepared to identify and support students with EBD, as they are highly likely to be served in the general education setting.

When defining EBD, the first thought that comes to mind is students with antisocial tendencies whose behaviors are aggressive, noncompliant, and defiant, posing significant challenges to adults and peers alike. Although these students with externalizing behaviors are the easiest to recognize, the EBD category also includes students with internalizing behavior disorders. Examples of internalizing behaviors include anxiety, depression, withdrawal, and eating disorders. Thus the term *EBD* includes students with externalizing, internalizing, and combined behavior patterns (Achenbach, 1991; Walker et al., 2004).

Although they are most often recognized for their behavioral excesses, students with EBD also have pronounced social and academic deficits. For example, they struggle to negotiate relationships with peers and teachers, exhibiting high levels of aggressive and coercive behaviors (Walker, Irvin, Noell, & Singer, 1992), as well as impaired social skills, that make it difficult for them to interpret social situations accurately. For example, students with EBD are likely to interpret a neutral experience, such as a pat on the back by a peer, as hostile. They may perceive it as "hitting" (Crick, Grotpeter, & Bigbee, 2002). Not surprisingly, students with EBD tend to respond sharply to such interactions, a response that can be shocking to their peers, resulting in strained peer relationships.

Furthermore, students with and at risk for EBD also struggle academically. Even if these students go on to receive special education support under the ED label (IDEA, 2004), they still experience less success than general education students and students in other disability categories (Landrum, Tankersley, & Kauffman, 2003). They often have broad academic deficits in reading, writing, and mathematics (Mattison, Hooper, & Glassberg, 2002; Nelson, Benner, Lane, & Smith, 2004; Reid, Gonzalez, Nordness, Trout, & Epstein, 2004) that tend *not* to improve over time. In fact, their academic skills may even decline (Nelson et al. 2004).

Not only do students with and at risk for EBD struggle in school, but also their outcomes do not improve when they leave school. They continue to struggle in their interpersonal relationships, experiencing high rates of divorce, unemployment, and use of mental health services (Kauffman & Brigham, 2009; Kauffman & Landrum, 2009; Wagner & Davis, 2006; Walker et al., 2004). In short, life is difficult for this population.

Primary prevention efforts hold promise for students with and at risk for EBD in that primary prevention programs can help level the playing field for students by subscribing to an instructional approach to behavior. In positive behavior support models, faculty and staff establish behavioral expectations to specify exactly what is expected in each key location in the school. Then the expectations are taught directly, just as academic skills are taught. Students are provided with opportunities to practice and receive reinforcement for meeting these expectations. Schoolwide data such as office discipline referrals, behavior screening tools (e.g., Systematic Screening for Behavior Disorders [SSBD], Walker & Severson, 1992; Student Risk Screening Scale [SRSS], Drummond, 1994), attendance data, curriculum-based measures, and standardized test scores are used to monitor student performance and determine which students may need additional supports.

For students with and at risk for EBD, this three-tiered model offers a comprehensive, data-driven approach to provide graduated support according to individual students' needs to (1) prevent the development of behavioral problems that may lead to EBD and (2) support students *with* EBD by implementing targeted supports (e.g., secondary and tertiary). In short, this model includes proactive components aimed at prevention (primary prevention programs), as well as reactive components aimed at remediation (secondary and tertiary prevention programs; Kauffman & Landrum, 2009).

TEACHERS' STRUCTURING

Ideally, all schools would have a comprehensive three-tiered model in place that would meet the multiple needs of all learners. Such a model provides tremendous support, clarity, and structure for students, as well as for teachers, administrators, and school-site support personnel, thereby allowing everyone to attend to the business of teaching and learning. However, even if a schoolwide plan is not in place, it is important for teachers, administrators, and school-site support personnel to have an extensive range of skills and competences in order to prevent and respond to problem behaviors. They need a proactive set of strategies and tactics to prevent problem behaviors from occurring and thereby facilitate instruction. More specifically, when a teacher can spend less time responding to problem behaviors in a classroom, he or she can spend more time on instructional tasks and student learning opportunities.

Also, it is important for teachers and other school-site personnel to understand the relationship between instruction and behavior: How we teach influences how students behave, and how students behave influences how we teach (Lane & Wehby, 2002). For example, if a math teacher is attempting to teach place value with the use of manipulatives yet is concerned about students using them as projectiles, the teacher may rely on techniques that are not as effective or engaging, such as using worksheets. In more extreme cases, a vicious cycle of negative reinforcement occurs in which teachers essentially (yet unintentionally) engage in a curriculum of noninstruction (Shores et al., 1993). In brief, teachers implicitly agree to avoid instructional tasks if students eliminate the aggressive, disruptive behaviors that occur when teachers introduce task demands. Essentially, the messages become (1) I won't bother you if you won't try to teach (student perspective) and (2) I won't try to teach if you don't misbehave (teacher perspective).

This book provides a comprehensive continuum of supports that can be used to prevent and respond to problem behaviors, ideally within the framework of a three-tiered model of prevention. It offers even more critical support for those who do not have the advantage of working within a schoolwide primary prevention model.

ORGANIZATION OF THIS VOLUME

Dealing with challenging student behaviors is one of the most difficult aspects of teaching. Teachers frequently report this to be among *the* most challenging tasks they encounter in their jobs, and many teachers indicate that they feel ill prepared to meet the behavioral challenges they experience in the classroom (Schumm & Vaughn, 1995). A thorough knowledge of proactive systems of behavior management provides teachers with powerful resources that allow them to be effective and confident educators. Teaching environments characterized by consistent, positive discipline approaches contribute to students' academic and social success. This volume begins with an explanation of three-tiered models of prevention that can be used to prevent behavior challenges from occurring, as well as to respond to existing cases. We then offer a continuum of strategies beginning with general proactive approaches that increase in intensity to address the most challenging behaviors (see Figure 1.1). We offer a straightforward, practical approach to preventing behavior challenges, as well as effectively managing those that do occur. In this volume, we offer a unique approach to preventing and managing behavior problems in the classroom. Whereas most texts emphasize general theories of

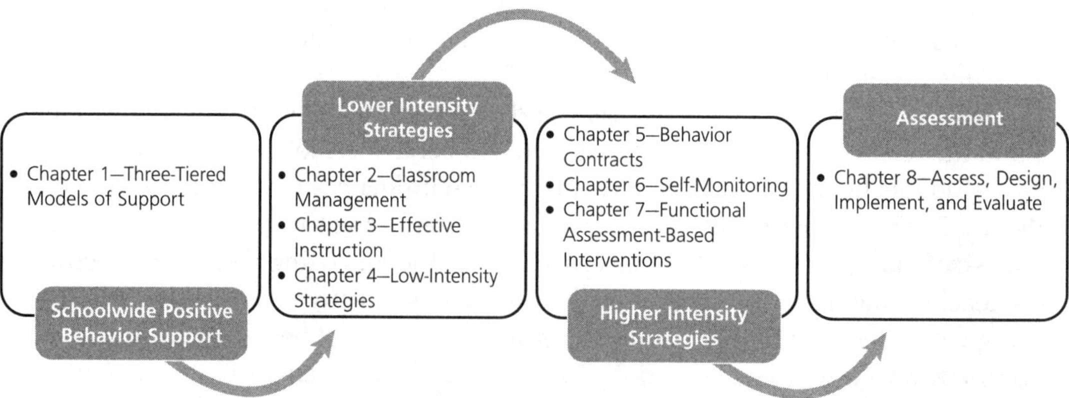

FIGURE 1.1. An overview of research-based practices for preventing and responding to behavior problems: Effective, practical strategies that work.

behavior management, we focus on specific techniques for proactive management. This information can be used by a range of individuals, including: (1) school-site personnel (e.g., teachers, administrators, school psychologists, behavior specialists, and paraprofessionals), whose main goal is to support instruction; (2) teacher trainers who are focused on preparing preservice teachers; (3) staff development trainers who are focused on supporting inservice teachers; (4) researchers who are interested in understanding and effecting change at the school-site level; and (5) parents who are interested in gleaning information that can help them to understand and support their child's learning and behavior within the school-site context.

We describe a continuum that begins with a broad-based approach to thinking about student behavior and ends with focused, intensive interventions to address more severe problems. We have organized this volume into three parts: Preventing Behavior Problems, Responding to Problem Behaviors, and Getting Started. In the paragraphs that follow, we provide a detailed overview of each chapter.

The first part addresses the systems that must be in place in order to provide effective instruction and avoid most behavior problems. The second part provides specific strategies for dealing with more challenging behavior. Each chapter includes an overview of the strategy, of the research supporting its use, and of the efficacy of the strategy with different populations (e.g., students with learning disabilities, students in general education, English language learners, and students at risk) and a detailed explanation of how to implement it. The final part looks at how to get started at the classroom level and includes an evaluation tool to help you decide where and how to focus your behavior changes.

Part I. Preventing Behavior Problems

In Part I, we focus on classwide strategies for preventing problem behaviors. Chapter 1 provides an overview of the continuum of supports available and describes a comprehensive three-tiered model of prevention. We explain how teachers can structure their own classrooms to align with schoolwide prevention programs.

The next three chapters are dedicated to secondary-level classwide supports designed to prevent problem behaviors from occurring by facilitating strong instruction and incorporating sound classroom management strategies. Chapter 2 focuses on classroom management, Chapter 3 on instructional delivery, and Chapter 4 on teacher behaviors with an emphasis on low-intensity strategies (strategies that take limited time and effort to implement).

In Chapter 2, *Classroom Management*, we review the elements necessary for a comprehensive approach to classroom management. Before teachers can address the behavior of individual students, they must establish classroom routines that ensure a productive learning environment for *all* students. This chapter includes topics such as physical room arrangement, classroom climate, student transitions, supervision and monitoring, approaches to discipline, and managing paperwork.

We review the supporting research conducted in elementary, middle, and high school settings. Then we provide information and recommendations for addressing these issues in the classroom, providing step-by-step directions, illustrations, and related resources.

In Chapter 3, *Instructional Delivery*, we address issues related to the delivery of curriculum and instruction. An important component of managing behavior is to create learning experiences that provide students with opportunities to work in their zones of proximal development. Behavior problems are more likely to emerge when schoolwork is either too easy or too difficult (Glick & Armstrong, 1996; Umbreit, Lane, & Dejud, 2004). Therefore, we begin by providing an overview of instructional delivery, emphasizing the following: appropriate curricula, engaging instruction, appropriate pacing, and choice and preferred activities. Then we provide information and recommendations for addressing these issues in the classroom, providing step-by-step directions, illustrations, and related resources.

In Chapter 4, *Low-Intensity Strategies*, we discuss how teachers can examine their own teaching styles and student–teacher interactions to be sure they are using a proactive approach to supporting positive student behavior. We begin by discussing how to plan for and implement intrinsically rewarding activities. Then we introduce strategies that teachers can employ to redirect, minimize, or prevent undesirable behaviors. The techniques include: (1) supervision, (2) proximity, (3) with-it-ness, (4) appropriate use of praise, (5) providing opportunities to respond, (6) instructive feedback, (7) choice and preferred activities, (8) token economies, and (9) formal teaching of prosocial behaviors. Then we provide information and recommendations for addressing these strategies in the classroom, providing step-by-step directions, illustrations, and related resources.

Part II. Responding to Problem Behaviors

In Part II, we focus on more intensive strategies for responding to existing problem behaviors. These chapters assist teachers and other professionals with students who manifest challenging behaviors in spite of strong classroom management, effective teaching, and an active awareness of how teachers' actions can support positive behaviors. In Chapter 5, we introduce behavior contracting; in Chapter 6, self-monitoring; and in Chapter 7, functional assessment-based interventions.

In Chapter 5, *Behavior Contracts*, we examine behavior contracting with individual students to address academic and behavior issues. We include an overview of behavior contracting, reviewing research to support the use of behavior contracts with different populations of elementary, middle, and high school-age students. Then we provide information and recommendations for designing, implementing, and evaluating behavior contracts in the classroom, some of which may involve the parent, and for monitoring implementation and outcomes. We also provide illustrations and related resources.

In Chapter 6, *Self-Monitoring*, we introduce self-monitoring procedures for use with individual students to address academic and behavior issues. We include an overview of self-monitoring strategies, supporting research for its use with elementary, middle, and high school-age students. Then we provide information and recommendations for designing, implementing, and evaluating self-monitoring interventions in the classroom. We offer step-by-step directions, illustrations, and related resources.

In Chapter 7, *Functional Assessment-Based Interventions*, we provide an approach to designing and implementing functional assessment-based interventions for use with individual students to address academic and behavior issues. Chapter 7 includes an overview of functional assessment-based interventions, focusing on one systematic approach developed by Umbreit, Ferro and colleagues (2007). We review the supporting literature for this approach as applied to use with students with and at risk for high-incidence disabilities (e.g., learning disabilities, emotional disturbances, and other health impairments; IDEA, 2004). Then we provide information and recommendations for designing, implementing, and evaluating functional assessment-based interventions in the classroom. We offer step-by-step directions, illustrations, and related resources.

Part III. Getting Started

In this final section, we focus exclusively on helping teachers and other individuals to make informed decisions about how to apply the strategies for preventing and responding to problem behaviors presented in this book. This section contains only one chapter, Chapter 8.

In Chapter 8, *Getting Started in Your Classroom*, we provide guidelines on how to get started. We include a self-assessment, practical suggestions for determining which procedures to employ, and feasible guidelines for monitoring outcomes. We also emphasize the importance of addressing schoolwide components and offer teachers, administrators, and other school-site support personnel suggestions for how to help start schoolwide programs as well.

At this point, we invite you to grab a latte (decaf, grande, nonfat, extra hot!) or a cup of tea and read on!

CHAPTER 2

Classroom Management

Good classroom management is what makes it possible to teach effectively. Without an orderly, purposeful environment, educators cannot establish a classroom climate that fosters learning and collaboration. Students require a predictable, yet engaging, routine that promotes their interests and contributes to their sense of well-being. It may seem too obvious to even mention, but creating a well-ordered classroom is surprisingly difficult. Although it is a challenging task for many teachers, taking the time to develop a well-run classroom is important, as it contributes greatly to a teacher's success in promoting high academic outcomes for students (Downey, 2008; Hall, Lund, & Jackson, 1968; Sutherland, Wehby, & Copeland, 2000), as well as to teachers' job satisfaction. Ingersoll and Smith (2003) examined the reasons that up to 50% of first-year educators leave the teaching profession. Although several factors contributed to this alarmingly high percentage, 35% of those who reported lack of job satisfaction as their primary reason for leaving the field cited student discipline as a major cause of their dissatisfaction.

A host of studies have demonstrated the relation between a teacher's ability to manage student behavior and student success on a number of indicators (Cameron & Pierce, 1994; Espin & Yell, 1994; Reinke, Lewis-Palmer, & Merrell, 2008). Most important, orderly classrooms help support student learning because they increase what Gettinger (1986) refers to as *academic learning time* (ALT). The amount of time that students spend in school is not equal to the amount of time they are actively involved in activities that promote learning. There is allocated time, which refers to the total amount of time devoted to an activity. Then there is engaged time, which is the amount of time students are actually on task. However, ALT occurs only when learning results from students' on-task behavior during the allocated time. You can see what a high standard ALT is. Teachers may have allocated adequate time, and students may participate, but if students have not learned something, then ALT has not been achieved (Gettinger & Seibert, 2002). Teachers must effectively manage the classroom to ensure adequate ALT. Although not every moment can be devoted to learning, it is essential to minimize the use of reactive behavior management strategies that result in nonproductive time for the majority of students. For example, if students do not know procedures for routine activities such as pencil sharpening or if teachers do not have effective methods for keeping students focused, then large amounts of time are squandered managing these types of events.

Classrooms are busy, lively places filled with high energy. Savvy teachers can avert a majority of disruptive behaviors by creating a system that establishes routines to address predictable events or needs. For example, over the course of a regular school day, students will need to sharpen their pencils, turn in work, ask questions of the teacher, interact with their peers, use the restroom, and go to lunch. It is necessary to anticipate such occurrences, to communicate how students should respond, to teach students routines, to provide opportunities to practice, and to offer reinforcement for meeting your expectations (Lane, Wehby, & Cooley, 2006). Ultimately this investment will provide students with the ability to manage most of their nonacademic needs independently, leading to increased instructional time. Too often students are expected to be passive in school, but teachers can capitalize on students' natural desire to participate actively in the classroom community. Such approaches enrich a student's school experience by making the classroom a stimulating, engaging environment.

Proactive, positive classroom management means that a teacher has the knowledge and ability to put a wide array of skills into action. It means creating an environment in which students know how to interact appropriately with the teacher and each other, feel valued for their work and contributions to the classroom community, and are intrinsically motivated to engage in learning.

ESSENTIAL COMPONENTS OF CLASSROOM MANAGEMENT

Although there are a number of strategies that promote a well-managed classroom, in this chapter we discuss five essential components, classroom climate, physical room arrangement, approach to discipline, routines and procedures, and managing paperwork.

Much of the literature on general classroom management discusses practices that are not yet evidence-based according to the current guidelines and recommendations for evaluating a given educational practice (Gersten et al., 2005; Horner et al., 2005). However, the information in this chapter is based on the seminal works of early researchers and theoreticians such as Haim Ginott and B.F. Skinner (see Table 2.1), who investigated how to effectively support students in becoming engaged and productive learners and to provide teachers, administrators, and other school-site support personnel with valuable tools for doing so. We also include information based on our collective experiences as general and special education classroom teachers across the K–12 continuum. Thus the information provided is research-based and/or practice-based.

TABLE 2.1. Classic Discipline Models

Reference	Main concepts
Glasser, W. (1969). *Schools without failure.* New York: Harper & Row. Glasser, W. (1985). *Control theory in the classroom.* New York: Perennial Library.	• Help students make good behavioral choices by demonstrating that good choices result in positive outcomes. • Classroom rules facilitate student and class achievement. • Consequences should carry weight but should also be reasonable and should never include ridicule or emotional or physical punishment. • Teachers should be both consistent and persistent in shaping positive student behavior. • Cooperative work is more motivating and enjoyable for students. It also fosters independence.
Kounin, J. (1977). *Discipline and group management in classrooms.* New York: Holt, Rinehart & Winston.	• Efficient transitions are critical for managing the entire classroom. • Whole-group lessons are effective only when *all* students are engaged. If just a few are participating, it is unlikely that sufficient learning is occurring. • Providing stimulating instruction promotes student engagement and reduces student boredom, which leads to misbehavior. • Teachers should be aware of what is going on in all parts of the classroom at all times.
Skinner, B. F. (1953). *Science and human behavior.* New York: Macmillan.	• Reinforce the behaviors you want students to display. • Be careful not to inadvertently reinforce negative behavior by rewarding the student with too much attention or the opportunity to escape an assigned task. • Extinguish undesirable behaviors by ignoring them or administering consequences. • Shape desirable behaviors by reinforcing frequently at first, then reinforce intermittently. • Reinforcers can be social (verbal praise, smiles), can consists of activities (free time) or can be tangible (edibles, pencils).
Ginott, H. (1971). *Teacher and child.* New York: Macmillan.	• Teachers should use what Ginott termed "sane messages," or language that describes the situation and does not judge the student's character. • Model the behavior you want students to demonstrate. • Invite the cooperation of your students instead of demanding it. This promotes students' independence and autonomy. • Use praise to describe students' actions, not their characters or personalities. For example, it would be appropriate for a teacher to say, "Anna, you did a good job of putting away your papers," rather than "Anna, you are such a good girl." • Acknowledge students' feelings instead of telling them how they *should* feel.

Classroom Climate

One of the fundamental aspects of classroom management is the climate or tone of a classroom. In other words, does the class have an energetic feel, with students actively participating? Do students interact respectfully with one another and their teacher? Does the teacher treat each student kindly and with patience? It is the teacher's responsibility to set the tone by making expectations clear and modeling how to put them into practice (Colvin, 2002). Ideally, this would be facilitated by the structure afforded by a primary prevention plan. However, even if such a schoolwide model is not in place, the teacher must still set the tone in his or her classroom.

Establishing a positive climate requires the teacher to think consciously about several factors. Teachers must consider student, teacher, and school variables to set a tone that works for the unique characteristics of each classroom. For example, students and teachers in rural areas are likely to have different concerns than do those in urban settings. Rural students may have to spend a considerable amount of time riding the bus to get to school, whereas urban students are apt to walk to their neighborhood school. As a result, teachers in rural and urban settings might tailor homework assignments to accommodate these differences. Thinking about the contextual and cultural factors that affect students helps the teacher to thoughtfully examine how to foster a climate that accommodates their varied needs while helping them feel empowered to learn.

Student Variables

These variables include things such as a student's cultural background and whether he or she is an English language learner (ELL) or has a disability or a health issue that impedes learning. Other variables could be family issues, such as divorce or after-school care. In addition, one should consider a student's socioeconomic status and how it might affect his or her outside learning opportunities.

Cultural values and learning styles of diverse groups (e.g., Mexican Americans) can vary greatly and manifest in a variety of cognitive styles and approaches to learning (Ramirez & Castaneda, 1974; Valenzuela, 1999). Teachers must be in tune with these multiple factors to create a respectful, positive classroom environment. When a teacher does not share a student's cultural background, he or she may erroneously interpret the student's actions as defiant or disrespectful when that may not be the case. Similarly, teachers may view students as less socially competent when they use patterns of interaction that are predominant in their home setting but are not congruent with school norms (Crago, Eriks-Brophy, Pesco, & McAlpine, 1997). Florio and Schultz (1979) relate the example of the Warm Springs Native American children who experienced school failure partly because they engaged in minimal talk. Teachers did not realize that this was a cultural pattern of interaction in the children's homes and instead saw students as deficient in their communication abilities.

Students should never be made to feel inadequate or in the wrong when their values or customs are not congruent with the dominant culture (Gay, 2006; Weinstein, Curran, & Tomlinson-Clarke, 2003). However, this does not mean that the teacher cannot establish common expectations that everyone in the classroom will strive to achieve. It does mean that some modes of interacting may have to be explained and explicitly taught, modeled, practiced, and reinforced. For example, some teachers may encourage a Socratic method of discussion, but depending on the interactional style a student is accustomed to, teaching and modeling of this method will be necessary.

It may also be the case that the teacher will decide that some degree of cultural accommodation on his or her own part is necessary. For example, Au and Carroll's study of the interactional style of Hawaiian students demonstrated that when majority teachers implemented instructional practices that were congruent with the cultural beliefs and styles of their students, the students performed better academically (Au, 1980; Au & Carroll, 1997).

The same reasoning holds when considering other student variables. For example, in a classroom with ELLs who need assistance as they acquire English, a climate of collaboration and helpfulness will make these students feel at ease. This, in turn, makes it easier for them to learn. The point is that teachers, administrators, or other school-site support personnel should gather and understand as much information as possible about their students and the school community. This type of information informs decisions so that teachers can leverage areas of strength, accommodate areas of weakness, and avoid areas of potential discord.

Teacher Variables

Teachers and other school-site support personnel must take stock of their own strengths and weaknesses, as well as those of their students (Gettinger & Kohler, 2006). How are expectations communicated? Is the teacher patient and polite? Does he or she provide adequate scaffolding so that students can reach the desired standards and expectations? Is the teacher accessible and friendly, but still firm and in charge? Are students provided with opportunities to practice the expectations that have been established? Are appropriate behaviors reinforced? Taking an honest, objective look at a teacher's behavior is important. For example, some teachers tell students that they are expected to raise their hands and wait to be called on but then respond to students who call out the answer, unintentionally reinforcing this behavior (Lane, Pierson, & Givner, 2003).

Your personal qualities and your own behavior patterns will be crucial in making students feel comfortable while instilling the importance of academic work (Landrum & Kauffman, 2006; Partin, 2009). The manner in which a teacher interacts with students sends the strongest signal about how students are expected to behave (Pianta, 1994; Silver, Measelle, Armstrong, & Essex, 2005). Being polite and genuinely interested in your students is a highly desirable model for them to emulate. And do not forget that a smile and a friendly manner go a long way in making students feel at ease; in the literature this is referred to as teacher warmth (Maggin, 2008).

Teachers should pay careful attention to the language they use. Rather than using judgmental language, teachers should attempt to be descriptive so that students have an opportunity to respond appropriately. Instead of saying, "You never listen, Michael! Get back in your seat," it can be more effective to remind Michael of the classroom procedures. "Michael, during silent reading I would like you to read to yourself at your desk." At first it can feel cumbersome to use descriptive language, but nonjudgmental language contributes to an atmosphere of shared work and learning, avoiding overreliance on reactive discipline (Pianta, 2006; Walker et al., 2004).

Equally important as the verbal messages a teacher sends are the nonverbal ones communicated by the teacher's actions. If you use challenging and threatening behavior, such as raising your voice or standing too close to a student when you are angry, it undermines your ability to establish a businesslike and calm environment. The emphasis should be on deescalating unwanted behavior in a matter-of-fact, proactive manner rather than in a reactive and negative one (Colvin, 2004). Understanding his or her own personality and patterns of interaction can help a teacher prepare for challenging situations.

School Variables

A supportive school environment can be of substantial assistance in establishing the right tone in the classroom. Some schools put considerable emphasis on topics such as character education, school safety, social skills, and/or positive behavior support. There may be a schoolwide plan in place to support one of these areas, which, in turn, will support teachers' efforts in the classroom (see Chapter 1). When schoolwide rules are in place, then all students know what the expectations are, no matter where they are in the building—in the hallway, classroom, cafeteria, or the bus. It is also very effective in promoting prosocial behaviors for students to receive additional reinforcement from adults other than the classroom teacher. A school that has an orderly environment in which students feel safe will underscore the efforts a teacher makes in his or her individual classroom (Walker et al., 2004).

Classroom climate is in part established through affective and sometimes hard-to-measure behaviors. However, setting the right tone is fundamental for successful classroom management. Understanding the needs of each unique group of students allows you to build a rapport that makes all other aspects of teaching easier. Understanding yourself will make you more sensitive to your own interaction style and how it affects your students. Finally, being aware of school resources (or lack thereof) allows you to make the most of them or helps you consider what other resources you might need to access (Lane, Kalberg, & Menzies, 2009).

Physical Room Arrangement

Before students even arrive in your classroom, you can establish order by carefully considering the physical layout of your classroom (Morrow, Reutzel, & Casey, 2006). The types of instructional activities a teacher plans to implement is key to efficient room arrangement. Will students work collaboratively? Will their work be differentiated, requiring them to use centers? Will there be areas devoted to materials that students can access independently? Each of these questions necessitates consideration of the flow of work, as well as of instruction. Thinking ahead about how your classroom will be used and being proactive about eliminating trouble spots and facilitating student movement can avert a substantial number of problems. Next, we consider the various activities and routines that are affected by room arrangement (Colvin, 2004; Evertson & Weinstein, 2006).

Classroom Flow

Sometimes disruption occurs when there is inadequate space for the physical movement that takes place in the classroom (Burgess & Fordyce, 1989; Maxwell, 1989). Think about how students will move around the classroom. There should be space to walk to desks and pull out chairs without bumping into one another. High-traffic areas should be free of obstructions. Consider this point as you examine the space (1) in front of your desk, (2) where you store materials, (3) where your pencil sharpener is located, and (4) in front of your doorway. Ideally, there should be enough room for students to pass freely by one another. Of course, this can be a challenge in undersized rooms or overcrowded schools. However, some teachers do not maximize the space they have because they have not considered how instructional activities and routine events such as lining up are affected by room arrangement.

Additionally, a teacher and support staff should be able to scan the room and see *all* students. Do not have areas that are blocked off from your view by bookcases or file cabinets; if you cannot see a student, you cannot keep him or her safe. It is possible to create inviting, comfortable spaces but still be able to see all parts of the classroom. You can also have a quiet space where students can "cool off" if they are feeling angry or overstimulated, but this area must be visible to the teacher. Similarly, students should be able to easily view the teacher during whole-class lessons. Desks need to be arranged so that students can see comfortably. If you have round tables or if students are seated in cooperative groups of desks, teach a procedure for moving chairs so students can maintain a clear sight line during whole-group instruction. If there are areas in the room where students will gather—for example, to hear a story, read from the author's chair, or conduct a musical performance—dedicate adequate space so students can sit next to one another without being squeezed together.

Dedicated Work Space and Materials Storage

Closely related to physical space is deciding where to locate materials, centers, and designated activity spots (Morrow et al., 2006). These areas are important structures and spaces that facilitate specific academic tasks and provide students with access to materials. Avoid making these areas trouble spots by anticipating potential problems. For example, it would not be wise to store journals directly by the entrance to the classroom, as this might cause students to bottleneck in the doorway as they pick up their journal for the starting activity. Also, this could potentially cause ambiguity in determining whether students are on time to the next class if they are waiting to get in the door.

Once you decide on the supplies and books students will have access to, locate them in convenient and easy-to-reach places. For example, many teachers have a single tub or bucket for students whose desks are arranged in a group. It may contain several items such as pencils, erasers, stapler, scissors, and markers so that students can get what they need with minimal disruption. Other options include stations that are stocked with paper or other supplies. When using an arrangement like this, be sure to specify procedures concerning how and when students replenish their materials. As another example, when students are encouraged to browse in a classroom library area or choose leveled texts, sufficient space should be available for students to examine books and easily reshelve them. Ideally, more than one student should be able to be in the area at a time. Teaching students procedures for accessing materials and activities is discussed in more detail in the next section, but first it is important to be sure that there is adequate space and that items are organized.

Teachers must also consider activity centers and other spaces in which all students will gather together at the same time (Paine, Radicchi, Rosellini, Deutchman, & Darch, 1983). Activity centers should have adequate seating for the number of students who will be using them. All materials for a center's activities should be stocked and accessible. Posting directions and procedures in each center will prevent unnecessary traffic back and forth from the center and promote student independence. In elementary settings, some teachers leave an open space near the front of the room in which students can sit on the floor for events such as stories or demonstrations. This area, too, should have adequate space for everyone. In primary classrooms (grades K–3), rugs with grid lines or different colored squares can be used to indicate where individual students sit. Examine the traffic patterns created by these areas so that students can access them easily and efficiently.

In middle and high school settings, it is important to consider work space relative to the content area. For example, in a middle school band classroom, it will be important to think about traffic patterns as students enter the room, retrieve their musical instruments (e.g., from a locker or a shelf), and move to the designated area. Remember, some classes—for instance, choir or drama—may not require seats. This will have implications for defining what is meant by being *on time to class*. In this case it might mean being in one's place on a riser or on the stage (Lane, Kalberg, & Menzies, 2009).

Room Decorating

An often overlooked component of room environment is how the classroom is decorated. The way your classroom looks communicates to students how much you value them and the work the class is engaged in. Admittedly, many teachers face challenges with the rooms allocated to them. Some classrooms are too small, have poor lighting, or may be painted drab or unappealing colors. Still, it is possible to display attractive and useful items that create a warm and welcoming environment for students. Tools such as schedules, word walls, periodic tables, time lines, or other materials are both useful and visually appealing.

Although student work should be showcased in the classroom, decisions need to be made regarding which work will be displayed and how. If only final products or correct work is posted, all students should have opportunities to have something exhibited. Some administrators and teachers elect to show "work in progress" but stamp it as a draft so that a perfect paper is not necessary before it can be displayed. Carefully consider what types of corrections or comments you want to have available for all to see. Displaying their work allows students to feel pride in their accomplishments. Yet we recommend not having teacher comments or grades visible for everyone to read. We believe that students, whether they are in kindergarten or 12th grade, should have the choice of whether this type of information is available for all to see. Grades and evaluative comments can be written on the back of a student paper so that they cannot be seen when the work is affixed to a wall or bulletin board. It is also important to be aware of your school and district policies concerning confidentiality in regard to grades and progress monitoring activities (see Chapter 8, this volume), which may preclude you from posting materials with grades that everyone can see (Lane, Kalberg, & Menzies, 2009)

Teachers and paraprofessionals should be aware of how their own desk areas look. Avoid clutter and disarray. The materials you need should be easily accessible and neatly stored. As space is a precious commodity in most classrooms, be sure not to use a disproportionate amount of it. We have seen teachers commandeer a desk and several tables because their paperwork management system was so disorganized. Also, beware of creating the impression of a barrier between you and the students.

Seating Arrangements

Depending on the size and shape of your classroom, a variety of seating arrangements may be possible (see Figure 2.1). After considering where high-traffic areas are likely to be, the types of activities you will need to accommodate, and the loca-

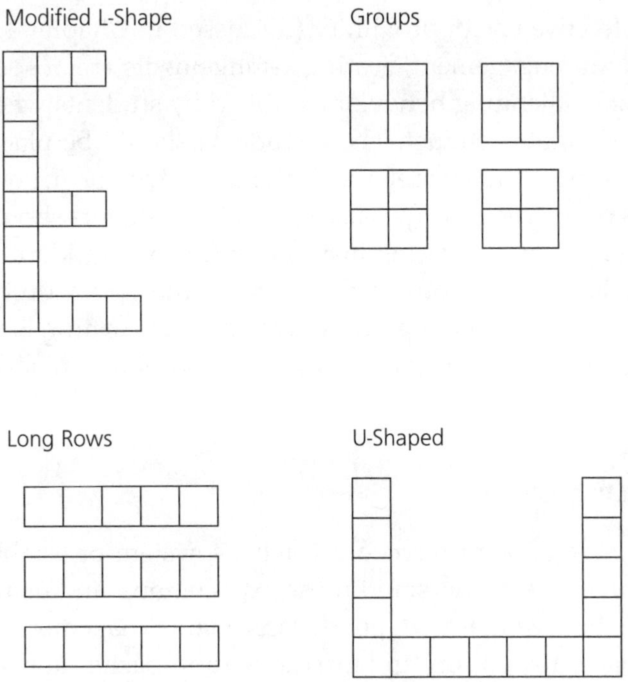

FIGURE 2.1. Room arrangements.

tion of your main teaching area, decide which type of seating arrangement best suits your teaching style and learning activities.

Some types of classroom arrangements offer more structure in a classroom. Seating students in traditional rows has a couple of important advantages. It provides the clearest sight line to the main blackboard, whiteboard (or smartboard), or projector screen. Rows also allow the teacher to supervise all students easily and minimize interaction among students. However, traditional rows do not preclude the use of cooperative groups or pairing up students. Procedures for moving desks or chairs together when required for various activities can be easily taught.

Many teachers prefer to group student desks in ways that facilitate ongoing cooperative group work, thus avoiding having to rearrange desks and creates more opportunities for student interaction. Alternately, a U-shaped design or several rows of desks that are adjacent to one another may combine aspects of cooperative groups with traditional rows.

For some teachers, such as those in a science laboratory or music class, room arrangement may be predetermined. Regardless of which arrangement you prefer, there are a few critical elements to be aware of when delivering instruction (Walker et al., 2004). First, determine whether students have sufficient space to get out of their seats and walk through the classroom. Overcrowding leads to students accidently bumping into one another, which is a catalyst for disruptive behavior. Also, teachers must have easy access to each student and be able to circulate near all desks to make effective use of proximity (discussed in Chapter 4, in this volume) to support academic engagement. Seating arrangements are of special importance when preventing challenging behavior exhibited by students who have difficulty maintaining appropriate conduct. These students should be placed in what Nelson, Benner, and Mooney (2008) refer to as the *action zone*, or "front and center relative to the focus of instruction" (p. 146). Finally, all students should be able to see the teacher or the person delivering instruction (e.g., the guidance counselor who is teaching a social skills lesson). If they cannot, the opportunity to circumvent some behaviors simply by making eye contact is lost. Learning is supported when each student can see what the teacher is saying and doing in addition to hearing his or her voice.

Approach to Discipline

We use the term *discipline* to refer to a teacher's system of establishing expectations, helping students to understand those expectations, and using consequences and rewards. We believe that with good classroom management skills, an engaging and appropriate curriculum, and instructive approaches to resistant behaviors teachers, administrators, and other school-site support staff will only occasionally need to rely on a discipline (or reactive consequence-based) system. A teacher's approach to discipline should be grounded in evidence-based practices shown to be effective. Research clearly demonstrates that positive and proactive systems of management are more successful, not to mention more humanistic, than reactive, punitive approaches (Lane, Kalberg, & Menzies, 2009). Teachers who use effective discipline combined with the other elements of good classroom management can devote the maximum amount of school time to teaching and learning rather than to reacting to inappropriate behaviors. In addition to being good for student learning and safety, this is also good for teachers in terms of job satisfaction and retention (American Psychological Association Classroom Violence Directed Against Teachers Task Force, 2009).

The first part of your discipline plan consists of a few positively stated rules. Ideally, the entire school staff should develop three to five positively stated expectations that the whole school will abide by (see Figure 2.2). Rather than inventing individual rules or systems, classroom teachers should display, teach, and reinforce schoolwide expectations consistently. These expectations are operationalized for each setting, including the classroom (see Figure 2.3). Choose expectations that cover a range of behaviors. For example, the expectation "Respect yourself and others" can be used to remind students not to bother other students, either verbally or physically. Using expectations that are more general avoids negatively stated rules such as "Don't get out of your seat without permission." Knowing when it is or is not appropriate to leave one's seat is a procedure that students should be taught (procedures are discussed in the next section), rather than a rule to be enforced.

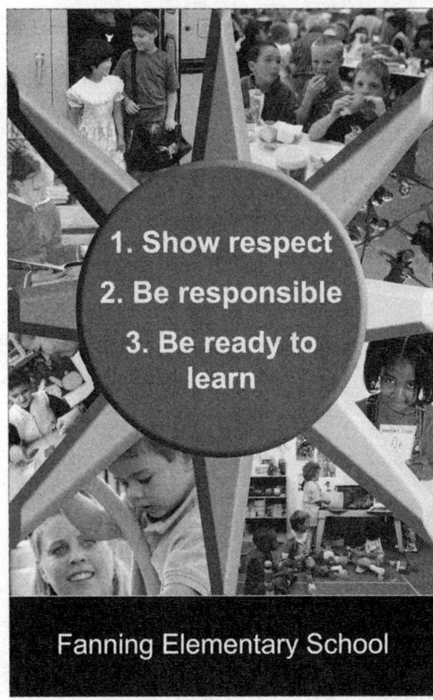

FIGURE 2.2. **Sample positive behavior support—elementary level.** Designed by Kylie Beck, Vanderbilt University Kennedy Center/National Institute of Child Health and Human Development Grant No. P30 HD15052. From Lane, Kalberg, and Menzies (2009). Copyright 2009 by The Guilford Press. Reprinted by permission.

Some teachers like to get student input when forming expectations. Whether you use the schoolwide expectations or—if schoolwide expectations have not yet been established—you create your own with student input, it is important to describe, demonstrate, and rehearse what each expectation looks like. It is not enough to tell students the expectations. Although it may seem time-consuming to explicitly teach each of them, this procedure ultimately saves time because all students understand the expectations right from the beginning. Teachers often assume that students already understand the teacher's definition of a behavior, yet this may not be the case. Explicitly and carefully teaching the expectations avoids this problem. Examples and non-examples of what they look like and do not look like in practice should be taught. Expectations should also be posted in the classroom where all students can see them. It is helpful to include pictures or icons that provide examples of prosocial behaviors to accompany the written expectations. This is particularly important for young students, as well as those with developmental disabilities (Lane, Kalberg, & Menzies, 2009).

After all the students understand the expectations, the next step is to find opportunities to positively reinforce students for following them. This contributes to a positive classroom tone and encourages students to be well behaved. Essentially, you are accentuating the positive rather than emphasizing the negative (the "Mary Poppins principle"). Students should be reinforced with verbal praise that

	Settings					
	Classroom	**Hallway**	**Cafeteria**	**Playground**	**Bathroom**	**Bus**
Respect	• Follow directions • Use kind words and actions • Control your temper • Cooperate with others • Use an inside voice	• Use a quiet voice • Walk on the right side of the hallway • Keep hands to yourself	• Use an inside voice • Use manners • Listen to and follow adult requests	• Respect other people's personal space • Follow the rules of the game	• Use the restroom and then return to class • Stay in your own bathroom stall • Little talking	• Use kind words toward the bus driver and other students • Listen to and follow the bus driver's rules
Responsibility	• Arrive to class on time • Remain in school for the whole day • Bring your required materials • Turn in finished work • Exercise self-control	• Keep hands to yourself • Walk in the hallway • Stay in line with your class	• Make your choices quickly • Eat your own food • Choose a seat and stick with it • Clean up after yourself	• Play approved games • Use equipment appropriately • Return equipment when you are done • Line up when the bell rings	• Flush toilet • Wash hands with soap • Throw away any trash properly • Report any problems to your teacher	• Talk quietly with others • Listen to and follow the bus driver's rules • Remain in seat after you enter the bus • Use self-control
Best Effort	• Participate in class activities • Complete work with best effort • Ask for help politely	• Walk quietly • Walk directly to next location	• Use your table manners • Use an inside voice	• Include others in your games • Be active • Follow the rules of the game	• Take care of your business quickly • Keep bathroom tidy	• Listen to and follow the bus driver's rules • Keep hands and feet to self

FIGURE 2.3. Expectation matrix: Orange Elementary School. Adapted from Walker, Ramsey, and Gresham (2004, p. 138). Copyright 2004 by Wadsworth, a part of Cengage Learning, Inc. Adapted by permission. *www.cengage.com/permissions.*

describes the prosocial behavior you are targeting (for you behaviorists, this is behavior-specific praise; Cooper, Heron, & Heward, 2007). For example, stating "I appreciate how Susan was polite and helpful by lining up when I asked" is much more powerful than reprimanding students who do not line up. Please keep in mind that what is reinforcing for one student is not necessary reinforcing for all students. The preceding statement is very appropriate for Susan if her behavior is maintained by attention. However, if Susan is not fond of social attention, this may actually be perceived as a punisher, which will yield a decrease in the desired behavior (Cooper et al., 2007; Umbreit et al., 2007).

In a behavioral model, students are described as either seeking access to or escape from social attention, activities or tasks, or sensory experiences. Students' whose behavior accesses these experiences or consequences is maintained by positive reinforcement. In contrast, students whose behavior avoids these experiences or consequences is maintained by negative reinforcement. Once the behavior is identified, the maintaining function is determined. In other words, why does the student display the behavior? For example, if a student consistently talks during work time and the teacher yells at him, he is receiving positive reinforcement. Of course, it is not what we would think of as positive reinforcement, but in behavioral terms the student is receiving attention. If a student gets in trouble every day during mathematics instruction and is sent to the office, she is receiving negative reinforcement because she escapes from her schoolwork. In the first case, the function of the behavior is to get the teacher's attention. In the second case, the function of the behavior is to escape work. Understanding the function of a behavior is critical in changing it; namely, it informs intervention efforts. We discuss this further in Chapter 7.

It may be necessary to offer a gentle prompt to some students to help them display the behavior you are encouraging. Focusing on the positive and supporting it will shape student behavior more effectively than will reprimands. Prompts help cue students to perform appropriate behavior without resorting to a disciplinary action. An example of prompting a student to be quiet and line up would be to say, "Alexis, please push in your chair and go stand quietly behind Javier." For those unused to using positive prompts, it may be difficult initially Reframing how one thinks of discipline techniques can require quite a bit of effort.

Of course, not every student will respond to proactive strategies every time. It is necessary to establish consequences for undesirable behavior. Consequences should be logical and natural (Cooper et al., 2007). They should be determined ahead of time, and students should be aware of the consequences. For example, the first consequence could be a warning, followed by the loss of a minor privilege. If these are not effective, it is a good idea to communicate with parents that you need assistance in supporting good behavior. If a student still does not respond, it may be necessary to intervene more directly or consistently. At each juncture, we encourage you to think back to the notion of function: What is maintaining this undesirable behavior (Umbreit et al., 2007)?

Consequences should be administered in a brisk and matter-of-fact manner. A teacher's display of anger will escalate negative feelings and make discipline seem personal rather than a consequence of not abiding by the school or classroom rules (Colvin, 2004).

In Chapter 4 we discuss several low-intensity strategies that can be used to avoid and minimize misbehavior. In Chapters 5, 6, and 7 we provide solutions to more intrusive or hard-to-manage misbehavior. However, the next element of classroom management we discuss here includes effective routines and procedures critical for avoiding problem behavior.

Routines and Procedures

Teaching procedures and establishing routines for the commonplace activities that occur in the classroom is essential in maximizing academic engaged time and minimizing disruptive behaviors. Procedures help students successfully participate in a host of activities because students understand the teacher's expectations and know exactly what to do (Lane, Pierson, & Givner, 2003; Lane, Pierson, Stang, & Carter, 2010). Rather than constraining students, procedures and routines free students and teachers to work efficiently and independently.

Procedures are the manner in which a teacher wants tasks and activities performed. Once these procedures become routines, they are performed efficiently and with a minimal disturbance. In particular, teachers should teach procedures for transitions from one activity to the next and for common events such as (1) going the restroom, (2) getting a drink of water, (3) accessing materials, and (4) turning in work. Teaching students how to signal the teacher for his or her attention is particularly important. This procedure may be different depending on whether the teacher and students are involved in a whole-group lesson, small-group instruction, or independent work (Walker et al., 2004).

Just as with schoolwide expectations, procedures need to be explicitly taught, modeled, practiced, and reinforced. First, each procedure should be defined and explained in concrete terms. Then the teacher should model each procedure so it is clear to students what it looks like. Students need to practice the procedure while the teacher watches and provides feedback (guided practice). Finally, students should be prompted to display the expected behavior when necessary and reinforced when they demonstrate it. Eventually, procedures will become routine, and it will become less necessary to prompt the behavior. Reinforcement will shift to an intermittent schedule to promote maintenance (Cooper et al., 2007). However, if over time students fail to follow a given procedure appropriately, it is important to provide a follow-up lesson (also called a booster session) and again prompt and reinforce until the behavior is performed satisfactorily.

One critical procedure concerns how students will enter the classroom in the morning and begin their first activity. It is critical to have a starter activity that all students engage in while waiting for classmates to arrive and for the teacher to take attendance (Evertson &Weinstein, 2006). Time that otherwise might be wasted can be used productively. This also reduces the chance of students misbehaving because their time is unstructured. Some teachers begin with independent reading, whereas others may choose vocabulary practice, journal prompts, logic problems, and so on. More important than the activity itself is that students are aware of *what* to do and *how* to proceed. See Box 2.1 for a narrative describing how Mr. Guzman instructs his students in a procedure.

Determining the routines you think are essential ahead of time will help you develop lessons for these procedures. Leaving the classroom for lunch, for assemblies, and at the end of the day are frequently occurring events you will want to address. Also consider in-class transitions such as moving from one lesson to the next. This is particularly applicable when changing instructional formats, such as from whole-group instruction to cooperative groups or center activities. Turning in papers, greeting visitors who enter the classroom, and responding to a teacher's signal for attention are all routine events that will occur in your classroom and for which procedures should be developed. Infrequently occurring events such as emergency drills need to be anticipated as well (Evertson &Weinstein, 2006).

Nelson et al. (2008, p. 148) make the following suggestions when managing transitions:

1. Be sure there are clear avenues for students to move to the designated instructional area.
2. Develop a signal to indicate an impending transition.
3. Secure students' attention and remind them of expectations regarding noise level, travel direction, and personal space issues.
4. Secure student attention to end a transition and designate the beginning of the next activity.

In addition, tools such as agendas or classroom schedules help facilitate transitions. Establishing procedures for transitions and other everyday events in a classroom creates a task-oriented and predictable environment with clear expectations. These are key to a well-managed classroom that reduces the occurrence of undesirable behaviors and promotes desirable ones.

Managing Paperwork

Attending to paperwork may not seem to be part of classroom management. However, the clerical tasks related to teaching need to be completed quickly, efficiently, and unobtrusively so most of a teacher's energy can be directed to students. Some teachers spend an inordinate amount of time collecting and returning papers, taking attendance, or simply getting ready to begin lessons. This impedes the flow of instruction, takes teacher's attention off students, and contributes to student behavior problems by not providing sufficient structure. Although a well-managed

BOX 2.1. Mr. Guzman Teaches a Procedure

Mr. Guzman is an easygoing, well-loved fifth-grade teacher. However, his relaxed nature is partly due to his well-managed classroom. Because Mr. Guzman spent the first days of school teaching the procedures he thinks are essential, his students are industrious and on task. One of the first routines he established was how to get ready to go to the cafeteria for lunch. Mr. Guzman teaches reading just before lunch, and he knows that by 11:45 his students are eager to eat and then play outside after several hours in the classroom. He always begins reading with whole-group instruction, and the last part of the session is devoted to small groups and independent reading. This is how he introduced the procedure that they follow every day:

> "Students, each day at 11:40 when you are working in your small group or reading a book quietly at your desk or in the reading center, I will stand up and turn off the lights to signal you that it is time to get ready to go to the cafeteria for lunch. This means that you should (1) stop what you are doing, (2) quietly put away your books and papers, (3) return to your seat, and (4) wait for me to give you the signal to line up."

Mr. Guzman used a PowerPoint with the four points typed out so that his students would have a visual aid in addition to listening to him. Then Mr. Guzman asked Lucia to model the directions for him. As the other students watched, Lucia pretended to be reading a book to herself at the reading center. Mr. Guzman turned off the lights for a moment and then said, "It's time to get ready for lunch." Lucia got up, went to her desk, put away her book, and then sat down in her chair. Mr. Guzman smiled broadly and said, "Thank you for getting ready to go to lunch so quickly and quietly, Lucia. You may line up."

Now it was time to practice with the entire class. Mr. Guzman asked his students to get into the reading groups they had been in the previous day. Once they were in their groups, he said to them, "Remember, when I turn off the lights you will (1) stop what you are doing, (2) quietly put away your books and papers, (3) return to your seat, and (4) wait for me to give you the signal to line up." Mr. Guzman turned the lights off, and they all practiced the procedure together. Mr. Guzman thanked individual students as they went to their desks quietly and put away their materials. Once everyone was ready, Mr. Guzman thanked the entire class. He reminded students that each day at 11:40 they would follow this procedure to end reading and to get ready for lunch.

Mr. Guzman has carefully considered and instructed his students in a procedure he knows will reduce chaos when ending one activity and getting ready to move to the next. The first thing he did was to explain exactly what the procedure was, then he and a student modeled the procedure, and finally the entire class practiced the procedure together. Mr. Guzman offered reinforcement by thanking students as they correctly displayed the appropriate behavior. He knows that the procedure will require some practice, continued reinforcement, and most likely some prompting before it becomes routine. However, he feels satisfied that students are clear about his expectations and that they have the information they need to perform the procedure correctly.

classroom should practically run on its own once everything is in place, it is critical that teachers are focused on continually promoting student engagement with the task at hand. In this way you can head off potential problems rather than having to react to them.

Teachers are typically concerned with two types of paperwork. The first includes student work and the accompanying grading and recording. The second includes administrative requirements such as attendance reports, report cards, special education documents, responses to e-mails, and site-specific activities.

Deciding ahead of time how to collect and distribute student papers and establishing procedures for doing so will greatly reduce the commotion related to these events. Avoid collecting and returning papers as a whole-class activity. If students are waiting with nothing to do except receive their papers, they are tempted to begin playing and talking, which leads to disruptive behavior. We are not saying that students should never have the chance to take a break or interact, but consider the context of the opportunities you provide for doing so. The nature of an activity sends different signals about the importance of student behavior. Sitting passively may seem like a waste of time to students, so playing might appear to be a reasonable option. If students are working, they know that playing is incompatible with completing the assigned task.

Papers can be returned to student boxes or cubbies or, if students are older, placed in hanging file folders. If you feel it is easier to turn back papers as a whole-class activity, develop efficient procedures, such as having designated student monitors quickly return papers to their owners. However, confidentiality must be ensured. One option is to staple papers so that grades are not visible to students returning the papers. Similarly, papers can be placed in baskets as students finish assignments or, if collected as a whole group, can be passed *across* rows so teachers can easily monitor students as they turn in their assignments (provided that the latter option does not violate a district or school policy). In either case, having a procedure will streamline the event and reduce the opportunity for misbehavior. Because teachers handle so many student papers, this is a more important consideration than it might seem at first.

A teacher's time with students should be used to actively monitor, teach, or facilitate student activities and not for grading. Because it can quickly become overwhelming to manage student papers and grades, planning ahead is essential. Teachers need to decide what types of papers to grade and the kind of feedback that is needed. Depending on the students' age, some types of assignments can be self- or peer-evaluated. Detailed but efficient feedback can also be provided through the use of rubrics.

Despite its importance, keeping track of administrative paperwork should not interfere with a teacher's active supervision or involvement with students. These are activities that require a teacher to develop routines for him- or herself. For instance, attendance should take no more than a few seconds, and there should be a procedure for submitting it to the office. Most official paperwork is now completed electronically, which can make it easier to create, store, and retrieve documents such as individualized education programs (IEPs) or report cards. Just as with paper files, create an organizational system so necessary items can be accessed easily and quickly. Teachers should not check e-mail or cell phones during class time, as an essential part of classroom management is being attentive to students and aware of what is happening in the classroom. Managing all types of paperwork should take as little class time as possible to allow a teacher to concentrate fully on students. Research shows that students have better academic outcomes when they are actively supervised by their teachers (Brophy, 1986c). Active supervision may improve safety in two senses: (1) it may help students to feel more certain of their physical safety if they feel confident that the teacher is attentive and fully aware of all classroom activities, and (2) it may also help students to feel more confident and safe in taking educational risks if they feel that the teacher is aware and in control of the class.

SUMMARY

In this chapter we discussed the five essential components of classroom management: classroom climate; physical room arrangement; approach to discipline; routines and procedures; and managing paperwork. Paying attention to each of these classroom dimensions creates a well-ordered teaching and learning environment (see Box 2.2). This is the first line of defense in preventing behavior problems. Teachers should not underestimate their role in supporting students' positive conduct. Not only does effective classroom management avoid a majority of discipline problems, but lack of good management actually contributes to them.

There are literally hundreds of books and other resources available to assist teachers, administrators, and other school-site personnel in establishing strong classroom management skills and practices. Table 2.2 presents a classroom management resource guide designed to provide you with information on a few classroom management books, websites, and refereed journal articles that can help you (1) guide your thinking about and planning of the topics discussed in this chapter and (2) construct your classroom management plan.

The next chapter focuses on the instructional side of the equation. An important component of managing behavior is to create learning experiences that provide students with opportunities to work in their zones of proximal development (Vygotsky, 1978). Behavior problems are more likely to emerge when schoolwork is either too easy or too difficult. In Chapter 3 we discuss how to choose appropriate curricula, as well as how to differentiate it to best meet students' needs. In addition, we introduce a variety of instructional delivery models that promote engagement and increase achievement.

BOX 2.2. Strategies in Practice

Ms. Flor has been teaching for several years, but at the beginning of every school year she mentally runs through her checklist for effective classroom management. She goes in a week early to get the **physical layout** of her room set up. Ms. Flor prefers to have students sit in desks that are clustered in groups of four. She finds this **seating arrangement** conducive to the collaborative activities she values for her students. She places the desks fairly close to the smartboard so that everyone can either easily see it or can quickly turn their chairs around to face it. Over the years she has experimented with different arrangements and now knows that having the desks near the front of the room, the activity centers near the back, and an open space in between them facilitates the traffic **flow**. Ms. Flor's own **materials** are neatly stored in a cupboard, and students have one basket per group on their desks with all the supplies they need throughout the day.

Classroom climate is very important to Ms. Flor, who has an upbeat nature and a sunny smile. She finds out as much as possible about her students before they arrive, and because she has been at the same school for several years, she is very familiar with the school community. On the first day of school, Ms. Flor is at the door to greet each student with a smile and handshake, and she instructs them to find the desks marked with their nametags. On each desk is a note welcoming students to their new classroom.

Of course, Ms. Flor takes the time to introduce and discuss the **schoolwide expectations**: (1) Respect yourself and others, (2) Work hard, and (3) Take care of your school. She explains to the students how the expectations help them work together productively, and she provides examples of what they do and do not look like. Ms. Flor gives the students opportunities to role-play with her, and they act out a few scenarios of respecting others and working hard. She and her students have fun doing this, but it also helps everyone understand the kinds of behaviors she expects. Ms. Flor has a poster with the expectations ready, and she tells the students she will hang it over the smartboard, where everyone can see it. She also lets the students know that they will be reviewing the schoolwide expectations every month throughout the school year.

Ms. Flor and the students also discuss **procedures**, such as when to sharpen pencils, how to get a drink, and how to turn in completed assignments. The students also learn how to **transition** from one learning activity to another and how to get ready for lunch, recess, and dismissal. Students feel reassured by Ms. Flor's warm but work-oriented manner. They already have a lot of information about what to expect and how they should behave, which provides a sense of security and helps them feel ready to learn. Ms. Flor knows she will have to remind students of the procedures, and in some cases reteach them, but she feels they are off to a good start.

Finally, not only has Ms. Flor organized her students, but she has also organized herself. Each day she is **prepared** with all the materials she needs for each lesson. As the year goes on, it gets much easier, as many of the lessons follow a predictable format. Ms. Flor has also created a **system for collecting and returning student papers.** Each group has a paper monitor who collects assignments throughout the day and puts them in a basket on Ms. Flor's desk. She prefers to return them at the beginning of each lesson as students complete a sponge activity. A sponge activity is a brief review activity that she finds to be a productive use of students' time and also signals the beginning of the new lesson.

Ms. Flor still has plenty of work to do after students leave for the afternoon, but when her day has gone smoothly because of her proactive approach to classroom management, she still has some energy left to tackle her **administrative paperwork**, assessment of student work, and lesson planning.

TABLE 2.2. Classroom Management Resource Guide

Reference	Description	Target group	Cost/retrieval information
	Books		
Barr, R. D., & Parrett, W. H. (2008). *Saving our students, saving our schools: 50 proven strategies for helping underachieving students and improving schools* (2nd ed.). Thousand Oaks, CA: Corwin Press.	This book focuses on effectively meeting the needs of at-risk students by supporting academic success and creating a positive classroom climate. Topics include (1) establishing priorities that focus on student learning; (2) creating a school and classroom climate of respect; (3) maintaining high expectations for academic performance; (4) relying on results-driven instructional and assessment practices; and (5) collaborating with parents and families.	Educators of at-risk students	*www.corwinpress.com/books* $40.95 paperback $80.95 hardcover
Canter, L. (2006). *Classroom management for academic success*. Bloomington, IN: Solution Tree.	The author explores classroom management as a way to improve student achievement and academic success. Topics discussed include motivating students to be academically engaged, building relationships with students and parents, and the "2-week turnaround program" to improve classroom climate in a disruptive classroom.	K–12 educators	*www.solution-tree.com/Public/Media.aspx?ShowDetail=true&ProductID=BKF209* $39.95
Emmer, E. T., Evertson, C. M., & Worsham, M. E. (2006). *Classroom management for secondary teachers* (6th ed.). Boston, MA: Allyn & Bacon.	With an emphasis on prevention, the authors provide a comprehensive discussion of classroom organization, management, and discipline for secondary school teachers. Example topics include organizing your classroom and materials, choosing rules and procedures, communication skills, and managing problem behaviors.	Secondary educators	*www.amazon.com/Classroom-Management-Secondary-Teachers-6th/dp/0205349951* $24.00
Kerr, M. M., & Nelson, C. M. (2010). *Strategies for addressing behavior problems in the classroom* (6th ed.). Upper Saddle River, NJ.: Pearson Merrill Prentice Hall.	Presents empirically sound research-based strategies for working with students with emotional and behavioral problems. In the first section, the authors focus on foundations of effective behavior management, discussing topics such as identifying and serving students with behavior problems and PBS. In the next section, strategies for specific behavior problems are addressed, such as handling disruptive and aggressive behaviors and improving social skills.	K–12 special and general educators	*www.mypearsonstore.com/bookstore/product.asp?isbn=0136045243&xid=PSED* $103.00

Marzano, R. J., Marzano, J. S., & Pickering, D. J. (2003). *Classroom management that works: Research-based strategies for every teacher.* Alexandria, VA: Association for Supervision and Curriculum Development,	The authors discuss the importance of classroom management to student engagement and achievement, effective strategies that teachers and schools can use to foster classroom management are presented, including topics such as rules and procedures, teacher–student relationships, getting off to a good start, the student's responsibility for management, and management at the school level. Concepts are based on more than 100 studies on classroom management.	All educators	*shop.ascd.org/productdisplay.cfm?productid=103027* $25.95
Wong, H., & Wong, R. (1998). *The first days of school.* Mountain View, CA: Harry Wong.	Designed for first-year teachers, including basic understandings for teachers, future understandings for professionals, and in-depth discussions of three characteristics, including positive expectations, classroom management, and lesson mastery.	Elementary and middle educators	*www.harrywong.com* $24.95
	Websites		
Epstein, M., Atkins, M., Cullinan, D., Kutash, K., & Weaver, R. (2008). *Reducing behavior problems in the elementary school classroom: A practice guide* (NCEE No. 2008-012). Institute of Education Sciences, U.S. Department of Education. Washington, DC: National Center for Education Evaluation and Regional Assistance.	What Works Clearinghouse practice guide for reducing behavior problems in the elementary classroom, with five recommendations for evidence-based practices. Compiled using stringent criteria for what is considered evidence-based practice by a review board assigned by the Institute of Education Sciences.	Elementary educators	*ies.ed.gov/ncee/wwc/publications/practiceguides*
Teachers.Net Classroom Management Chatboard	A chat room devoted to classroom management issues. The site is sponsored by Teachers.Net. All resources on the site are available for free, but the site contains commercial advertising.	K–12 educators	*teachers.net/chat/?*
IRIS Center	This site is developed by Vanderbilt University and Claremont Graduate University. It has several interactive modules that introduce various behavior management plans for the entire class, as well as those that address individual students.	K–college educators	*iris.peabody.vanderbilt.edu/index.html*
Intervention Central	Offers free tools and resources to help school staff and parents to promote positive classroom behaviors and foster effective learning for all children.	K–12 educators; parents	*interventioncentral.org*

(cont.)

TABLE 2.2. *(cont.)*

Reference	Description	Target group	Cost/retrieval information
	Refereed journal articles		
Brownell, M. T., & Walthe-Thomas, C. (2001). Stephen W. Smith: Strategies for building a positive classroom environment by preventing behavior problems. *Intervention in School and Clinic, 37*, 31–35.	Documents an interview with Dr. Stephen W. Smith, an expert on working with students with behavior disorders and classroom management. Topics include preventative strategies that individual teachers can use to prevent behavior problems in their classrooms, strategies teachers can use to teach students more appropriate behaviors when problem behaviors occur, working with parents to improve classroom behavior, and how individual teacher efforts can be a part of schoolwide behavior management.	Elementary educators; may be useful for all grade levels	*Intervention in School and Clinic* is published by Pro-Ed, Inc. *isc.sagepub.com/cgi/pdf_extract/37/1/31*
Smith, R., & Lambert, M. (2008). Assuming the best. *Educational Leadership, 66*(1), 16-20.	With a strong emphasis on prevention and proactive classroom management, authors describe how assuming that students want to be in school, participate, and learn appropriate behavior underpins successful classroom management. The focus is on being positive and caring for students. Highly practical strategies presented include using volume, tone, and posture; implementing the 2-by-10 strategy; breaking things into small steps; using behavior rubrics; and using visuals.	K–12 educators	*Educational Leadership* is published by the Association for Supervision and Curriculum Development (ASCD). *www.ascd.org/publications/educational_leadership/sept08/vol66/num01/Assuming_the_Best.aspx*
Reinke, W., Lewis-Palmer, T., & Merrell, K. (2008). The classroom check-up: A classwide teacher consultation model for increasing praise and decreasing disruptive behavior. *School Psychology Review, 37*(3), 315–332.	Presents the classroom checkup (CCU), a classroom consultation model for improving teachers' classroom management skills, which consist of assessing the classroom, providing feedback, presenting a menu of intervention options, choosing an appropriate intervention, and self-monitoring of treatment integrity. Results of an evaluation study of the CCU are reported, indicating that use of the CCU paired with performance feedback resulted in improved teacher classroom management strategies (e.g., increased rates of total praise and behavior-specific praise and decreased use of reprimands), as well as reduced student disruptions.	K–12 educators (participants in study were elementary teachers)	*School Psychology Review* is published by the National Association of School Psychologists. *www.pubmedcentral.nih.gov/articlerender.fcgi?artid=2603055*

Bond, N. (2007). Questioning strategies that minimize classroom management problems. *Kappa Delta Pi Record, 44*(1), 18–21.	Provides 12 specific techniques for asking questions that teachers can use to minimize classroom problems and maximize student learning. Techniques are designed to reduce student dissatisfaction or boredom and clarify expectations for students to reduce problem behavior or classroom management problems. Examples of strategies include writing out some questions when planning the lesson, asking questions that are at the appropriate level for each student, providing students with sufficient wait time after asking a question and before responding to their comments, and varying the way students respond to questions.	K–12 educators	The *Kappa Delta Pi Record* is published by Kappa Delta Pi. *www.kdp.org/teachingresources/pdf/classrmmgmt/12_Questions_that_minimize_classrm_mgmt_problemsRecord_F07_Bond.pdf*
Parish, T., & Mahoney, S. (2006). Classrooms: How to turn them from battlegrounds to connecting places. *Education, 126*, 437–440.	Discusses things educators can do to create a more need-fulfilling classroom environment by connecting with students (rather than being tough, which doesn't work). Strategies that teachers can use to enhance student motivation (e.g., showing students they care and treating them with courtesy and kindness) are included, as well as things students can do to enhance their own motivation (e.g., treating classmates and teachers with respect, which will help students feel respected in return).	K–12 educators; particularly relevant for grades 4–12 and beyond	*Education* is published by Project Innovation, Inc. *www.highbeam.com/doc/1G1-145681735.html*
Simonsen, B., Fairbanks, S., Briesch, A., Myers, D., & Sugai, G. (2008). Evidence-based practices in classroom management: Considerations for research to practice. *Education and Treatment of Children, 31*, 351–380.	The authors report the findings of a comprehensive literature review in which they identified 20 evidence-based classroom management practices. These practices were grouped into five categories, including (1) maximizing structure (physical arrangement), (2) posting, teaching, reviewing, monitoring, and reinforcing expectations, (3) actively engaging students in observable ways, (4) using a continuum of strategies for responding to appropriate behaviors, and (5) using a continuum of strategies to respond to inappropriate behaviors. Suggestions for implementing and assessing these practices in the classroom are included.	K–12 educators	*Education and Treatment of Children* is published by West Virginia University Press. *muse.jhu.edu/login?uri=/journals/education_and_treatment_of_children/v031/31.3.simonsen.pdf*

CHAPTER 3

Instructional Delivery

In Chapter 2 we provided information on the necessary tools for creating a well-managed classroom, including resources to provide you with additional direction on the concepts presented. In Chapter 3 we focus on choosing and teaching curricular content in a way that maximizes student engagement. Student engagement is directly related to behavior (Brophy, 1986a, 1986b; Sutherland & Wright, in press), so it is the next logical step in promoting prosocial behavior and reducing undesirable behaviors that impede the instructional process. Students with high rates of engagement experience a host of positive outcomes. They tend to enjoy school more, persist at difficult tasks, have higher achievement, are less likely to drop out of school, and are more likely to continue with their education after high school (Greenwood, Horton, & Utley, 2002; Klem & Connell, 2004; Skinner & Belmont, 1993). When students are engaged in their work, they have less opportunity (and need) to display undesirable behaviors (Walker et al., 2004).

A number of researchers have examined the factors that contribute to student motivation and engagement in school. Although it is beyond the scope of this chapter to address all of these factors, in the pages that follow we highlight a few essential factors and provide teachers, administrators, other school-site personnel, and university instructors with resources to explore other factors (see Table 3.6 at the end of the chapter).

For example, Brophy's (1986b) review of the literature provided strong evidence that several factors influence student learning, some of which include (1) rapid pacing of instruction; (2) adequate ALT (see Chapter 2 for a definition); (3) providing students with feedback; and (4) active teaching, which includes modeling and systematic, focused presentation of concepts, as well as active supervision during learning activities. Newman (1991) suggested that student engagement is increased when students (1) have some autonomy over their learning, (2) are engaged in authentic tasks, (3) have opportunities to collaborate with their peers, and (4) can showcase their strengths.

Another critical factor is a teacher's ability to adjust instruction so that it is sensitive to the student's instructional level, making certain that it is neither too difficult nor too easy (Gickling & Armstrong, 1978; Skinner & Belmont, 1993; Umbreit et al., 2004). Learning experiences should be designed so that students can work in their zones of proximal development (Vygotsky, 1978). Students are optimally engaged when academic tasks are just slightly beyond what they can do on their own. A knowledgeable teacher designs learning experiences so that students can draw on their current skills as they work with the teacher or their peers to tackle new concepts or tasks. The teacher scaffolds instruction by providing students with sufficient individualized support and close guidance so that each student can learn new material without frustration (Vygotsky, 1978).

Behavior problems tend to occur when school work is either too easy, too difficult, or boring; in other words, when it is not in the student's zone of proximal development (Dunlap, Foster-Johnson, Clarke, Kern, & Childs, 1995; Gickling & Armstrong, 1978). When schoolwork is too easy, students do not need to pay attention or be involved with the task to learn the concept or complete the assignment. Similarly, when academic tasks are beyond a student's ability and he or she is not provided with scaffolding to access or approach the assignment, a student is apt to disengage from the work because he or she is frustrated. This sense of frustration can manifest in withdrawal or acting out (Colvin, 2004).

Similarly, boredom can be the result of inappropriately delivered content. For example, lengthy discussions or a lecture format are inappropriate for second graders, and having fifth graders learn about the water cycle solely by reading the textbook is ineffective. These activities are not sensitive to the students' learning needs, nor do they engage students' interest in the topic. In short, students will act out to get out of tasks that are not appropriate for their instructional level (Lane, 2007).

Teachers and school-site personnel (e.g., reading specialists) who choose appropriate curricula, deliver instruction so that it engages students, pace their lessons accurately, and offer choice and preferred activities and are able to create classrooms in which misbehavior is less likely to occur (Brophy, 1986a, 1986b). This chapter examines each of these approaches and provides examples of what it might look like in the classroom. It also provides information about instructional models that have been shown to increase student achievement.

CHOOSING APPROPRIATE CURRICULA

In most schools the grade-level curriculum is already determined. Each state offers standards that detail the specific content to be taught in kindergarten through 12th grade in each academic area. Standards are developed in conjunction with policy makers, textbook publishers, content-area experts, national curriculum associations (see Table 3.1), teachers, and parents, among others. Districts often produce their own curriculum guides based on state standards. Curriculum guides are an invaluable resource for teachers, administrators, and other school-site personnel; however, they represent just one step in determining how to approach instruction. Each teacher must make a variety of decisions about the best way to present content to his or her students.

As professionals, school-site personnel who deliver instruction should carefully consider several factors when planning instruction, including student skill

TABLE 3.1. Examples of Curriculum Standards from National Organizations

Organization	Standard	Description
National Council of Teachers of Mathematics *www.nctm.org*	Algebra standard for grades PreK–2	Understand patterns, relations, and functions: In prekindergarten through grade 2, all students should sort, classify, and order objects by size, number, and other properties.
National Council of Teachers of English *www.ncte.org*	English/language arts for grades K–12	Students apply knowledge of language structure, language conventions (e.g., spelling and punctuation), media techniques, figurative language, and genre to create, critique, and discuss print and nonprint texts.
National Center for History in the Schools *nchs.ucla.edu*	History standard for grades K–4	Understand selected attributes and historical developments of societies in Africa, the Americas, Asia, and Europe.
National Academies of Science *www.nationalacademies.org*	Physical science standard for grades 5–8	As a result of their activities in grades 5–8, all students should develop an understanding of properties and changes in properties of matter, motions and forces, and transfer of energy.
National Association for Sport and Physical Education *www.aahperd.org/Naspe*	Physical education standard for grades K–12	A physically educated student understands that physical activity provides opportunities for enjoyment, challenge, self-expression, and social interaction.
Consortium of National Arts Education Associations *artsedge.kennedy-center.org/teach/standards/contents.cfm*	Visual arts standard for grades 9–12	Students reflect on how artworks differ visually, spatially, temporally, and functionally and describe how these are related to history and culture.
Consortium of National Arts Education Associations */www.menc.org*	Music standard for grades K–4	Students sing independently, on pitch and in rhythm, with appropriate timbre, diction, and posture, and maintain a steady tempo.

Note. These are not federally mandated standards. Rather, these are voluntary standards created by national organizations to serve as guidelines for nationwide use.

and strategy level, readiness, prior knowledge, and interest. They must also give thought to the materials, space, and time available to devote to a topic. Additionally, teachers must reflect on their own skill levels in the content area, as well as in pedagogy. All of these factors shape the designated curriculum into the curriculum that students actually experience. So, although it may seem that teachers have limited decision-making power in choosing a curriculum, in reality they exert a huge influence on what is taught and what students access. To make effective curricular choices, teachers and others who deliver instruction need to be aware of this fact and to make informed, conscious decisions about how they manage content.

APPROACHING THE CURRICULUM

Simmons and Kame'enui (1996, p. 1) defined *curriculum design* as "the way information in a particular domain (e.g., social studies, science, reading, mathematics) is selected, prioritized, sequenced, organized, and scheduled for instruction within a highly orchestrated series of lessons and materials that make up a course of study." Related to curriculum design is *instructional design*, which consists of the activities and materials used to deliver the curriculum. One way to approach both curriculum and instructional design is to use the *big ideas* framework (Coyne Kame'enui, & Carnine, 2007; Simmons & Kame'enui, 1996). It consists of six concepts: (1) big ideas, (2) conspicuous strategies, (3) mediated scaffolding, (4) strategic integration, (5) judicious review, and (6) primed background knowledge (see Table 3.2). In the sections that follow, we describe each of these constructs. For those readers interested in learning more about these six concepts, we have included additional resources (see Table 3.6 later in the chapter).

Big ideas refers to the process of identifying the most important concepts and ideas in the content. These are the things that *all* students need to learn. For exam-

TABLE 3.2. Framework for Planning for Instruction

Concept	Definition
Big ideas	Identifying the most important curricular concepts that students need to learn and around which instruction will be planned.
Conspicuous strategies	Teaching students strategies that will help them learn the content.
Mediated scaffolding	Deciding on the types of support a student will need to master the task or assignment.
Strategic integration	Opportunities for students to use the target skill in other activities.
Judicious review	Opportunities for adequate and sustained practice of the concepts.
Primed background knowledge	Using students' prior knowledge as a springboard for new learning.

Note. Based on Coyne, Kame'enui, and Carnine (2007).

ple, if the topic is the American Revolution, you may decide that it is critical for all students to be able to identify the reasons the war was fought. You may also want them to know the names and dates of decisive battles, but that might be secondary to your selected big idea. This exercise in identifying the big ideas helps teachers decide how much time to devote to particular aspects of the curriculum. It is also essential in determining the instructional strategies you will use. Perhaps the class will watch a single video or view a PowerPoint presentation about the battles and corresponding dates, but learning about the reasons for the war may require students to be involved in several activities that necessitate the use of higher order thinking skills.

Some students find it easier to learn content if they are taught strategies for tackling the materials. Thinking about *conspicuous strategies* means that you will decide beforehand whether students would benefit from strategies instruction to help them learn the content they will encounter. Strategies instruction (which is described fully later on in this chapter) makes explicit the steps for learning or monitoring a task. For example, if students will be required to memorize specialized vocabulary, you may want to introduce the *keyword method*, an elaborated strategy for remembering vocabulary meanings (Uberti, Scruggs, & Mastropieri, 2003). Identifying prerequisite skills students will need is critical to making the material accessible. We should also point out that sometimes people confuse the terms *strategies instruction* and *instructional strategies*. Instructional strategies are a teacher's repertoire of effective practices. For example, teachers make use of a variety of instructional approaches, such as direct instruction, small-group instruction, lecture, and cooperative learning. Strategies instruction refers to specific techniques that can be taught to students to help them become independent, self-regulated learners, which we discuss later in this chapter.

Mediated scaffolding is the level of support a learner needs when embarking on a new learning task (Vygotsky, 1978). Of course, the intensity of support needed will vary depending on the skill level or readiness of the student. Some students will require greater assistance than others. At first a student may need substantial scaffolding, but as he or she begins to master the task, less assistance is necessary. The goal is to help students to become able to complete tasks independently and also to provide enough support so that they can learn skills and concepts without frustration. For example, identifying the beginning, middle, and end of a story is a common comprehension technique used with early readers. Initially students will require repeated modeling of the task. The teacher will read multiple stories and explicitly identify their beginnings, middles, and ends. Then she or he may show students how to use a graphic organizer (Kim, Vaughn, Wanzek, & Wei, 2004) to record the three parts of a story as they work in pairs. Subsequently students may practice the target skill by using the graphic organizer independently when reading a book. With sufficient modeling and practice, students will be able to identify the beginning, middle, and end of a story without any support at all (see Dixon-Krauss, 1996, for additional information on mediated scaffolding in literacy instruction).

Strategic integration helps students connect the task to other concepts, ideas, skills, or experiences. Making these connections helps students understand the material at a deeper level. For example, students may have been taught to identify story elements such as setting, characters, and plot. Asking students to compose a narrative with those elements provides strategic integration of the target skill into the complex skill of writing. As opposed to simply identifying the elements of a story, writing a narrative demands that students understand the elements at a higher level (see Harris, Graham, Mason, & Friedlander, 2008, for research-based information; see also *www.teachervision.fen.com*).

Students must be provided with ample time to practice newly learned material. However, simply having massed practice directly following the introduction of the material is not enough. Practice should consist of what Simmons and Kame'enui (1996) called *judicious review*. They suggest the following guidelines for providing practice opportunities: Opportunities for practice should be distributed over time and should be offered for relatively short periods of time with intervals between practice sessions (Bloom & Shuell, 1981; Jameson, McDonnell, Johnson, Riesen, & Polychronis, 2007). Target skills and concepts should be integrated into more complex tasks so that students can use them in a meaningful way and not just in rote practice. Practice should include diverse tasks so that students are required to demonstrate their understanding in various ways. Finally, practice opportunities should be generous enough that students can eventually perform tasks fluently, without hesitation (Hunter, 1976).

Primed background knowledge requires that teachers determine the related or prerequisite information students already have about a task or topic, as well as how students are able to tap into and use that information. Helping students use what they already know to understand new concepts and tasks increases their acquisition of novel material. However, students need different amounts of prompting to retrieve and take advantage of the relevant information they already possess. For example, students with learning disabilities often have difficulty with memory processes and may not spontaneously make connections between related concepts already in their repertoire (Stichter, Conroy, & Kauffman, 2008). Even students without disabilities will learn new material with varying degrees of skill. The previous example of teaching students to identify the beginning, middle, and end of a story also can be used to illustrate primed background knowledge. If students can identify parts of a narrative, then they can be *primed* to learn the new skill of summarizing, as the two tasks are related. The teacher reminds students of the skills or strategies they have already acquired, explains how they are related to the new skill or strategy, and then demonstrates how to summarize a story through modeling and providing examples. Intentionally reminding students of what they know and how it relates to the new task at hand ensures that students have made the connection rather than leaving it to chance. Some students may need brief reminders (prompts), whereas others will benefit from more elaborated explanations.

Simmons and Kame'enui (1996, p.11) made the following suggestions for priming background knowledge:

1. Identify essential preskills or background knowledge most proximal to the new task.
2. Once proximal tasks are identified, determine whether the background knowledge needs to be primed or taught.
3. Provide the priming necessary to elicit the correct information or ready the learner by focusing attention on a difficult task or component of a task.

Similar to the Simmons and Kame'enui model is the *planning pyramid* developed by Schumm, Vaughn, and Leavell (1994). This model helps teachers plan content for students with a diverse range of abilities and skills. Just as with the big-ideas framework, teachers must decide which content *all* students need to master. A three-tiered pyramid is used to represent this planning model (see Figure 3.1). The base of the pyramid is the material that a teacher identifies for all students to learn. Explicit instruction, adequate practice time, and a variety of activities are devoted to the base content to ensure that each student achieves the targeted skills and concepts.

The second tier of the pyramid identifies the content that *most* students will learn. The material may be extensions of the initial content or may be related con-

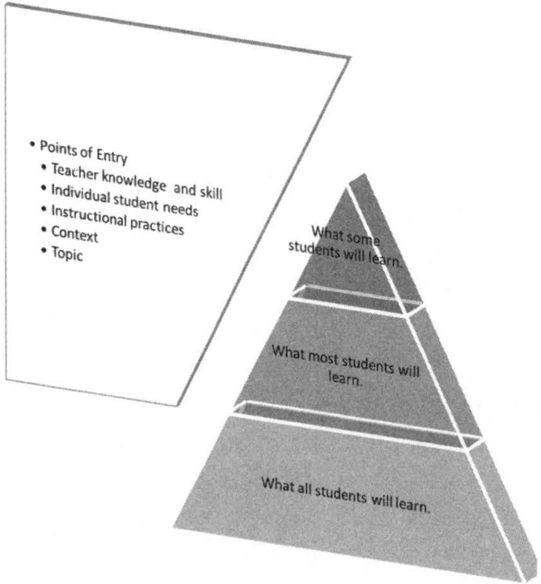

FIGURE 3.1. Planning pyramid. From Schumm, Vaughn, and Leavell (1994). Copyright 1994 by the International Reading Association. Reprinted by permission.

cepts. Less exposure to these ideas may be provided, and students are not required to learn them to mastery. The top level of the pyramid consists of supplementary material. Only a *few* students may be expected to acquire this content, and the least amount of time is devoted to it. For example, centers or independent activities are made available to students who are proficient in the content of the lower tiers or want to further explore the topics.

In addition to deciding which content to teach, the planning pyramid also encourages teachers to consider issues referred to as "points of entry" (Schumm et al., 1994, p. 612). Using a list of provided questions, teachers examine the curricular topic, their own teaching skill, available resources, the context (e.g., classroom environment, students' social skills), and instructional strategies. See Table 3.3 for the entire list of questions.

TABLE 3.3. Questions to Consider When Planning for Instruction

Domain	Planning questions
Teacher	• Have I taught this material before? • What prior knowledge do I have of this topic? • How interesting is the topic to me? • How much time do I have to plan the lesson or unit? • What resources do I have available for this lesson or unit?
Topic	• Is the material new or review? • What prior knowledge do students have of this topic? • How interesting is the topic to individual students? • How many new concepts are introduced? • How complex are the new concepts? • How clearly are concepts presented in the textbook? • When considering the overall curriculum, how important is this topic?
Context	• Will a language difference make comprehension of a particular concept difficult for a student? • Will students with reading difficulties be able to function independently in learning the concepts from text? • Will a student with behavior or attention problems be able to concentrate on the lesson? • Are there likely to be students with high interest in or prior knowledge of these concepts who would be anxious to explore the topic in greater breadth or depth or to share their knowledge with classmates? • Do my students have the vocabulary they need to understand the concepts to be taught?
Instructional practices	• What methods will I use to motivate students and to set a purpose for learning? • What grouping pattern is most appropriate? • What instructional strategies can I implement to promote learning for all students? • What textbook adaptations can I implement to assist individuals or subgroups of students? • What literacy processes must I teach to promote learning of content? • What learning strategies do my students know nor need to learn that will help them master these concepts? • How will I monitor students' learning on an ongoing, informal basis? • How will I assess student learning at the end of the lesson or unit?

Note. Adapted from Schumm, Vaughn, and Leavell (1994). Copyright 1994 by the International Reading Association. Adapted by permission.

These frameworks assist teachers and other school-site personnel who deliver instruction in thinking through the prescribed curricula in order to shape instruction in a way that best meets the needs of their particular students. Although the content is provided by the district and state, it is the teacher who uses his or her expertise in curriculum and instructional design to provide optimal learning opportunities so students achieve a high degree of understanding of that content. Most important, when the curriculum is thought through in a detailed and critical manner, it can be adjusted to meet the needs and strengths of a teacher's current students.

DIFFERENTIATING THE CURRICULUM

The big-ideas framework and the planning pyramid both provide structures to help teachers think through their content. Tomlinson's (2005) work on differentiation of curriculum includes related topics that will help teachers consider a variety of activities and instructional practices to adapt content to best meet students' needs. Although all students may be exposed to the same content, differentiation allows for variations in delivery of that content to match it to the learning preferences, skill levels, or interests of differing students. Although whole-group lessons can be an effective instructional practice, the majority of classroom learning time should not be devoted to whole-group, undifferentiated instruction. Undifferentiated instruction is unlikely to meet the needs of all students, as each will not be working in his or her individual zone of proximal development (Baker, Clark, Maier, & Viger, 2008). Consequently, the result is that students are less likely to be engaged, a situation that is associated with lower levels of academic achievement (Sutherland & Wright, in press; Urdan & Schoenfelder, 2006).

To differentiate instruction for students, teachers make choices about three parts of the educational process: the content, the way students learn the content, and the product, or the ways in which students demonstrate understanding of the content. Offering multiple approaches to each of these elements is at the heart of differentiation. Next we discuss how to differentiate curriculum using the three elements as a guide (for a full explanation of differentiation, see Tomlinson, 2005, and Tomlinson & McTighe, 2005).

Content

A teacher's first consideration is *what* to teach. Tomlinson offers several approaches to deciding which parts of the curriculum to focus on. The first is called *concept-based teaching*. Rather than thinking about content as *covering* a multitude of facts, such as definitions, dates, events, and vocabulary, a teacher can use critical concepts and principles to guide student learning. For example, one of the history/social science standards for California's fourth graders is to "understand the structures, functions, and powers of the local, state, and federal governments as described in the U.S. Constitution" (California Department of Education, 2000). *Covering* this material might mean that a teacher has students learn what is in the text of the U.S. Constitution and that they are able to list the shared powers of the federal, state, and local governments. But an activity that takes a conceptual view would have students learn how different states' laws are shaped by their local histories. For example, students could learn about states that enacted Jim Crow laws to legalize the separation of blacks and whites, the subsequent court case to abolish school segregation, and the role of the Civil Rights Act of 1964 and the Voting Rights Act of 1965 in eradicating Jim Crow laws. This topic examines the fourth-grade standard by looking at the tension between state and federal rights and the role of the judicial, legislative, and executive branches in negotiating those respective rights.

Conceptualizing the content this way allows for a deeper understanding that is more likely to be remembered in comparison to subject matter learned in a rote fashion. A rich and complex consideration of curriculum also allows for a wide range of differentiation. A differentiated curriculum provides the opportunity to study ideas and events as diverse as current-day restrictions on voting, the heroism of Rosa Parks, or the anti-Chinese legislation of California in the late 1800s. Seeing history and specific topics as dynamic and complicated makes the curriculum engaging and more likely to be of interest to students than if they are taught history as dry facts divorced from the lived experience of real people. Subsequently, more students are able to take in and retain the material presented (Gersten, Baker, Smith-Johnson, Dimino, & Peterson, 2006).

In addition to content standards for history, California also specifies that students are able to demonstrate *analysis skills*. A concept-based approach allows teachers to be more efficient because they can address several standards at once. For example, the Jim Crow topic teaches the content standard and also requires students to use skills that address the following analysis skill: "Students explain the central issues and problems from the past, placing people and events in a matrix of time and place" (California Department of Education, 2000, p. 22).

Another approach to differentiating the content is called *curriculum compacting* (Reis & Renzulli, 1992). Students who may have considerable knowledge of or exposure to a topic are excellent candidates for this strategy. First, teachers assess a student's knowledge about the subject to be studied. If a student has mastered an area of the curriculum that is going to be presented as a whole-group lesson, then the student is excused from that activity. Instead, the teacher will decide which of the yet-to-be-learned concepts or skills the student should focus on. That information is then used to design a learning plan that the student will engage in while other students are participating in the whole-group lessons. By discovering areas of inconsistency or incompleteness in students' knowledge, teachers may be able to provoke curiosity in the topic (Lepper, 1988) and allow students to go above and beyond what they already know. In some instances a student may work independently or in a small group, but in other cases the student may join another teacher's class to access information. Providing students with opportunities for a deeper rather than a wider understanding of content may be one way to keep especially knowledgeable students motivated and engaged. It is also important to consider students' behavioral patterns as well when differentiating instruction (Kalberg, Lane, & Menzies, 2009). For example, if the behavior screening data that are collected as part of regular school practices (e.g., the Strengths and Difficulties Questionnaire; Goodman, 1997) suggests that a student has a high level of hyperactivity, then that student may also need a self-monitoring intervention (see Chapter 6 in this volume) to help him or her stay focused on this more differentiated learning opportunity.

Although Tomlinson (2005) offers several suggestions for differentiating content (see Table 3.4), the last illustration we present here is the use of *mini-lessons* (Tomlinson, 2005, p. 76). Mini-lessons are an important vehicle for reteaching skills or concepts to students who need additional time to fully understand or master them. After whole-group instruction on a topic, students should be assessed to see who would benefit from additional instruction. Because not all students will require reteaching, mini-lessons provide an opportunity for more intensive instruction. Lessons are tailored to student needs and delivered in a small-group or one-on-one format. Furthermore, students who do not require additional instruction on the topic then have the opportunity to pursue an activity matched to their interest or readiness level. For struggling students who often lack the intrinsic motivation necessary to navigate tasks or topics that appear too difficult (Stipek, 1993), mini-lessons provide the necessary help they need to avoid frustration and the desire to give up.

TABLE 3.4. Content Differentiation Techniques

Technique	Description
Concept-based teaching	Using critical curricular concepts and principles to guide planning.
Curriculum compacting	Using assessment data to excuse students from previously learned content and to design activities to access new concepts.
Using varied materials	Planning instruction with a wide variety of materials in mind, including media, computer applications, video, magazines, texts, audio files, and field trips.
Learning contracts	Students create a plan that indicates what they will study and how they will tackle the content. Student and teacher discuss the plan together to reach agreement on its goals and activities.
Mini-lessons	Development of short, focused lessons for reteaching or enrichment.
Varied support systems	Use of a variety of supports such as graphic organizers, advance organizers, peer buddies, adult mentors, reading partners, highlighting of important text, and study sheets.

Note. Based on Tomlinson (2005).

Process

In addition to addressing content, teachers must also examine the instructional activities they provide for students. The instructional process is what Tomlinson (2005, p. 79) refers to as a "sense-making activity." These are the instructional events a teacher plans so that students can learn or *make sense of* material. In many classrooms, all students engage in the same type of process. For example, the teacher may have taught a lesson on double-digit multiplication and then had all students complete 10 practice problems. However, differentiating the process based on students' learning preferences, skill levels, or interests involves choosing from a rich array of process activities (see Figure 3.2). Some examples include a "hands-on" activity in which students use manipulatives to represent written multiplication problems, a cooperative group activity in which students work together to create a "cheat sheet" on how to approach a double-digit multiplication problem, or the use of computer software to practice the newly introduced algorithm. Incorporating different process activities into the curriculum provides additional opportunities for students to make sense of the content.

Teachers can offer the richness of process activities either simultaneously or sequentially. Simultaneous-process activities involve providing several options that are available at the same time for students. In a classroom this would be a mix of centers, independent activities, and small-group work during a class period. Providing sequential-process activities means that all students are involved in the same activity, but more than one activity is planned so that all students experience several ways of processing the content.

In addition to differentiation based on interest or learning preference, skill level is also an important consideration. Students are unlikely to engage in activities they deem as too easy or too difficult (Gickling & Armstrong, 1978; Stipek, 1993; Umbreit et al., 2004). Although Stipek termed this the *principle of optimal challenge*, it is similar to Vygotsky's (1978) zone of proximal development, with the implications for practice being the same. Students learn best when they work just beyond their current level of achievement; essentially, when they are stretched (but not too stretched). Most teachers will acknowledge, however, that differentiating instruction based on skill level for a classroom of 30 students is no easy task. This

- Cooperative learning groups
- Computer-assisted instruction
- Learning centers
- Writing activities
- Creation of graphic organizers

FIGURE 3.2. Examples of process activities.

requires teachers to really know their students' abilities. By familiarizing themselves with the previous year's curriculum, talking to students' prior teachers, and administering both formal and informal preassessments, teachers and other individuals who deliver instruction (e.g., paraprofessionals, guidance counselors, and librarians) can obtain the knowledge necessary to differentiate based on skill level. This knowledge should be used to provide students with activities within their zones of proximal development. For example, students with no prior knowledge about a topic may need to focus on knowledge- or comprehension-related activities (e.g., naming, describing, outlining, predicting). A moderately knowledgeable student may be better suited for application- or analysis-related activities (e.g., solving, constructing, classifying, comparing, investigating), whereas a student who has already mastered a topic is likely ready for synthesis or evaluation activities (e.g., inventing, proposing, judging, recommending, debating).

Differentiating process activities based on students' skill levels, interests, or learning preferences enhances a teacher's ability to engage students in their academic work. In turn, it promotes student learning and achievement. Students who are provided with opportunities to participate in activities that are of interest to them and that offer a moderate challenge will likely experience a greater intrinsic desire to learn (Stipek, 1993)—the ultimate goal.

Product

A *product* is the tangible evidence of a student's understanding of a topic, skill, or concept. It is the concrete representation of what he or she knows. Products are not simply the final activity at the end of a unit. Rather, they are a mechanism to help students engage with the material in a complex and multifaceted manner. Teachers should assign products that provide opportunities for students to think deeply about the target skill or concept. Using products also offers an extended time line for students to work with material in a way that regular class assignments do not. Based on our own experiences in the classroom, these products often become a source of pride for students, and they are eager to see them displayed and shared (see Figure 3.3 for a list of suggested products).

- PowerPoint presentation
- Theater production
- Readers' Theatre performance
- Models
- Demonstration
- Essay
- Research paper
- Experiment
- Brochure
- Simulation
- Painting/drawing
- Musical performance
- Dance performance
- Game creation

FIGURE 3.3. Examples of products.

Differentiation of products is probably the easiest of the three elements (content, process, and product) to implement. However, too often *all* students are expected to complete the *exact* same product. And, oftentimes, such products are assigned as homework (e.g., making a model of a California Mission building; as former elementary teachers in California, two of the authors [K. L. L., H. M. M.] have seen hundreds of model Mission buildings). By using some basic guidelines, teachers can make it easier for students to choose how they would like to represent their knowledge, feel confident that all students are engaged, and still keep planning and task completion manageable. First, teachers must decide the central expectations or standards that students must address in their products: What are the facts, concepts, or skills to be demonstrated? Second, the required elements of a product should be delineated. For example, if the product is a PowerPoint presentation, it may need to include an introductory slide, references, and photos, in addition to the core content it covers. Providing structure will help students create better products and learn from and enjoy the experience more. Essentially, choice is important: Allow students to select the method by which they will "show what they know." It is also possible to allow students the option of choosing the sequence of tasks to be completed, a strategy that has been effective in reducing problem behaviors within the classroom setting (Kern, Mantegna, Vorndran, Bailin, & Hilt, 2001).

Another way to offer structure is to support students in expanding their ideas and skills. Tomlinson (2005) suggested holding brainstorming sessions to generate ideas, or workshops to instruct students in skills they may need (e.g., researching in the library). Students will also benefit from time lines and grading guidelines (e.g., rubrics). As with content and process, differentiation of products is a valuable tool for meeting the interests, learning preferences, and skill levels of a variety of students.

We realize that teachers cannot differentiate *all* content, processes, or products, and certainly not all of the time. Yet increasing one's repertoire of curricular and instructional skills is an important step in fostering high levels of student engagement. Next, we look at some research-based, specific instructional practices that are effective methods of delivering content. We encourage you, as a good teacher, to use a mix of these strategies and to use them contingent on both the unique demands of the content and the needs of your students.

INSTRUCTIONAL DELIVERY MODELS

Teachers have many choices when deciding how to present the curriculum to students. The previous discussion on how to differentiate curriculum encouraged you to consider content in a way that allows the various needs, interests, and readiness levels of students to be addressed. This is a critical process, as some instructional delivery practices are more effective with certain students or with a particular content, and they can even be more or less effective depending on the time of day.

Some teaching practices may be good for introducing new material (e.g., explicit teacher-directed instruction), whereas the use of cooperative groups may be better suited to enhancing depth of understanding. In this section, we discuss instructional practices that result in higher academic achievement. We begin with those that are predominately teacher-led and then discuss more student-centered practices. As always, the focus is on maximizing student engagement to reduce problem behaviors and increase achievement.

Direct and Explicit Instruction

Direct instruction conjures up pictures of students sitting passively at their desks while the teacher talks on and on and on. However, lecture or other teacher-dominated instruction is erroneously assumed to be direct instruction when, in fact, it is not. There are two types of direct instruction. One has its roots in specialized, focused curricula developed for students with special needs. This is usually referred to as *Direct Instruction* with a capital *D* and a capital *I* (Kinder & Carnine, 1991). The second type of direct instruction is what would more accurately be called *explicit instruction* (Miller, 2008). One example of explicit instruction is Madeline Hunter's work on lesson design (Hunter, 1976), an instructional model with seven components: (1) objectives, (2) standards, (3) anticipatory set, (4) teaching (e.g., input, modeling, checking for understanding), (5) guided practice/monitoring, (6) closure, and (7) independent practice. Although we do not follow Hunter's exact model, our discussion of explicit instruction is closely related.

Explicit instruction is highly organized and teacher directed, and it provides a step-by-step sequence for teaching content. It requires careful planning and includes six procedures: (1) introduction of an advance organizer, (2) instruction and modeling of the target skill or concept, (3) opportunities for guided practice, (4) opportunities for independent practice, (5) the use of a postorganizer, and (6) assessment of the skill or concept acquisition (see Figure 3.4). An in-depth explanation of each of these elements follows.

Advance organizers are used to help students understand the purpose of lessons and how they are related to what they already know. Advance organizers provide a way to tap into students' prior knowledge to provide scaffolding for the content.

- Use of an advance organizer
- Instruction and modeling of the target skill or concept
- Opportunities for guided practice
- Opportunities for independent practice
- Use of a postorganizer
- Assessment of skill or concept acquisition

FIGURE 3.4. Elements of explicit instruction.

There are several ways to provide students with an advance organizer. In the most simple form, an advance organizer involves verbally stating the objective of a lesson and briefly informing students of how they will learn the new material. A more sophisticated organizer would connect the new lesson to a previous one and explain how it is related to what was learned before. Providing an explanation of *why* students will engage in a lesson is also a type of advance organizer. Students process information better when teachers provide some background or explanation for the activities and instruction students are expected to participate in (Hartley & Davies, 1976). The type of organizer used (e.g., verbal, graphic) and the time devoted to it will depend on the content, its complexity, and students' previous exposure to it. Not only do advance organizers provide a context for lessons, but they also increase student interest and engagement (Ausubel, 2000).

After beginning lessons with an advance organizer, teachers should introduce the *target skill or concept* step by step. This is a structured and extremely detailed approach to teaching the material. In addition to clearly delineating each step for students, it is necessary to accompany the explanation with an illustration or to model the process so students can see exactly what each step looks like. Pairing the verbal explanation with a demonstration is much more effective than relying on a verbal explanation alone. Teachers should use an overhead projector, liquid crystal display (LCD), or interactive whiteboard when modeling or demonstrating, rather than standing with their backs to students as they write on the whiteboard or blackboard. This makes it possible to see whether students are on task and understand the lesson. Standing at a board facing away from students makes it difficult to spot and proactively address behavior problems.

When introducing and modeling new skills or concepts, teachers should make use of *think-alouds*. In a think-aloud, a teacher verbalizes thoughts about the learning process—especially thoughts students themselves are likely to have as they tackle novel material. In this way the metacognitive processes involved in learning something new can be explicitly taught. For example, when showing students how to get ready to write an essay, the teacher might say, "I know the first step in writing is to think about what I want to say, so I'll just brainstorm some of my ideas and write them down." The teacher would next model by writing ideas down on the overhead, thinking out loud as she or he arrives at each one at them. This is also referred to as cognitive modeling, a process by which the teacher verbalizes the thoughts that he or she or has in relationship to the task at hand. Cognitive modeling is most beneficial when the cognition (thoughts) and behavior (writing) are modeled together during the actual task rather than presenting the cognitive component *after* the behavior (e.g., "Here is what I was thinking when I had trouble figuring out what to write"; Graham & Harris, 2005).

The next procedure for providing explicit instruction is *guided practice*, or providing students opportunities to perform tasks under the teacher's supervision. Guided practice allows teachers to correct student errors and offer prompts and reminders of how to complete the task. Guided practice is an example of scaffolding, as it makes the teacher or more experienced peer available to offer support to students as they learn how to perform tasks on their own. In the beginning students may need a substantial amount of support. Guided practice with decreasing support should continue until students can complete the task independently. It is important to provide sufficient time for guided practice so that students can learn the skill correctly and develop confidence in their ability to perform it independently.

Independent practice gives students the chance to become more fluent and accurate in completing tasks or understanding concepts. Once they have had sufficient guided practice and demonstrated mastery over a topic or skill, independent practice should be used to develop automaticity and promote a high level of accuracy in the target area. The teacher or other school-site instructors will need to decide on the criterion level for demonstrating independence. Typically, this ranges from 95 to 100% accuracy. After students have demonstrated the required level of accuracy when completing the task, they can move on to increasing speed or fluency.

Postorganizers wrap up lessons or units for students. In the busy day-to-day routines of the classroom, it can be easy to omit a postorganizer, but providing one helps bring closure to lessons. Postorganizers provide a schema for the entire learning sequence. They can be a simple verbal reminder of what students have learned, why it is important, how they will use the information in the future, and how it may be connected to future learning. Furthermore, including such a closing activity also provides structure to the learning process, which also supports positive behavior during instruction (Walker et al., 2004).

Assessment is not necessarily the final element of explicit instruction because it should be integrated throughout. Short, informal assessments are critical tools for providing formative information that helps teachers decide how to adjust instruction for effective learning. It is unproductive to get to the end of an instructional unit and then find that students have not mastered the essential concepts. *Progress monitoring* is a type of curriculum-based assessment that provides frequent information about a student's progress derived from short probes. It is used predominately in the areas of early reading (Wayman, Wallace, Wiley, Ticha, & Espin, 2007) and mathematics (Foegen, Jiban, & Deno, 2007). In Chapter 8 we provide information on different types of curriculum-based academic measures, such as Dynamic Indicators of Basic Early Literacy Skills (DIBELS; Good, Gruba, & Kaminski, 2002) or AIMSweb, that you might want to adopt for use in your classroom if your district or school has not yet institutionalized such procedures to monitor student progress.

Although a strict progress monitoring program based on the principles of curriculum-based measurement (CBM; see Deno, 2003) is unnecessary for all content, such programs can be adapted into a useful assessment tool for any subject matter. Basically, progress monitoring uses brief, sensitive probes directly linked to the curriculum to gauge student understanding of the concept. With this information, areas of weakness that require reteaching or additional practice time can be identified. Because the assessments are administered throughout the learning sequence, the teacher knows immediately and consistently which students are having difficulty with particular elements of the unit or lesson and can adjust instruction accordingly.

Explicit instruction is an effective strategy for teaching specific skills. In particular, it is useful when the skills are complicated or need to be learned in a precise sequence. However, explicit instruction should be just one of several models of teaching used to deliver content. Next, we discuss two other powerful instructional models: strategies instruction and cooperative learning. These models can be used to promote achievement and maintain student interest in learning, which will facilitate engagement and prevent disruption.

Cooperative Learning

When structured correctly, cooperative learning is one of the most engaging, productive forms of instruction (Johnson & Johnson, 1999). It provides a setting in which students can think about, verbalize, and then refine their ideas about a topic through interactions with their peers. It maximizes the time that students are actively involved in learning and minimizes passivity. Cooperative learning can also counteract the implicit (and sometimes explicit) competitiveness that pits students against each other in many classrooms. A competitive approach to learning creates a situation in which some students will never be able to win. An overly competitive classroom ensures that a certain number of students will not want to participate and can lead to behavior problems. Very few of us persist in activities in which we are unlikely to succeed, so it is no surprise that students would not want to, either. Teachers, administrators, and other school-site personnel should be aware that even something as seemingly straightforward as asking who knows the answer to a particular question can promote a competitive environment. Some students are more likely than others to know the answer and are more likely to be called on, and consequently they will receive a disproportionate amount of positive attention. Instead, discussion questions are posed to each group or to dyads; then all students have the opportunity to talk about the answer. Thus *all* students engage in the material.

There are many different types of cooperative learning structures or activities that teachers can use (see Table 3.5 for a partial list). However, three important elements characterize all types of cooperative learning. These include (1) group goals, (2) individual accountability, and (3) interpersonal and small-group skills. We discuss each of these and then introduce Jigsaw II, a versatile cooperative learning activity (see Slavin's [1995] seminal text for a detailed look at cooperative learning).

Cooperative learning is premised on establishing group goals that all group members must work toward. In achieving those goals, the group depends on the contribution and participation of everyone. This promotes prosocial norms for both

TABLE 3.5. Cooperative Learning Activities

Activity	Description
Jigsaw II	This popular cooperative learning activity is good for narrative material from which concepts rather than discrete skills are to be learned. The teacher provides the designated assignment. Students leave their original teams to go work in expert teams to learn portions of the assignment in depth. They return to their original teams, and each member then teaches the entire team the portion of work in which he or she is an expert. In this way, the entire group learns all of the different sections of the original assignment.
Team product	Teams work together to produce a specific product such as a learning center, a PowerPoint presentation, a performance, a worksheet, etc. To increase accountability, all group members should be responsible for a specific tasks as well as for the final product.
Think–pair–share	This informal method of cooperative learning pairs students in advance. During instruction they will be asked to *think* of an answer on their own, *pair* with their partners to discuss their answers, and then *share* their consensus with the rest of the class.
Numbered heads together	This is another informal method of cooperative learning that can be used with other modes of instruction. Groups are previously assigned so students know who to confer with when given directions to do so. During a lesson the teacher can say, "Consult with your group," and the students will talk together. They know that the teacher expects that all group members will have discussed the question and arrived at an answer. The teacher will call on only one representative for the group to provide the answer, so all members must be ready.
Student teams—achievement divisions (STAD)	This form of cooperative learning includes class presentations, teams, quizzes, individual improvement scores, and team recognition. The teacher presents the material in a lecture or presentation format, and then heterogeneous student teams work together to learn the material. Achievement is tracked through individual quiz scores. The team is motivated to ensure that each team member earns high scores so that the entire team wins recognition.
Teams–games–tournaments (TGT)	TGT is similar to STAD, but instead of quizzes, academic tournaments are held during which each individual team member represents his or her entire team in a different challenge. This encourages the team to prepare all members so that that their team will earn the most points.

Note. Based on Slavin (1995).

over- and underachieving students. Because individual success is tied to group success, the stigma of being a "brainiac" is reduced, while at the same time students who are low achievers are more likely to be supported than scorned. Rather than the teacher providing reinforcers such as praise or grades, peers reinforce each other as they work toward a mutual goal.

Group goals do not simply promote positive norms; they also stimulate intellectual growth. The use of cooperative groups is another way to optimize students' ability to learn in their zones of proximal development (Vygotsky, 1978). Rarely can a teacher interact with every student on a given task in the space of a lesson, but cooperative activities allow for a greater number of students to be engaged and to work with more experienced peers. For students who are more knowledgeable, interactive group work gives them the chance to elaborate their understanding of skills or concepts as they lead those with less expertise. Research has demonstrated that cooperative learning increases achievement for both low and high achievers (Sharan et al., 1984).

Individual accountability is another critical element for effective cooperative learning. If every student in the group is not held accountable for some portion of the work, some students will feel resentful, as they are left with an unfair amount of work. Further, some students will not adequately learn the designated material. Accountability ensures that all students participate equally. This does not mean that all students have to do the same thing; most likely they will have ownership of different tasks. But it does mean that all students have commensurate responsibilities. It is the teacher's duty to design cooperative learning activities so that each student is assigned a specific task that leads to the group's goal and on which he or she will be evaluated. For example, in a history class students may stage a performance of a historical event. Some students may do the initial research, others may write the script, and some may perform. Group goals and individual accountability work in tandem to create the incentive for all students to work collaboratively and help one another.

The final critical element for successful cooperative learning is to determine whether students have the prerequisite social skills for engaging in small-group work (Gresham, 2002c). If not, effective skills for working together must be taught. In all cases the expectations for behavior should be reviewed. Students should be taught or reminded how to listen carefully to one another's ideas, how to provide feedback in a respectful way, and how to ask for clarification. Additionally, students should know how to self-monitor their level of participation to be sure that they are neither dominating the activity nor contributing insufficiently.

Types of Cooperative Learning Activities

Different cooperative learning activities can be chosen depending on the purpose of the lesson. Some are designed to have students review a lesson that was first introduced by the teacher, whereas others can be used to have students specialize in a particular aspect of a topic and then work together to share their collective information. Some cooperative learning activities are designed for specific content areas, such as the cooperative integrated reading and composition (Stevens, Madden, Slavin, & Farnish, 1987) and team accelerated instruction in mathematics (Slavin & Karweit, 1985) models.

Jigsaw II (Slavin, 1986) is a popular cooperative learning activity that can be used to help students tackle written material. It is better suited for use when students need to acquire or review broader concepts rather than learning specific skills. Students work in heterogeneous groups in which each student is assigned a portion of the text or topic to be covered. Using graphic organizers to help guide them, each team member reviews his or her assigned material and records (and learns) the pertinent information. Students then meet with their *expert* teams, composed of students who were each assigned the same material. The expert groups discuss their shared understanding of the material and record additional notes as necessary. Then expert members meet with their original groups and each student teaches the novel information he or she learned to the rest of the group. Students can then be assessed on the material, and the scores that each group member receives contribute to a team score. This builds incentive for students to be sure that all team members learn the material well enough to perform adequately on the assessment.

Cooperative learning has a positive impact on many student and classroom variables, including self-esteem, social dynamics, students' locus of control, on-task behavior, altruism, perspective taking, and, of course, academic growth (Slavin, 1995). It is a dynamic, active form of learning that encourages students to participate positively in the classroom community. As a result, cooperative learning is an effective strategy for promoting student engagement and minimizing misbehavior.

Strategies Instruction

Another instructional practice that results in high academic achievement and that supports behaviors that facilitate the instructional process is strategies instruction. As you may recall from your high school and college days, a strategy is a tool, plan, or technique that you use to accomplish a task, solve a problem, or engage in other self-determined behaviors (Wehmeyer & Field, 2007). For example, if your instructor or administrator assigned you this book to read, you might (1) set goals regarding the number of pages or sections that you will read each day, (2) develop a system for monitoring your progress on these daily goals, (3) construct mnemonics to remember some of the information covered, and (4) develop a plan to reinforce yourself when you master the overall goals of completing the book and learning some new instructional strategies. Strategies instruction is the process by which you teach students about strategies (Harris et al., 2008). This includes how to and when to use specific strategies, determining which strategies work best for the students as learners, and incorporating strategies as part of their everyday learning activities. Some learners will learn such strategies with less explicit instruction (e.g., by watching their parents, teachers, and peers take on and accomplish new tasks). Other learners (particularly those who struggle academically, behaviorally, or socially) may require more explicit strategies instruction. Although many administrators, teachers, and other school-site personnel are concerned about adding new instructional topics to the school day, taking time for strategies instruction is well worth the investment.

Providing students with the tools to monitor their own learning and teaching them specific strategies for tackling various activities can promote academic achievement, as well as a sense of self-control and increased feelings of self-efficacy

(Schunk, 1985). Students are also more independent and self-directed when they know strategies that they can employ when faced with a task. This means that they do not have to wait for the teacher to assist them, which minimizes dependence on the teacher and maximizes participation in class activities.

There are strategies that can be used to improve writing (Harris et al., 2008), reading comprehension (Pressley, Johnson, Symons, McGoldrick, & Kurita, 1989), vocabulary (Beck, McKeown, & Kucan, 2002), mathematics (Jitendra, 2002), assignment completion, and even behavior (Menzies, Lane, & Lee, 2009). One critical aspect of teaching a strategy is to use an explicit instruction model when first introducing new skills. Step-by-step instruction in the strategy (including the use of cognitive modeling) is essential, followed by guided and independent practice until students are fluent. The strategy must be nearly effortless to ensure that students can use it to learn other concepts or complete assigned tasks. Next, we provide an example of how to use strategy instruction in writing.

Self-regulated strategy development (SRSD; Santangelo, Harris, & Graham, 2008) is a teaching process that addresses strategies for writing composition as well as strategies for self-regulation. It has been shown to improve the writing abilities of students in grades 2–12 (Graham, 2006; Graham & Perin, 2007; Lane, Harris, et al., 2008) by helping them plan, compose, critique, and revise their written work. The teacher first evaluates which strategy would be most effective to have the student use. For example, young students might be taught a general method such as POW (Pick my idea, Organize my notes, Write and say more) or WWW What = 2 How = 2 for story writing (Tracy, Reid, & Graham, 2009), whereas upper-grade students may benefit from specific instruction in writing reports (MacArthur, Schwartz, Graham, Molloy, & Harris, 1996). Other types of strategies include persuasive writing (Little et al., 2010) and revising expository text (De La Paz & Graham, 2002). Regardless of the specific strategy targeted, the SRSD process is highly flexible, consisting of six recursive stages that can be used to introduce and develop writing and self-regulation knowledge and strategies (Sandmel et al., 2009; Santangelo et al., 2008). Before introducing these strategies, we emphasize that these steps are not linear as they are in the direct instruction process. Furthermore, they are not time based. The teacher or person delivering the instruction subscribes to a criterion-based focus, devoting the necessary time to master each stage. To this end, a teacher can revisit previously taught stages with the frequency and intensity needed to ensure mastery. It is quite possible that one or more days will be devoted to each instructional stage depending on how students respond.

The first stage is to *assess and develop students' background knowledge*. It is important to determine which skills students already have and what they know about the topic. For example, with report writing, the teacher might lead students in a discussion of what report writing is, how it differs from other types of writing, and why they are going to learn how to use it.

The next stage is to *discuss the strategy*. This stage motivates students to want to learn and use the new strategy. The teacher prompts a discussion of students' perceptions of their existing writing processes. The strategy is then introduced as a tool students can use to improve or refine their writing performance. Then the purpose and steps of the strategy are explained.

In the third stage of SRSD, the teacher explicitly *models use of the strategy.* As discussed previously in this chapter regarding explicit instruction, think-alouds and cognitive modeling are effective in helping students understand the strategy. The think-aloud can address the *why* and *how* of the strategy's implementation. Cognitive modeling introduces the cognitive (occurring thoughts) and behavioral (writing) tasks in real time and in tandem so that the student can see the instructor's thoughts ("Man, I am having trouble finding the right word to show how this character is feeling! But, I am going use the word *confused* for right now and just keep on going with the story") in conjunction with the behavior (writing the sentence, "Katie Lane was confused by the fact that her chocolate chip cookie was missing from her lunch box"). Students should also be encouraged to discuss the strategy and to identify how they might adapt it to make it most effective for their own use. Students should also set goals (Santangelo et al., 2008) by identifying specific areas in which they would like to improve. It is important for teachers to be involved in the goal-setting process, making certain that the goals contain three properties: specificity, difficulty, and proximity (Harris et al., 2008). Specifically, the students' goals should include (1) an explicit statement of what is required for the task (specificity); (2) a reasonable level of difficulty so that the goal is neither too easy nor too hard (difficulty); and (3) a time frame for completion that is not in the too distant future (proximity; see Harris et al., 2008, p. 34 for additional information). Once goals are established, students can self-assess their progress toward the goal as they use the new strategy. As we mentioned, it is likely that some stages—particularly this third stage—may require more than 1 day of instruction. We again emphasize that multiple demonstrations based on the students' instructional needs and corresponding progress can and should be provided. Understanding each stage of the strategy is critical for students' subsequent ability to use it.

Next, students must *memorize the strategy.* To use the strategy independently, students need to be able to remember each of its steps. This process of memorizing the strategy steps actually begins in the first stage, when the strategy is introduced. Students can be taught a mnemonic, with emphasis placed on the meaning and importance of each step. If a particular student has difficulty with memorization, he or she can be given a cue card. While students memorize the strategy, they should be given multiple opportunities to *use the strategy with teacher support* (*Support it*) and supervision. This provides the scaffolding necessary for students to become proficient with the strategy.

The final stage is *independent use* of the strategy. Students should also be encouraged to think of other settings or academic tasks in which the strategy can be used.

Writing is one of the most difficult school-related tasks for students. Teaching specific writing strategies using the SRSD framework empowers students to be successful, independent, and autonomous. These are characteristics that promote student engagement and decrease behavior problems. The same is true in other content areas. Once students have the strategies (and the resulting self-confidence), they can tackle the assigned academic task. They can remain more engaged and be more productive in their work (Wehmeyer & Field, 2007).

OTHER CONSIDERATIONS

In this chapter, we offered a variety of approaches for examining curricula and designing instruction. A final issue related to instruction that contributes to teacher effectiveness (and subsequently to student achievement) is evaluating teaching practices to determine whether instruction is presented as an integrated whole that provides an optimal experience for students. Based on our experiences as teacher trainers and mentor teachers, we have learned that teachers can have all the individual elements right but that orchestration of them can distinguish excellent teachers from those who are merely adequate.

Once a teacher has made decisions about the content, considered instructional approaches, and designed the necessary lessons, he or she must also monitor and assess how that instruction is offered. First, do all students have the prerequisite skills or strategies needed before encountering the new content? Perhaps some or all students need a booster or more intensive instruction on a particular skill or topic. Second, is there an appropriate mix of direct instruction, group work, and independent work planned? Will students have adequate practice time to master the skills?

Before delivering any lesson, it is essential that teachers secure students' attention prior to giving instruction and check their understanding of the task before they are asked to begin the lesson. One classwide strategy is to give each student a ring with three colors of cards: green, yellow, and red. After explaining the task, the teacher can check for understanding by calling on individual students and then ask all students to arrange their cards to indicate their level of understanding. If a student places a green card on top, this is an indication that he or she is ready to begin (go) the task. A yellow card on top indicates that the student has a few questions but can get started. A red card on top indicates that the student is stopped and cannot begin the task without further instruction. After students have arranged their cards, teachers can take a quick scan of the classroom to see which students (those with red) need assistance right away. Also, if the majority of the class have placed a yellow or a red card on top, this is a signal to the teacher that the directions were not clear and that it is necessary to clarify the lesson with the whole class (see Stahr, Cushing, Lane, & Fox, 2006).

The next step is to scrutinize how each particular lesson is delivered. Will it be introduced with an advance organizer so that students understand the general ideas or objectives before getting started? If it is a continuation of a previous lesson, a brief orientation to the time that will be devoted to the lesson or tasks that will be completed may be all that is required. At the beginning of and throughout a lesson, it is crucial to determine whether all students are paying attention. Elements such as pacing or providing clear and focused instruction affect how closely students listen. For example, some teachers have difficulty with pacing because they are not prepared for the lesson. If time is lost searching for materials or because of false starts when introducing the content, students' attention will wander. Overelaboration, a lack of clarity, or redundancy will also cause students to lose interest in the lesson. Effective teachers use instructional cues that help students know which information is important ("Be sure to include this in your notes") or understand how to approach the material ("This might take you a while to complete"). Such cues help students attend to lessons and be more efficient in their learning.

Frequently checking for student understanding throughout a lesson is also important for ensuring engagement. This helps students avoid confusion and provides the opportunity for on-the-spot reteaching of concepts that prove to be more difficult to acquire. There is no sense in devoting an hour to a lesson before realizing students were lost halfway into it. Checking for understanding can be accomplished through effective questioning skills. Questions should be unambiguous and asked one at time (Brophy & Good, 1986). Teachers also need to provide adequate *wait time* to give students enough time to think about and respond to the question (Rowe, 1986).

Offering feedback during lessons is an important way to encourage students' positive participation. Rosenshine and Stevens (1986) identified four types of student responses that can help a teacher determine what type of feedback to provide: (1) correct and unhesitating, (2) correct but hesitant, (3) incorrect due to carelessness, and (4) incorrect due to lack of knowledge. A correct and unhesitating response simply requires acknowledgement such as "Yes, that is correct." When addressing a hesitant response, the teacher should acknowledge its accuracy but then provide a brief recap or explanation as to why it is correct. If an answer is incorrect due to carelessness, the teacher should point out that it is incorrect and move on with the lesson. Prompting or cuing can be used to shape an incorrect answer that is the result of a lack of understanding or knowledge (Cooper et al., 2007). Prompting should be rapid, and the teacher can provide the correct answer to avoid bogging down the lesson. All feedback should be nonjudgmental and constructive.

SUMMARY

In Chapter 3 we examined how to make curricular decisions, utilize powerful instructional methods, and employ effective teaching strategies. This builds on the information presented in Chapter 2 about how to create a well-managed classroom. Used in tandem, a well-managed classroom and engaging curriculum and instruction will prevent the majority of behavior problems. Table 3.6 presents other resources that you may find helpful as you seek to refine your instructional repertoire. Specifically, you will find other books, websites, and refereed journal articles that will provide you with other research-based information on the topics presented in this classroom. Furthermore, in Chapter 8 you will find a series of self-assessments that can assist you in evaluating your own knowledge, skills, and confidence in the use of the content presented in both Chapters 2 and 3. We encourage you to take a moment to complete these few surveys in Chapter 8 before moving forward to Chapter 4.

In the next chapter we introduce several low-intensity strategies to address the needs of students who require additional support to be well behaved. Specifically, in Chapter 4, we discuss how teachers can examine their own teaching style and student–teacher interactions to be sure they are actively utilizing a proactive approach to supporting positive student behavior. We begin by discussing how to plan for and implement intrinsically rewarding activities. Then we introduce a host of strategies that teachers can employ to redirect, minimize, or prevent undesirable behaviors. The techniques include (1) active supervision, (2) proximity, (3) overlappingness and with-it-ness, (4) pacing, (5) appropriate use of praise, (6) providing opportunities to respond, (7) instructive feedback, (8) choice and preferred activities, (9) token economies, and (10) formal teaching of prosocial behaviors. Then we provide information and recommendations for addressing these strategies in the classroom, providing step-by-step directions, illustrations, and related resources.

TABLE 3.6. Instructional Delivery Resource Guide

Reference	Description	Target group	Cost/retrieval information
	Books		
Tomlinson, C. A. (2005). *How to differentiate instruction in mixed-ability classrooms*. Upper Saddle River, NJ: Pearson Education.	This text provides extensive information on how to differentiate curriculum for diverse learners.	K–12 educators	*www.amazon.com* $23.00
Hoover, J. J., & Patton, J. R. (2005). *Curriculum adaptations*. Austin, TX: Pro-Ed.	This text includes information on how to adapt curriculum for students with learning and behavior problems.	K–12 educators	*www.proedinc.com* $32.00
Hariman, M., & Toth, M. (1994). *Inspiring active learning: A complete handbook for today's teachers* (2nd ed.). Alexandria, VA: ASCD.	This text details strategies for maintaining student engagement, for motivating students, and for using routines to make efficient use of class time.	K–12 educators	*www.ascd.org* $34.95
Slavin, R. E. (1995). *Cooperative learning* (2nd ed.). Needham Heights, MA: Allyn & Bacon.	This text includes detailed instructions on how to implement a variety of cooperative learning activities, including those in Table 3.5.	K–12 educators	*www.amazon.com* or *www.pearsonhighered.com* $51.00
National Council of Teachers of Mathematics. (2000). *Principles and standards for school mathematics*. Reston, VA: Author.	This text by the National Council of Teachers of Mathematics details student development in mathematics from kindergarten to grade 12. It includes the Council's standards for each grade level.	K–12 mathematics educators	*www.nctThm.org* $54.95
National Council of Teachers of English. (1996). *Standards for the English language arts*. Newark, DE: International Reading Association.	This text by the National Council of Teachers of English details the Council's standards in the following areas: reading, writing, speaking, listening, viewing, and visually representing.	K–12 English/ language arts educators	*www.ncte.org/store/books/standards/105977.htm* $18.00

Harris, K. R. Graham, S., Mason, L. H., & Friedlander, B. (2008). *Powerful writing strategies for all students*. Baltimore: Brookes.	The authors provide highly effective 20 to 50-minute lesson plans to supplement the general writing curriculum for teaching elementary or middle school students who struggle with writing. Teaching strategies are based on the authors' self-regulated strategy development, a strategy with a substantial research base.	K–8 educators	*www.brookespublishing.com/store/books/harris-67052/index.htm* $39.95
	Websites		
Strategic Instruction Model	This website on strategy instruction is sponsored by the University of Kansas.	K–12 educators	*www.ku-crl.org/sim/index.shtml*
Cooperative Learning	This website on cooperative and collaborative learning is sponsored by the Educational Broadcasting System.	K–12 educators	*www.thirteen.org/edonline/concept2class/coopcollab*
National Institute for Literacy	This federal agency supports a website that provides a host of information on a variety of literacy-related topics to improve reading outcomes for adults and K–12 students.	K–12 educators interested in improving reading performance.	*www.nifl.gov*
Exploratorium: The Museum of Science, Art, and Human Perception at the Palace of Fine Arts, San Francisco, CA	The Exploratorium offers an online education page that has several interactive units for students to engage with, as well as podcasts with teaching tips for educators.	K–12 science educators	*www.exploratorium.edu/explore/handson.html*
Math Forum at Drexel University	This site's mission is to improve math learning, teaching, and communication. It includes resources for parents and teachers, as well as interactive games and learning activities for students.	K–12 mathematics educators	*mathforum.org*
U.S. Department of Education	This federal agency offers a webpage with extensive links to other educational resources.	K–12 educators	*www.free.ed.gov*

(cont.)

TABLE 3.6. *(cont.)*

Reference	Description	Target group	Cost/retrieval information
	Refereed journal articles		
Gersten, R., et al. (2006). Eyes on the prize: Teaching complex historical content to middle school students with learning disabilities. *Exceptional Children, 72*, 264–280.	This article introduces a history unit designed to improve achievement of students with *and* without learning disabilities. It illustrates the use of several strategies that were effective in helping students learn the target concepts in a high-engagement format.	K–12 social studies and history educators	*Exceptional Children* is published by the Council for Exceptional Children. *www.cec.sped.org/AM/Template.cfm?Section=Publications1*
Feldman, K., & Denti, L. (2004). High-access instruction: Practical strategies to increase active learning in diverse classrooms. *Focus on Exceptional Children, 36*, 2–12.	This article details high-engagement strategies that can be used every day in the classroom. It also includes information on several common classroom practices that are ineffective despite their popularity.	K–12 educators	*Focus on Exceptional Children* is published by the Love Publishing Company. *www.lovepublishing.com/catalog/focus_on_exceptional_children_31.html*
Conroy, M., Sutherland, K., Snyder, A., & Marsh, S. (2008). Classwide interventions: Effective instruction makes a difference. *Teaching Exceptional Children, 40*, 24–30.	This article discusses several easy-to-implement interventions that are effective for a whole class.	K–12 educators	*Teaching Exceptional Children* is published by the Council for Exceptional Children. *www.cec.sped.org/Content/NavigationMenu/Publications2/TEACHINGExceptionalChildren/default.htm*
Sandmel, K. N., Brindle, M., Harris, K. R., Lane, K.. L., Graham, S., Nackel, J., et al. (2009). Making it work: Differentiating tier two self-regulated strategies development in writing in tandem with schoolwide positive behavior support. *Teaching Exceptional Children, 42*, 22–33.	The authors describe outcomes of two studies that evaluated self-regulated strategy development with students with problems with writing and behavior who attended a school with a universal model of positive behavior support. Illustrations are used to describe this approach for teachers to use in their classrooms.	Educators of students with behavior or writing concerns	*Teaching Exceptional Children* is published by the Council for Exceptional Children. *www.cec.sped.org/Content/NavigationMenu/Publications2/TEACHINGExceptionalChildren/default.htm*

CHAPTER 4

Low-Intensity Strategies

As we discussed in Chapters 2 and 3, many (if not most!) behavior problems can be prevented when the teacher and other instructional leaders provide a stimulating curriculum and supportive instruction in the context of a well-managed class. Yet some students will require additional support to demonstrate appropriate behaviors. This chapter introduces low-intensity strategies that teachers and other school-site personnel can use to redirect, minimize, and prevent behaviors that interfere with running an orderly classroom. These strategies and techniques are the next components in a proactive approach to supporting positive student behavior.

Before introducing the strategies, we start with a discussion about how to develop a student's intrinsic motivation to do well in school. Based on our professional experience in schools, we have noticed that oftentimes teachers tend to enjoy most those students who are intrinsically motivated by school tasks. However, many students are not a good *fit* with school and do not find satisfaction in school-defined goals and values. Additionally, many find it difficult to conform to the structure of the school setting and need extra help to do so. A behavioral approach is an effective, efficient way of managing student performance (Cooper et al., 2007). Yet long-term success often depends on moving from external reinforcement by teachers and parents to an internal desire on the part of the student to maintain his or her new mode of interaction.

In the second part of this chapter we introduce several strategies that should be part of a teacher's toolbox for supporting good behavior, as well as addressing misbehavior. As noted in Chapter 2, a positive climate is imperative for establishing a classroom community in which students *want* to work together to be productive and help one another, as well as the teacher. To establish such a climate, teachers should avoid overreliance on a reactive discipline system. These discipline systems tend to work against a harmonious feeling in the classroom because they do not focus on motivating students and validating them for what they do correctly. Instead, we encourage you to establish a balanced approach to classroom management that involves both (1) an instructional approach to behavior that is proactive in nature and (2) a reactive component that allows you to respond respectfully and effectively when problem behaviors do occur (Lane, 2007; Lane, Kalberg, & Menzies, 2009).

The low-intensity strategies presented here are both research- and practice-based, with evidence to suggest that using these strategies increases a teacher's ability to implement a proactive, supportive behavioral plan. They include active supervision, proximity, overlappingness and with-it-ness, pacing appropriate use of praise, providing opportunities to respond, and instructive feedback. Also discussed are slightly more intensive strategies—including use of choice and preferred activities, token economies, and formal teaching of prosocial behaviors—that are supported by an even more extensive research base.

THE IMPORTANCE OF DEVELOPING INTRINSIC MOTIVATION

Motivation can be described as either intrinsic or extrinsic. *Intrinsic motivation* is defined as engagement in activities for their own sake and without coercion (Alderman, 1999); essentially, participation in a task serves as its own reward (Pintrich & Schunk, 2002). For example, a student taking piano lessons may choose to practice every day because he or she simply enjoys playing and wants to get better. On the other hand, a piano student who is extrinsically motivated may practice not because he or she enjoys it but instead to please the piano teacher, who may then lavish praise on the student. Or perhaps the child's parent rewards the student with a treat of some kind after each hour of practice. Hence *extrinsic motivation* is the engagement in activities to attain rewards (e.g., praise, grades, special privileges, tangibles; Alderman, 1999). Yet increasing a student's motivation is not an entirely simple formula, because students may be both intrinsically and extrinsically motivated at the same time. In short, these types of motivated behavior are not mutually exclusive.

Teachers strive to help students achieve an intrinsic love of learning. Yet we know that some students feel incompetent to learn, others are afraid of failure, and some are simply uninterested in some academic content areas. So for many teachers, getting students to love learning may seem like an extremely difficult task. Although multiple factors (e.g., feelings of self-efficacy, autonomy, parental involvement) influence a student's motivation to learn, teachers *can* play a major

TABLE 4.1. Elements of Instruction That Promote Intrinsic Motivation

Control

When students are able to exert some autonomy during learning activities, they become more intrinsically motivated.

Challenge

Students who work just beyond their current achievement level experience the best opportunity for success and satisfaction. When provided with appropriate support, the work is then neither too challenging nor too easy.

Curiosity

Humans are innately wired to gain pleasure from activities and events that are surprising, incongruous, complex, or discrepant with their expectations or beliefs. Educational activities that arouse student's curiosity are intrinsically motivating.

Contextualization

Students need to both see and experience the real-world functionality of the content they are learning.

Note. Based on Lepper (1988) and Pintrich and Schunk (2002).

role in creating a classroom environment that fosters the intrinsic motivation necessary to achieve the love of learning they desire in their students. Many classroom motivation experts (Lepper, 1988; Pintrich & Schunk, 2002; Stipek, 1993) point to *the four C's—control, challenge, curiosity,* and *contextualization*—as sources for enhancing intrinsic motivation (see Table 4.1). In this section, we describe each source of intrinsic motivation and how it may be fostered within the classroom.

Control

Students have an innate need to feel autonomous. In other words, they want to feel that they are participating in activities by their own will rather than just to access or avoid some type of stimulus or experience, such as obtaining a letter grade or receiving a detention (deCharms, 1976, 1984; Deci, 1975, cited in Stipek, 1993; Deci & Ryan, 1985). Further, students want to feel that outcomes are within their own control. As a result, students are more likely to exert effort in school when they attribute their successes and failures to factors over which they have control (Ormrod, 2000, p. 497). Attributions for success or failure may include students' own ability, their effort, other people, task difficulty, and even luck (Ormrod, 2000). Weiner (1985) contended that these attributions had three distinct characteristics: locus, stability, and controllability. First, in terms of locus, students may attribute outcomes to internal factors (within themselves) or external factors (outside themselves; Ormrod, 2000). For example, a student with an internal locus may believe his or her good grade is a result of hard work. On the other hand, if the student believed the good grade was just pure luck, then this student has an external locus. Second, stability refers to factors that may or may not change (Ormrod, 2000). For example, a student who believes that he or she did not do well on a test because of his or her lack of intelligence is attributing the outcome to relatively stable cause (i.e., intelligence). In a related way, believing that failing a test was due to lack of sleep the night before is attributing the outcome to an unstable factor (i.e., lack of sleep). Finally, students attribute outcomes to controllable or uncontrollable factors (Ormrod, 2000). Controllable factors include things students can influence and change, such as effort. Conversely, students have no influence over uncontrollable factors. Essentially, when students believe their own behavior is the cause of outcomes they can control, they become more intrinsically motivated (Stipek, 1993). Although the locus, stability, and controllability of attributions may vary by the classroom situation, the instructional activity, and the teacher–student dynamic, we are certain that students with an internal locus make greater efforts toward mastery than those with an external locus (Pintrich & Schunk, 2002; Pressley & McCormick, 1995).

Teachers, administrators, and other school-site personnel can cultivate positive attributions and foster autonomy by providing students with choices and activities that create a sense of control over their own academic outcomes. Although we are not encouraging anyone to take a laissez-faire approach to instruction such that students run the classroom, we do encourage teachers and other instructional leaders to loosen the reins in planning instruction and procedures. This can be accomplished in both behavioral and academic domains. For example, oftentimes school-site personnel spend a substantial portion of the first week of school going over schoolwide expectations and classroom procedures. Ideally, these expectations and procedures should be the same in each classroom. Additionally, teachers and other personnel who deliver instruction may need to generate rules and procedures specific to their classrooms that align with the schoolwide expectations (see Chapter 1). For example, a science teacher may need safety procedures for his or her laboratory experiments, whereas an ethics teacher may need procedures specific to facilitating healthy class discussions. Both sets of procedures may fall under the schoolwide expectations "be respectful" or "be responsible." To develop some of these more specific procedures, the teacher could elicit suggestions from students. For example, the ethics teacher could ask students to propose some guidelines for classroom discussions, such as what students should do when they do not agree with a controversial opinion or what their body language should be when someone else has the speaking floor. The teacher and students could also consider rewards and consequences that are linked to the schoolwide plan for following the classroom discussion guidelines (e.g., giving a certain number of positive behavior support tickets paired with behavior-specific praise for students who met expectations during the class discussion). The whole class could discuss them, vote on them, and post them in the classroom (Stipek, 1993). In doing so, they are creating a "social contract" with everyone in the class such that each student can develop a sense of personal responsibility for meeting the classroom discussion guidelines of the entire class. By facilitating ownership in the classroom experience, the teacher is helping to foster student autonomy and a sense of control.

From an academic standpoint, Stipek (1993) proposed five ways to foster autonomy and perceptions of control. Students can: (1) participate in the design of academic tasks, (2) choose how tasks are completed, (3) be allowed some discretion about when they complete tasks, (4) correct some of their own assignments, and (5) set personal goals. Teachers who differentiate curriculum and instructional tasks for their students (see Chapter 3) already provide a firm basis for supporting intrinsic motivation.

First, in participating in the design of their academic tasks, students may be asked to generate a list of topics, key words, or questions to be studied. Each student chooses to become a classroom "expert" on a selected topic (or key word or question). Then other students might consult with the expert to obtain the necessary information, or the expert could present to the whole class. Regardless, the expert is given a sense of control over the activity. For low-achieving students, this may provide an opportunity they might not otherwise have.

Students may also choose how tasks are completed. For example, after reading about alternative energy sources, students may choose from a list of possible ways to demonstrate their knowledge. These assignments might include designing a trifold pamphlet highlighting the three best alternative energy sources, writing a letter to the president encouraging him or her to consider various energy sources, or building an alternative energy source (e.g., a solar panel) and describing why it might be a better alternative than other energy sources.

In addition to choosing *how* tasks are completed, students may also choose *when* they are completed (Stipek, 1993). Of course, these choices have to fit within the teacher's time frame. If given a list of tasks to complete, some students may choose to complete either the harder or easier task first. Or they may choose to begin with a shorter rather than a longer task. Either way, the students are allowed some control over order of completion, thus increasing their sense of control (Kern et al., 1998).

Students could also have the opportunity to correct their own assignments. On a daily basis, this might include such things as correcting spelling words, math problems, daily oral language, or general worksheets. For long-term projects, students could be given a rubric and asked to evaluate their own projects. By asking students to evaluate their own work, teachers help promote autonomy and increase self-awareness.

Finally, students who set goals can enhance their feelings of self-control. Teachers can work with students to set both short-term and long-term goals. These goals should be both specific and challenging (Stipek, 1993). As discussed in Chapter 3, students need to be challenged just beyond their current level of achievement so that they are working within their zones of proximal development (Vygotsky, 1978). Thus setting goals that are either too hard or too easy to achieve will not enhance motivation. Teachers and students must work together to find the goal in the correct range. Further, the goal should be specific. *Study spelling words* will not suffice. Rather, the goal might be *practice 10 spelling words each night until the test.*

(See guidelines for goal setting presented in Chapter 3, this volume (Strategies Instruction); Harris & Graham, 1996b).

There may be a variety of additional ways to provide students with a sense of control, and the implications of doing so are clear. Students are more motivated to engage in activities when they perceive that their actions have some influence on the outcomes (Pintrich & Schunk, 2002).

Challenge

People have a natural preference for novel or moderately difficult tasks (Cooper et al., 2007; Stipek, 1993). Students are not intrinsically motivated to engage in easy tasks because these tasks will not increase their skills or level of understanding, and they are also unlikely to practice skills that they have already mastered. Ultimately, each of us desires to work on tasks that are neither too easy nor too hard, but rather those that are novel or somewhat difficult. Perhaps this is what makes video games so enticing for people. Generally, the player starts the video game at an easy level. As the player achieves success at early levels, the challenge gradually increases, presenting the player with new but attainable challenges or levels. Thus video game players are constantly striving to reach the next level. Essentially, the video game is grounded in the behavioral principle of shaping (Cooper et al., 2007). Stipek (1993) termed this desire for tasks that are new or moderately difficult the *principle of optimal challenge.* The implications for practice parallel those of Vygotsky's (1978) zone of proximal development in that students who work just beyond their current achievement level will experience the best opportunity for learning and success.

We encourage teachers and other school-site personnel involved with instructional activities to provide challenging activities and to adjust the level of difficulty as students master and develop skills, similar to the way video games adjust levels based on success (Pintrich & Schunk, 2002). Successful completion of difficult tasks and development of new skills will result in increased feelings of efficacy (White, 1959). Again, this concept speaks to the importance of differentiated instruction (see Chapter 3). Differentiating instruction may initially seem like a daunting challenge for teachers. However, failing to differentiate may present even greater challenges, both academically and behaviorally. For example, students who are presented with tasks that are impossibly hard may fall behind academically and have greater difficulty catching up as time goes on. Additionally, they may give up on schoolwork and spend their time disrupting other students and presenting a behavior management challenge in the classroom. In a related scenario, students who are never challenged and always earn high grades may become bored with the content and exhibit disruptive behavior (see Umbreit et al., 2004). In both cases, if the students were presented with novel or somewhat challenging tasks, they would be intrinsically motivated to engage in the work and less likely to disrupt others. Refer to Chapter 3 for extensive examples of how to differentiate instruction and academic tasks.

Lepper (1988) argued that for an activity to be optimally challenging to students, it must provide meaningful goals about which there is (1) uncertainty about success yet (2) clear performance feedback regarding one's progress to help maintain the student's interest. Further, students must be aware of their progression in attaining the performance goals. This awareness may result from both self-evaluation and teacher-provided feedback.

Curiosity

In addition to the natural human desire to meet challenges and feel autonomous, some theorists believe that humans are wired innately to gain pleasure from activities and events that are surprising, incongruous, complex, or discrepant with their expectations or beliefs (Berlyne, 1966; Hunt, 1965; Kagan, 1972, cited in Stipek, 1993). This may explain why many children enjoy cartoons and video games (Stipek, 1993), why some adults enjoy reading romance novels or watching soap operas, or why some people are addicted to Sudoku or crossword puzzles. In each case, stimuli that are moderately discrepant will arouse interest, whereas those that are not novel or discrepant from an individual's expectations will *not* arouse interest (Cooper et al., 2007). However, discrepancies that are too wide may result in anxiety or may simply be ignored (Stipek, 1993). This perspective is similar to the principle of optimal challenge in that a novel stimulus may elicit engagement in a challenging task. Curiosity about a task may result from its novelty or from the challenge that it offers (Cooper et al., 2007). A person may be inclined to satisfy his or her curiosity to reduce the discrepancy (Stipek, 1993). When the discrepancy is resolved, competency and, in turn, intrinsic motivation increase.

In school, activities that highlight inconsistency or incompleteness of a student's knowledge will prompt curiosity (Lepper, 1988). These activities may present students with information or ideas that are discrepant with their current beliefs or that are unexpected (Pintrich & Schunk, 2002). As previously stated, students are then motivated to resolve these discrepancies. However, not all activities that take place in the school setting will elicit curiosity for all students. Teachers cannot always rely on natural curiosity to spark interest and engagement. For some students, studying Watson and Crick's discovery of DNA does not mean *deoxyribonucleic acid,* but rather, **D**oes **N**ot **A**pply to me. Thus teachers must continually seek ways to provoke curiosity for the content. This can be accomplished in several ways.

First, teachers can make the topic or activity pertinent or relevant for students. How many times do students ask, "What does this have to do with me?" or "When am I ever going to use this?" Teachers should be prepared to answer these questions. This is why advance organizers or anticipatory sets used to introduce lessons or topics (see Chapter 3) are effective. An advance organizer anticipates this need. Second, teachers can add suspense to a topic by beginning lessons with thought-provoking questions (Stipek, 1993) such as "Can anyone name something that goes up but doesn't come down?" or "Would you ever want to be President of the United States? Why or why not?" Similarly, teachers can ask students to speculate about possible solutions to a problem or to predict answers to questions (Stipek, 1993) such as "What do you think will happen if you breed a red snapdragon with a white snapdragon?" Finally, teachers can encourage students to ask questions, which may raise curiosity. However, we recommend this technique with caution. As Pintrich and Schunck (2002) pointed out, if students have no prerequisite knowledge on a topic, asking questions may make students feel that the gap in their knowledge is unmanageable. Consequently, teachers should provide some background knowledge prior to prompting questions. Essentially, the goal is to stretch students (as we mentioned in Chapter 3). If the gap between the current and desired level of performance or knowledge is manageable, curious students may feel more motivated to learn than they will if the gap is more pronounced (Pintrich & Schunk, 2002).

Contextualization

The final *C* source of intrinsic motivation is contextualization, which involves highlighting the functionality of an activity by presenting it in either a naturalistic or a fantasy context (Lepper, 1988). Lepper contended that students need to both see and experience the real-world functionality of the content they are learning. Unfortunately, the classroom is often a *decontextualizing* environment in that students fail to see (or teachers fail to show) how content and activities relate to a bigger picture. To combat decontextualization, teachers can present topics in their natural context. For example, students who are learning to measure speed could be asked to plan the trip of their dreams in which they measure the distance (miles) from location to location, use a bus or plane schedule to find the time (hours) it takes to travel, and then calculate the speed (miles per hour).

In addition to natural contexts, activities can be presented within a fantasy context. There is evidence that fantasy can enhance learning as compared with instruction presented without fantasy elements (Pintrich & Schunk, 2002). Fantasy contexts can be created through simulations or games in which students become hands-on participants rather than just listeners or observers. Some examples of simulations include reenactments (e.g., Continental Congress, Kennedy–Nixon debates) or mock trials. Students can wear costumes or make props to make the simulation more real. The World Wide Web is another source for simulations in which students can access the technology to perform a frog dissection or even fly an airplane. Both simulations and games can make an otherwise boring activity both meaningful and motivating (Pintrich & Schunk, 2002). Although fantasy contexts can create a positive experience for students, fantasy elements such as costumes, props, technology, and other embellishments must not distract from the overall purpose of the activity and thereby inhibit learning (Pintrich & Schunk, 2002). Accordingly, teachers and other school-site personnel involved with instruction should ensure that the fantasy elements are truly linked to developing students' skills. Also, it is imperative that teachers, administrators, and others attend to students' safety, which is often not considered when interacting in virtual worlds. With careful and thoughtful planning, it is possible to incorporate both fantasy and natural contexts in activities that promote intrinsic motivation in students.

Now, please keep in mind the previous information regarding how to develop students' intrinsic motivation to do well as we shift toward a discussion of low-intensity strategies to support behaviors that facilitate instruction. The strategies we introduce next are grounded in research, as well as experience, providing teachers, administrators, and other school-site support staff with a range of tools to prevent and respond to low-level behavioral challenges that can interfere with instruction. Our intent in this chapter is to provide you with an overview of each strategy, including the rationale behind it. It is not our intent to provide you with an extensive literature review of the studies to support these strategies. But, for those reading this chapter who would like additional information, we have included a resource guide that contains recommended books, websites, and peer-reviewed articles for each of the low-intensity strategies discussed in this chapter (see Table 4.5 at the end of the chapter).

LOW-INTENSITY STRATEGIES: BEGINNING WITH THE BASICS

The following strategies are effective because they help students avoid negative behaviors. Rather than imposing a consequence for undesirable behavior, these strategies allow teachers and other school-site personnel to create opportunities for positive student responses and avert problem situations before they occur (Walker et al., 2004). The low-intensity strategies we address next include active supervision, proximity, overlappingness and with-it-ness, pacing, appropriate use of praise, opportunities to respond, and instructive feedback. See Table 4.2 for an overview of all low-intensity strategies addressed in this chapter.

Active Supervision

To preempt student misbehavior, teachers must actively supervise their students. Generally speaking, supervision can be categorized into three types of events. The most common need for supervision occurs during instructional time in the classroom, the next most common occurs during major transitions, which include instances in which students leave the classroom to go to another location such as the playground, lunchroom, or bus. Finally, teachers may be responsible for supervising students during recess or special events (e.g., assemblies or field trips). Each

TABLE 4.2. Low-Intensity Strategies

Strategy	Description
Active supervision	Visually scanning, moving about, and interacting with students while supervising a classroom or other designated area.
Proximity	Standing in close physical proximity in order to cue a student to appropriate behavior. Do not stand so close as to appear threatening.
Overlappingness and with-it-ness	Attending to more than one classroom event at a time and communicating to students, verbally or nonverbally, that the teacher is monitoring all students' activities.
Pacing	Moving through a lesson with appropriate momentum. Instruction should be smooth and focused and should eliminate common teacher behaviors that slow down the pace.
Appropriate use of praise	Using specific, appropriate, and contingent praise to provide feedback to a student on his or her behavior or work.
Opportunities to respond	Creating frequent opportunities for students to respond to teacher inquires. Teachers should provide approximately four to six opportunities to respond per minute. The response can be individual, choral, verbal, written, or indicated through a gesture or signal.
Instructive feedback	Providing more efficient learning for students by providing information about student responses. Once a student has responded, the teacher can present new or additional information or emphasize already learned concepts. The information is not necessarily corrective.
Choice and preferred activities	Offering students the opportunity to choose which instructional activity they would like to complete. This increases on-task behavior and decreases problem behaviors.
Token economies	A classwide system to systematically reinforce students for positive behavior.
Formal teaching of prosocial behaviors	Teaching specific social skills in either a small-group or whole-class format to address deficits in social skills. Teachers can purchase prepackaged curricula or develop their own.

of these situations requires what is called *active supervision* (Colvin, Sugai, Good, & Lee, 1997), which includes teacher actions such as scanning, escorting, and interacting with students to prevent problem behaviors. Active supervision should be used in conjunction with precorrections or altering, which are verbal reminders or the modeling and rehearsal of appropriate behaviors. Precorrections are effective because they are delivered shortly before a problem behavior is likely to take place and in the actual setting in which it typically occurs. When lining up to go to the cafeteria, a teacher delivers a precorrection when he or she says, "Students, remember that we keep our hands to ourselves and walk quietly on our way to lunch." The reminder specifically addresses the behavior the teacher is looking for (keeping hands and feet to oneself), and it occurs right before students are expected to display it (on the way to lunch).

To be good at active supervision, you need to physically move around the students' designated area instead of remaining in one place. Teachers who are typically seated at their desks or standing in one area on the playground or classroom make it more likely that students will misbehave. Also, frequent visual scans are critical, particularly in areas that encompass a large space, such as a playground or auditorium. Finally, interacting briefly with students helps keep them on track with positive behavior. In the behavioral literature, this is referred to as providing noncontingent attention (Cooper et al., 2007). In other words, the student does not have to do anything (good or bad) to acquire teacher attention; attention is given freely. For example, teachers can greet students on the playground or lunchroom; check in with them during class time and ask them how a task is going; gesture a directive or a hello; and (importantly) remind students when they are getting off track by cheerfully prompting them to engage in the desired behavior. Consistent use of these strategies results in a decrease in inappropriate behaviors and an increase in prosocial behaviors that lead to improved academic engagement time and more positive social relationships with adults and peers (Colvin et al., 1997; De Pry & Sugai, 2002).

Proximity

Related to active supervision is *physical proximity*. Moving closer to a student who is off task or who appears to be having difficulty staying focused can be an effective means of prompting the student to engage in an appropriate behavior rather than an undesired one. Almost all teachers have had the experience of walking close to two students who are talking during a lesson and then noticing that the talking stops. The mere presence of the teacher is enough to remind students what they should and should not be doing. Proximity has been shown to increase student engagement with school tasks, as well as to decrease maladaptive behavior (Ervin et al., 2000). However, proximity is a highly context-dependent strategy, meaning that a variety of factors must be taken into consideration in order to use it effectively (Conroy, Asmus, Ladwig, Sellers, & Valcante, 2004).

Proximity should be used in a nonthreatening manner so that it does not set off or escalate negative behavior. Proximity is a prompt to good behavior, not a punishment. A teacher must know his or her students well enough to be able to predict how proximity will work with a particular individual. It may be that proximity actually reinforces some students for off-task behavior if they strongly desire the teacher's attention. When used appropriately, proximity can be a quick, efficient way to remind a student to stay on task.

"Overlappingness" and "With-it-ness"

Kounin and his colleagues (Kounin, Friesen, & Norton, 1966; Kounin & Obradovic, 1968) were among the first researchers to systematically examine teacher actions that promoted good behavior in students with and without behavior disorders. Although it was acknowledged that personality traits such as patience, understanding, and flexibility were key to good classroom management, the specific *actions* that constituted good classroom management skills had not been previously identified. Two of those critical skills are called *overlappingness* and *with-it-ness*. These two skills work in concert to provide teachers with the ability to quickly identify and prevent behavior issues.

Overlappingness is a teacher's ability to attend to more than one classroom event at a time. Teachers who have "eyes in the back of their head" are more likely to be successful in a busy classroom with many students. For example, if a teacher is listening to a small group read, he or she must be able to pay attention to those reading while simultaneously noticing and correcting a disruptive student in another part of the room. Overlappingness indicates that a teacher can address a disruptive student but at the same time maintain the engagement of those working. Overlappingness can be a difficult skill to develop. It is hard not to focus all one's attention on a misbehaving student and the situation he or she has created, but a teacher does so at his or her peril. Once students think the teacher is focused on one thing and unaware of the rest of the class, then a lack of with-it-ness is signaled.

Whereas overlappingness is the action of paying attention to the entire class, with-it-ness is the teacher's ability to *communicate* to students that he or she is aware of what is going on and is in control of the entire classroom. A teacher or instructional support staff member indicates he or she is not *with-it* when he or she appears unaware of the entire classroom dynamic. This can also happen when a teacher addresses a minor behavior (talking) but lets a more serious one (throwing something) escape notice, or when a teacher intervenes too late and the misbehavior has increased in seriousness or spread to other students. Teachers with high levels of with-it-ness have classrooms with significantly lower rates of student misbehavior and higher rates of student engagement. This is true for general education students as well as those with emotional and behavioral disorders (EBD; Kounin et al., 1966). A corollary effect is that teachers who efficiently manage the behaviors of the entire class are able to develop a climate that actually suppresses the maladaptive behavior of students with behavior issues. These teachers are more successful at preventing such students from disturbing their classmates.

Pacing

Moving through a lesson with appropriate momentum facilitates student involvement (Englert, 1984; Miller, 2008). Generally, lessons that are quickly paced help students stay on task. However, we do want to mention that optimal *pacing* (moving neither too quickly nor too slowly through instructional tasks) tends to vary across students, particularly those with exceptionalities (e.g., learning disabilities, EBD). Therefore, it is important to consider issues related to differentiation of curriculum mentioned in Chapter 3.

Kounin and Obradovic's work (1968) provides insight into the obstacles that impede a teacher's instructional pace (see Table 4.3). They categorize several teacher actions as *overdone* when they interfere with the movement within and between lessons. The first is called *behavior overdone,* which occurs when a teacher does too much "nagging, preaching, or moralizing about the behavior of the class or a particular child" (p. 132). The next is *prop overdone* and occurs when a teacher talks too much about how to proceed with the materials needed for a lesson, such as where students are to put their pencils and papers. *Task overdone* refers to explanations that are overly elaborated and exceed what is necessary to understand the task. *Sheer overtalk* refers to excessive teacher talk on any subject, whether it is directions or instruction. Each of these overdone behaviors unnecessarily slows down a lesson and encourages students to start paying attention to distractions or creating other diversions—particularly for students who already struggle with learning and behavioral difficulties (Walker et al., 2004).

TABLE 4.3. Teacher Actions That Slow Instructional Pacing

Behavior overdone	Unnecessarily or extensively lecturing the class or a particular child about behavior during instructional time. It is perceived by students as nagging or badgering.
Prop overdone	Talking too much about how to proceed with the materials needed for a lesson.
Task overdone	Providing explanations that are overelaborated and exceed what students need to understand the task.
Sheer overtalk	Excessive teacher talk on any subject, whether it is the directions, instruction, or something not even related to the lesson.
Dangles	Beginning an activity, abruptly leaving it to address something else, and then eventually returning to it.
Thrust	Interrupting a student's response in a way that indicates the teacher is not listening to what the student is saying.
Truncation	Abruptly leaving an activity before it is completed and neglecting to return to it.
Stimulus-bounded	Reacting to and becoming immersed in a nonintrusive event rather than the task that the teacher and class are engaged in together.

Note. Based on Kounin and Obradovic (1968).

Other teacher actions can also hamper students' involvement in lessons, thereby slowing the pace. *Dangles* occur when a teacher begins an activity but then abruptly leaves it to address something else (e.g., going to the desk to look at the attendance roster after asking students to answer a question). A *truncation* is related to a dangle, but in this case the teacher does not return to the initial activity after leaving it. A *thrust* occurs when the teacher interrupts a student's response to impose her or his own message in a way that indicates that she or he is not listening to what the student is saying. Similarly, *stimulus-bounded* refers to a teacher reacting to and becoming immersed in a nonintrusive event rather than the task that the class is engaged in together. For example, a teacher who is writing math problems on the overhead may entirely stop the math lesson for a few minutes to lecture a student who is slouched in his or her chair.

A teacher might be excellent at planning interesting and appropriate curricular activities, but an inability to sustain the appropriate pace during lessons can make it difficult to keep students engaged. Overdones and dangles result in disjointed, confusing instruction. The behaviors identified by Kounin and Obradovic (1968) provide a good starting point for teachers to examine their own teaching styles. The actions that slow instructional pacing can be recognized and eliminated.

The skills discussed in Chapters 2 and 3 will also support your instructional pacing. For example, students who have been taught routines and procedures (Chapter 2) will know what to do with materials and thus assist the teacher in avoiding prop overdone. Similarly, teachers who understand the elements of direct instruction (Chapter 3) have a planning structure to rely on that helps eliminate task overdone.

Appropriate Use of Praise

The vast majority of students value teacher recognition and appreciate teacher feedback that acknowledges their hard work and compliance. In fact, even students who instigate negative interactions may be indicating that they want their teacher's attention (Sutherland & Wright, in press; see also Chapter 7, this volume). Accordingly, *praise* is a highly effective, efficient strategy for shaping student behavior. It can be used to promote desirable academic and social behavior in classrooms (Gable, Hester, Rock, & Hughes, 2009). Although praise is an easy strategy to implement and requires no preparation, research indicates that teachers should be aware of some basic premises when using praise to motivate students (Sutherland & Wright, in press).

First, teachers should determine the type of praise each student responds to best. Some students bask in the glow of public praise, whereas others prefer teacher praise to be a more private interaction. You might recall our discussion in Chapter 3 about the fact that students have different motives for behavior. Some students want to access attention, activities or tangibles, or sensory experiences, these are referred to as positive reinforcement. Other students want to avoid these things;

avoiding them is called negative reinforcement (Umbreit et al., 2007). Praise can be either nonverbal (e.g., a smile and a nod) or verbal (e.g., "I appreciate your hard work on that assignment"), and students will have different preferences here (Burnett, 2001). It may also be that a student does *not* want to be praised. In such cases, using praise would be counterproductive, as it may make the student uncomfortable or cause him or her to react hostilely (e.g., if the student's behavior is motivated by the desire to escape teacher attention). The tricky thing about determining the reinforcing value of praise is that you cannot know for sure whether praise is a reinforcer until you see how the rate of behavior changes in the future. If the frequency of the behavior you praised increases in the future, then you can know that your praise was a reinforcer (Cooper et al., 2007).

Praise should also be specific and provided in response to a particular action (Good & Grouws, 1977; Paine et al., 1983). Praise should include the student's name and be descriptive, sincere, and varied in format (e.g., do not always say, "Good job!"). Furthermore, praise should be delivered in such a manner that it does not interfere with the flow of instruction (Paine et al., 1983). For example, rather than saying "Serena, you are a good girl," it is more effective to say "Serena, you have done an excellent job helping Robert with his math." This way a student knows exactly what behavior the teacher thinks is worthy. Students are acutely aware of praise that is either insincere or unearned, which makes it ineffective. However, they do value praise for effort (Johnson, 1998). Praise is also more effective when it is delivered in close proximity to the student, and it may also be more effective when combined with increased *opportunities to respond* (OTR; Sutherland, Wehby, & Yoder, 2002). Giving students multiple opportunities to respond to teacher inquiries and requests affords more occasions for authentic praise. Next, we discuss how teachers can increase OTR in their classrooms.

Opportunities to Respond

Providing students with a high number of opportunities to answer or actively respond to academic requests promotes good behavior in students with even the most resistant behavior problems. A number of studies have shown that opportunities to respond (OTR) can increase engagement and correct responding, improve academic outcomes, and decrease disruptive behavior in a range of learners, including those with EBD (e.g., Conroy et al., 2008; Sutherland, Alder, & Gunter, 2003). Given the ease of increasing OTR, this is an effective and efficient tool for shaping student performance in classrooms.

An optimal schedule for OTR needs to be achieved, with some experts recommending four to six responses from each student per minute (Council for Exceptional Children, 1987; Gunter, Hummel, & Venn, 1998). The difficulty level of the opportunities provided should allow the student to get at least 80% of the answers correct. Responses can be verbal, written, a signal, or even choral. By combining OTR with other strategies, such as praise and proximity, teachers create a classroom environment that supports positive student–teacher interactions. These strategies allow students many opportunities to be well behaved and, equally important, *support* them in displaying appropriate behavior. The interaction between teachers and students is transactional. Therefore, when teachers create OTR and offer support for students and students respond, a constructive cycle of interaction is initiated (Sutherland & Wright, in press).

Instructive Feedback

Because the pace of a school day is so rapid, it can be challenging for teachers, administrators, and other school-site personnel to interact individually with all students. This is especially problematic if students receive insufficient information about their academic performance during instruction. *Instructive feedback* is a technique designed to provide more efficient learning for students by providing information about student responses. The aim of instructive feedback is to teach more in the same amount of time. A teacher can do this by capitalizing on interactions with students after they respond to questions or directives. Once a student has responded, the teacher can present new or additional information or emphasize already learned concepts. The information is not necessarily corrective, although it can be (see Chapter 3 for a discussion of corrective feedback). For example, during a discussion in English class, a teacher might ask for an illustration of descriptive language. When a student provides an example, the teacher could add, "Yes, and that descriptive phrase is an example of a simile." This extends and scaffolds the interaction. It is brief but, as we say, instructive.

Research indicates that even though the interaction is short, students do retain the new, additional, or reiterated information (see Werts, Wolery, Holcombe, & Gast, 1995, for an extensive review of instructive feedback). Instructive feedback has been shown to be effective whether delivered through one-to-one instruction or in small- or large-group instructional arrangements. It is also effective with a range of learners from preschoolers to secondary students, including those with disabilities. One suggested use for instructive feedback is to introduce new concepts that will be taught in the future. This provides students with prior knowledge on the topic, again making it an efficient teaching strategy. Just as with praise and OTR, instructional feedback is a quick, easy strategy that provides positive opportunities to interact with students. Increasing the number of positive interactions with students helps them enjoy school more and supports improved social and academic outcomes.

LOW-INTENSITY STRATEGIES: SCALING UP

The strategies discussed thus far (active supervision, proximity, overlappingness and with-it-ness, pacing, praise, OTR, and instructive feedback) are both efficient and effective, and they can be implemented by teachers and other instructional support staff on the spot. Using them contributes to a well-managed classroom in which teachers avoid potential problems and also makes students feel supported and engaged in classroom activities. The next research-based strategies we discuss are *choice and preferred activities, token economies*, and the *formal teaching of social skills*. Although these strategies are more time-consuming, learning to incorporate them into everyday instruction will address the behaviors of students who do not respond to the basic good teaching practices already introduced.

Choice and Preferred Activities

Incorporating *choice* into classroom activities is the hallmark of an expert, sensitive teacher (Dunlap et al., 1994; Kern, Delaney, Clarke, Dunlap, & Childs, 2001; Kern & Manz, 2004). Offering choice communicates that a teacher has respect for students' interests and abilities. It also indicates the teacher's ability to differentiate curriculum and plan for a variety of instructional activities (see Chapter 3). Schooling too often offers few or no opportunities for students to make their own choices or exert control over their activities. This can make school an undesirable place to spend so many hours a day. In fact, some evidence shows that lack of choice increases learned helplessness and may contribute to individuals' seeking out dangerous behaviors (Guess, Benson, & Siegel-Causey, 1985; Seligman, 1975). Further, as discussed earlier in the chapter, choice contributes to the development of intrinsic motivation so that students do not rely solely on extrinsic rewards to prompt them to engage in school tasks.

Offering choice in academic tasks reduces behavior problems and promotes on-task behavior. For example, Cosden, Gannon, and Haring (1995) showed that when students were allowed to choose from 10 activities, such as word problems, writing exercises, or answering science questions, their rate of accuracy increased as compared with occasions on which the teacher did not provide a choice of assignments. Another study demonstrated lower levels of disruptive behavior when students with emotional problems were allowed to choose the assignment they wanted to complete out of six to eight possibilities (Dunlap et al., 1994). Evidence also shows that simply providing the choice of which tasks students tackle first results in decreased problem behavior and increased on-task behavior (Kern, Mantegna, Vorndran, Bailin, & Hilt, 2001). In this study by Kern and colleagues, students were able to decide what to do first but still had to complete all tasks. In other words, it is not that the students were motivated by being able to avoid one or more tasks. They were motivated by the option of getting to decide how (e.g., in what order) to tackle the work.

Kern, Bambara, and Fogt (2002) provided a good example of how a classroom teacher incorporated both choice and high-interest activities to decrease problem behaviors and increase engagement of students with emotional disturbances. The science teacher provided choice in two ways. First, she allowed the class to vote as an entire group on which of two activities they preferred to do. For example, one of the choices was to begin either a land pollution experiment or an air pollution experiment. Another was either to review the posttest for the ecology unit or to take the pretest for the pollution unit. The next level of choice was at the individual level and pertained to how students would complete their individual work. Sometimes students were given the choice of practicing concepts either with a peer or at a computer. They were also offered a choice of topics within lessons, such as deciding whether to take notes on predators or on prey.

In addition to choice, the teacher included activities that were based on her prior observations of student preferences. Some of the examples of high-interest activities were "hands-on experiments, identifying pollution in the students' own neighborhoods, and developing their own trivia questions pertaining to the unit topics" (Kern et al., 2002, p. 321). Combining choice and high-interest activities decreased problem behaviors from an average of 8% to none by the final phase of the intervention. It increased engagement from an average of 57–89%. This rate of improvement was achieved with a population of students whose behaviors were extremely resistant to intervention. The teacher indicated that the intervention was acceptable in terms of the amount of time and planning that it took. Using choice as part of an approach to instruction can be an effective component in supporting positive classroom behavior.

Token Economies

A *token economy* is a classwide intervention used to promote specific student behaviors. When a student displays a behavior previously identified by the teacher as desirable or appropriate, he or she can earn a token that can later be exchanged for a reward (also known as a backup reinforcer). Token economies are a relatively easy way to systematically reinforce students for the prosocial behaviors teachers want to develop in their classrooms. Some teachers do not like to implement token economies because they feel students should not be rewarded for things they are already expected to do. However, many students (particularly those lacking the intrinsic desire to succeed) respond well to the extrinsic motivation that token economies offer. If you have a schoolwide positive behavior support (SWPBS) plan, we encourage you to avoid adding an additional token economy in the classroom. The intent of the schoolwide plan is to level the playing field for all students. Adding another system unnecessarily complicates the proactive behavior component of the schoolwide plan (Lane, Kalberg, & Menzies, 2009).

A token economy can be an effective means of shaping and supporting positive behavior. Eventually, displaying these behaviors becomes a habit, and extrinsic reinforcement can be decreased. Such an intermittent reinforcement schedule is a highly effective method of maintaining any behavior that has been acquired (Cooper et al., 2007). Token economies are a proactive, rather than reactive, way to address problem behaviors that are resistant to less intensive methods. They are effective with students ranging from preschool (Filcheck, McNeil, Greco, & Bernard, 2004) to college age (Boniecki & Moore, 2003) and are useful with a variety of populations, including general education students, as well as those with disabilities (Matson & Boisjoli, 2009).

If you do not have a schoolwide plan in place and you decide to implement a classwide token economy, consider the following steps. First, target behaviors must be identified and clearly defined. Common target behaviors include: (1) raising one's hand and waiting to be recognized, (2) sitting quietly, (3) coming to attention when asked, (4) walking appropriately in halls and classroom, (5) participating in and completing classwork and homework, and (6) being respectful to peers. Students should be provided with examples and non-examples of both desirable and undesirable behaviors. Students also need to know how many tokens each behavior earns. When students perform or exhibit a target behavior, they are rewarded with the requisite number of tokens.

A system for exchanging tokens must be established. First, the teacher decides what objects serve as tokens. Tokens should be eye-catching and easy to carry and store (as well as to give out). Students should not be able to counterfeit tokens. Some teachers make their own "bucks" and print them each week. It is critical to teach students how to receive and store tokens with minimal disruption. If there are no procedures or routines in place to make the system run smoothly, it is possible that a token economy itself can lead to misbehavior. Tokens are exchanged for tangible items, activities, or privileges at a regularly designated time (e.g., Friday afternoons). For example, some teachers may allow students to enter the student store at the end of the week, where they can exchange their tokens for pencils, erasers, and related items. Some teachers hold an auction at which students bid on items. Tokens should not be taken away once they have been earned—this action is what behaviorists refer to as *response cost*, which is a punishment procedure (Cooper et al., 2007). For a general intervention such as a token economy, response cost may work against eliciting prosocial behaviors. We recommend that, if a student has demonstrated a prosocial behavior, he or she deserves the reward he or she earned. If a student subsequently demonstrates an undesired behavior before the reward is received, other strategies can be used or different consequences (e.g., a note home) applied.

The success of a token economy depends on how desirable students find the rewards. Remember, not all students are tangibly motivated. Students are more motivated to work for tokens if they know they can be exchanged for something they highly desire. It has been our experience that some of the most motivating reinforcers are those that cost the least. For example, at one school we worked with, the most popular reinforcer was the opportunity to eat a brown-bag lunch with the teacher. Students simply desired more time with the teacher (elementary level) and with their peers (middle school). See Figure 4.1 for a list of reinforcer ideas, which also includes suggestions for reinforcing faculty, staff, and teachers, as well as students.

		Persons		
Function	**Type**	**Students**	**Faculty and Staff**	**Parents**
Seeking *Positive reinforcement*	Social attention	• Lunch with friend • Lunch with staff member of choice • Preferential seating • Reading time with adult • Meeting with the principal • Tutor/mentor younger class • Award given in front of class/school • Being featured in a positive behavior support video/skit • Praise postcard sent home	• Preferential parking spot • Award given during faculty meeting • Recognition during assembly • Being featured in a positive behavior support video/skit	• Student featured on school webpage • Student featured in newsletter or bulletin board • Phone call home from principal/teacher • Praise postcard sent home • Being featured in a positive behavior support video/skit
	Activity/Task	• Lunch with a friend • Lunch with staff member of choice • Movie (on campus) • Preferential seating • Being class helper • Extra reading time • Participating in or attending a positive behavior support assembly • Additional computer time • Additional recess time • Game of choice • Ticket to school event (e.g., sports, dance, play) • Extra basketball time • Feature spot in positive behavior support video	• Drawing winning positive behavior support ticket during assemblies • Ticket to school event (e.g., sports, play, dance) • Feature spot in positive behavior support video	• Ticket to school event (e.g., sports, dance, play) • Feature spot in positive behavior support video

	Tangible	• School supplies • Food coupon • School T-shirt or sweatshirt • Bike, radio, i-Pod • Candy, soft drinks • Gift cards (e.g., movie, stores, restaurants) • Discounted yearbook, dance ticket, sporting event	• Free yearbook • Gift certificate to local restaurant • Gift cards (e.g., movies, stores, restaurants) • Candy, soft drinks • School T-shirt or sweatshirt • School supplies • Car wash coupon	• Gift certificate (e.g., movies, stores, restaurants) • Postcard sent home regarding student's exemplary behavior • Bumper sticker for car • School T-shirt or sweatshirt
Avoiding *Negative reinforcement*	Social attention	• Lunch in private area with peer and staff member of choosing • Extra computer time • Quiet time in the library • Get-out-of-class-participation pass • Get out of physical education • Preferential seating during school event	• Supervision at the positive behavior support assembly • Before/after school supervision • Hallway monitor	• Phone conference instead of on-campus conference • Get out of classroom support duty
	Activity/ Task	• Extra computer time (avoiding class time) • Homework pass • Front-of-the-lunch-line pass • Additional free time • Extra library time • Preferred parking (avoiding the long walk to class!)	• Extra planning period • Relief from bus duty • Relief from lunch duty	• Phone conference instead of on-campus conference • Get out of classroom support duty
	Tangible	• Certificate to drop lowest grade	• Certificate to avoid walkie-talkie duty in the hallway	• Certificate to avoid supervision duty at extracurricular activities

FIGURE 4.1. Reinforcer menu: Suggested reinforcers based on the function of the behavior. Reprinted from Umbreit, Ferro, Liaupsin, and Lane (2007). Copyright 2007 by Pearson Education, Inc. Reprinted by permission.

Setting the price of a reinforcer requires a delicate balance. If a particular reinforcer is highly attractive, it should be more expensive. However, if the reinforcer supports students in acquiring a skill, it should be less expensive. If the value of reinforcers is set too low, students will be less motivated to earn the tokens to purchase them because they will perceive them as less valuable or too easy to attain. If the value is set too high, students may become discouraged or lose interest as the goal seems unobtainable. The system should be developed so that students have to put forth effort to earn tokens and so that all students have the opportunity to earn some tokens that can be exchanged for a reinforcer.

The most effective token economies are those that are implemented evenly and consistently. All students should be rewarded when they demonstrate the target behavior, and the rewards should be equal. If students feel the system favors some students over others, they will be less willing to participate. Still, a particular student's behavior can be shaped by the teacher's making a point to catch him or her meeting expectations. However, teachers should avoid giving one student 100 tokens for a behavior for which other students receive only 10 tokens. It is also a good idea to periodically evaluate how well the system is working and to fine-tune it if necessary. The goal is to reach a balance at which students are well behaved with the least amount of reinforcement. Again, we would like to emphasize the importance of a schoolwide primary prevention plan. It is more efficient and effective for teachers, students, and administrators alike to have one unified plan across all school settings. If given the option between a schoolwide or a classwide focus, we respectfully urge you to focus on the former (Lane, Kalberg, & Menzies, 2009).

Formal Teaching of Prosocial Behaviors

The last low-intensity strategy we discuss is the *direct teaching of social skills*. This can be done in either a small-group or whole-class format, depending on student needs. Teachers often assume that students already possess the social skills they want them to display. However, that may not be the case. It is more efficient to determine whether students have the identified skills, and to teach them if they do not, than to unsuccessfully attempt to manage a host of behavior issues related to a lack of social skills. Further, because teachers differ on the skills they think that students need to be successful in school, different teachers are likely to have different expectations—particularly if there is no primary prevention plan in place. For example, special education teachers are more likely to think that social skills that lead to self-control are more important than do general education teachers (Lane, Wehby, & Cooley, 2006). As a result, teachers should think about the skills that they value the most and then determine whether or not all students can perform them. This can be accomplished through assessment and intervention packages such as the Social Skills Improvement System (SSIS; Elliott & Gresham, 2007).

When students are not able to perform the identified or desired skill, we call it an *acquisition deficit* (a "can't do" problem). No amount of M&Ms is going to make the behavior occur, as it is not in the student's skill set (Gresham, 2002b; Lane, Kalberg, & Menzies, 2009). If students do have the skill in their repertoire but do not use it, we call it a *performance deficit* (a "won't do" problem). Reinforcing positive behavior through low-intensity strategies is effective only (1) if students know how to display the skill and (2) if the focus of the intervention is behavioral in the sense that the goal is to arrange antecedent conditions and to maintain consequences to prompt and reinforce the new, more desirable behavior (Umbreit et al., 2004). Otherwise, it makes sense to provide instruction that supports students in acquiring the desired behavior. Various studies have demonstrated the effectiveness of teaching social skills to improve behavior (see systematic reviews of empirical studies by Cook et al., 2008; Quinn, Kavale, Mathur, Rutherford, & Forness, 1999). Improving social skills that facilitate instructional experiences (referred to as academic enablers) also has the collateral effect of improving academics (Caprara, Barbaranelli, Pastorelli, Bandura, & Zimbardo, 2000; DiPerma & Elliott, 2000). A number of commercial packages can be purchased for use in the classroom, such as PeaceBuilders, Second Step: A Violence Prevention Program (SSVP; Committee for Children, 2007), or the SSIS. Depending on the curriculum, the focus is on a different aspect of social skill development. See Table 4.4 for a list of commercial social skills and violence prevention programs. The advantage to using a commercial curriculum is that all materials and lesson plans are provided, which is much easier than designing your own. Furthermore, many of these commercially available studies have been well researched, and sufficient evidence supports the utility of the program when implemented as designed (or with treatment integrity; Gresham, 1989).

Yet some students may need more customized instructional assistance. When working with schools, we have developed customized schoolwide social skills programs based on the work of Frank Gresham and Stephen Elliott. Prior to the introduction of the SSIS, we used Elliott and Gresham's (1991) *Social Skills Intervention Guide: Practical Strategies for Social Skills Training*. It offers predesigned lessons, but teachers can (1) choose from a wide variety of social skills and teach the ones they feel are most critical or (2) use a more data-based approach to identifying the skills their faculty and staff view as essential for success and then focus instruction on those identified skills. Next, we provide a step-by-step description of how this guide can be used in a classroom.

The curriculum includes 43 social skills that are divided into five domains: Cooperation, Assertion, Responsibility, Empathy, and Self-Control. For example, the Cooperation unit offers lessons on paying attention and following directions, and the Responsibility unit includes a lesson on how to ask permission to use someone else's property. Each lesson follows the same instructional model and includes the following steps: (1) *Tell*, (2) *Show*, (3) *Do*, (4) *Follow Through*, and (5) *Generalization*.

TABLE 4.4. Primary Prevention Programs

Name	Description	Representative supporting research	Target group	Cost/contact information
Promoting Alternative Thinking Strategies (PATHS; Greenberg, Kusché, & Mihalic, 1998)	PATHS is intended to reduce aggression and behavior problems. The program focuses on emotional literacy, self-control, social competence, interpersonal problem-solving skills, and positive peer relations.	Greenberg, M. T., Kusché, C. A., Cook, E. T., & Quamma, J. P. (1995). Promoting emotional competence in school-aged children: The effects of the PATHS curriculum. *Development and Psychopathology, 7*, 117–136.	K–6	Costs range from $15.00 to $45.00 per student per year. Channing Bete Company One Community Place South Deerfield, MA 01373-0200 800-477-4776 e-mail: *custsvcs@channing-bete.com* *www.channing-bete.com/prevention-programs/paths* *www.prevention.psu.edu/projects/PATHS.html*
PeaceBuilders (Molina & Molina, 1997)	PeaceBuilders is a violence prevention program. Programs include lessons to teach violence prevention and additional materials.	Vazsonyi, A. T., Bellison, L. M., & Flannery, D. J. (2004). Evaluation of a school-based, universal violence prevention program: Low-, medium-, and high-risk children. *Youth Violence and Juvenile Justice, 2*, 185–206.	K–5	Heartsprings, Inc. P.O. Box 12158 Tucson, AZ 85732 800-368-9356 520-298-7670 *www.peacebuilders_intl.com*
Caring School Community (CSC; originally the Child Development Project)	The CSC program focuses on strengthening students' ties to school and aims to reduce drug use, violence, and delinquency. It emphasizes the view of schools as caring communities.	Solomon, D., Watson, M., Battistich, V., Schaps, E., & Delucchi, K. (1996). Creating classrooms that students experience as communities. *American Journal of Community Psychology, 24*, 719–748.	K–6	Costs are approximately $185.00 per grade level. Each grade-level curriculum includes an overview of the program, 30 lessons, and supplementary materials. The Developmental Studies Center *www.devstu.org/programs.html*
Second Step: A Violence Prevention Program (SSVP; Committee for Children, 2007)	SSVP teaches social and emotional skills for violence prevention. Skills focus on four main areas: empathy, anger management, impulse control, and problem solving.	McMahon, S. D., & Washburn, J. J. (2003). Violence prevention: An evaluation of program effects with urban African-American students. *Journal of Primary Prevention, 24*, 43–62.	Preschool–9	Grade-level kits range from $169.00 to $400.00. Materials include staff training video, family guide, curriculum, posters, grade level kits, etc. Committee for Children 568 First Avenue South, Suite 600 Seattle, WA 98104-2804 800-634-4449, ext. 6223 e-mail: *clientsupport@cfchildren.org* *www.cfchildren.org*
Responding in Peaceful and Positive Ways (RIPP)	RIPP is a universal violence prevention program designed especially for middle school students. The curriculum	Meyer, A., & Farrell, A. (1998). Social skills training to promote resilience in urban sixth-grade students: One product of an	Middle school	Prevention Opportunities, LLC 12458 Ashland Vineyard Lane Ashland, VA 23005 804-301-4909

	develops students' social and cognitive skills so they can utilize nonviolent conflict resolution and positive communication.	action research strategy to prevent youth violence in high-risk environments. *Education and Treatment of Children, 21*, 461–488.		e-mail: *contact@preventionopportunities.com* *www.preventionopportunities.com/index.html* *www.has.vcu.edu/RIPP/phil.htm*
PREPARE	The PREPARE curriculum focuses on teaching prosocial behaviors to reduce aggression, reduce stress, and address prejudice. The curriculum manual includes procedures, materials, and supplementary exercises.	Colvin, G., Kame'enui, E. J., & Sugai, G. (1993). Reconceptualizing behavior management and school-wide discipline in general education. *Education and Treatment of Children, 16*, 361–381.	Designed for use with middle and high school students but can be adapted for younger students	The manual by Arnold Goldstein detailing the program is available through Research Press for $39.95. *www.researchpress.com*
Olweus Bullying Prevention Program (BPP; Olweus, 2001)	BPP is a universal intervention for elementary, middle, or high school students designed to reduce or prevent bullying. It includes schoolwide, classroom, and individual components.	Olweus, D. (1991). Bully/victim problems among schoolchildren: Basic facts and effects of a school-based intervention program. In D. J. Pepler & K. H. Rubin (Eds.), *The development and treatment of childhood aggression* (pp. 411-448). Hillsdale, NJ: Erlbaum.	K–12	In addition to an on-site coordinator, the program costs $200.00 per school for the questionnaire and software and $65.00 per teacher for classroom materials. Marlene Snyder, PhD Institute on Family and Neighborhood Life Clemson University 158 Poole Agricultural Center Clemson, SC 29634 864-710-4562 e-mail: *nobully@clemson.edu* *www.clemson.edu/olweus*
Bully-Proofing Your School (BPYS; Creating Caring Communities, 2008)	BPYS is a comprehensive program designed to reduce and respond to bullying in the school setting. It has multiple components that include staff and student training, as well as individual intervention and victim support.	Garrity, C. B., Jens, K., & Porter, W. W. (1997). Bully proofing your school: Creating a positive climate. *Intervention in School and Clinic, 32*, 235–243.	K–12	Bully-Proofing Your School materials are available through Sopris West Educational Services. 800-547-6747 *www.sopriswest.com* For training and other information contact *www.bullyproofing.org*
Midwestern Prevention Project (MPP; Pentz, Mihalic, & Grotpeter, 1998)	MPP is a comprehensive program to prevent adolescent drug abuse. It includes school-, community-, and family-based components. The school program uses modeling, role playing, and discussion to provide students with skills that help them avoid drug use.	Pentz, M. A., Mihalic, S. F., & Grotpeter, J. K. (1998). *Blueprints for Violence Prevention, Book 1: The Midwestern Prevention Project*. Boulder: University of Colorado, Institute of Behavioral Science, Center for the Study and Prevention of Violence.	Middle through late adolescence	Not commercially available. Costs are approximately $175,000 for 1,000 students, over 3 years. Karen Bernstein USC Norris Comprehensive Cancer Center University of Southern California 1441 Eastlake Avenue, MS-44 Los Angeles, CA 90089-9175 323-865-0325 e-mail: *karenber@usc.edu*

(cont.)

TABLE 4.4. *(cont.)*

Name	Description	Representative supporting research	Target group	Cost/contact information
Life Skills Training (LST; Botvin, Mihalic, & Grotpeter, 1998)	LST is a 3-year school-based program targeting middle school students. It is intended to prevent or ameliorate gateway drug use, including tobacco, alcohol, and marijuana. Students learn self-management skills, social skills, and information specific to drug use prevention.	Griffin, K. W., Botvin, G. J., Nichols, T. R., & Doyle, M. M. (2003). Effectiveness of a universal drug abuse prevention approach for youth at high risk for substance use initiation. *Preventive Medicine, 36*, 1–7.	Middle school students	Costs are approximately $7.00 per student, not including a minimum $2,000.00 per day fee for training. Princeton Health Press, Inc. 711 Westchester Avenue White Plains, NY 10604 800-293-4969 914-421-2007 *www.lifeskillstraining.com*
Project Toward No Drug Abuse (TND; Sussman, Rohrbach, & Mihalic, 2004)	TND provides information about the negative effects of drug use and promotes coping skills, stress management, effective communication, and ways to counteract risk factors.	Sun, W., Skara, S., Sun, P., Dent, C.W., & Sussman, S. (2006). Project Towards No Drug Abuse: Long-term substance use outcomes evaluation. *Preventive Medicine, 42*, 188–192.	High school students ages 14–19	Program materials include a teacher's manual ($70.00) and student workbooks. Optional materials are available, as is a 2-day training ($2,500.00). Jim Miyano USC Institute for Prevention Research 1000 South Fremont Avenue, Unit 8 Alhambra, CA 91803 800-400-8461 e-mail: *miyano@usc.edu* *www.tnd.usc.edu*
Good Behavior Game (GBG; Embry, Straatemeier, Lauger, & Richardson, 2003)	The GBG is a behavior modification program intended to decrease aggressive or disruptive behaviors. It is introduced as a classroom game that helps to reduce aggressive behavior and promote positive social skills.	Embry, D. D. (2002). The Good Behavior Game: A best practice candidate as a universal behavioral vaccine. *Clinical Child and Family Psychology Review, 5*, 273–297.	Early elementary	Hazelden Publishing and Educational Services 15251 Pleasant Valley Road P.O. Box 176 Center City, MN 55012-0176 800-328-9000 or 651-213-4200 e-mail: *customersupport@hazelden.org* *www.hazelden.org*

Note. See Center for the Prevention and Study of Violence (2004) for additional information about these programs. Reprinted Lane, Kalberg, and Menzies (2009).

The "Tell" section introduces each skill and helps students to understand what the skill is, generate ideas about ways they could use it, be aware of feelings they have concerning the skill, and recall times when they have had to use it. The teacher also points out why it is important to use the skill and what the benefits are from doing so. The last part of the "Tell" section is to identify and discuss each of the skill steps.

The "Show" section has teachers model the skill or has students demonstrate it through role play. The skill is enacted using each of the steps introduced in the "Tell" section. Adequate time should be given to this step, as it helps students understand what the skill looks like and how they can display it themselves.

The "Do" section provides students with additional practice of the skill. Students define the skill, reiterate its importance, list the skill steps, and then practice using the skill in small groups or pairs. This step gives them adequate time to practice the skill so they can easily display it in the appropriate situation.

"Follow Through" provides students with an opportunity for review at a later time or through homework assignments (which are provided in the curriculum). The final step, "Generalization," prompts students to use the skill in other settings or with other students. This helps them internalize it and recognize what it might look like in other contexts. The skill becomes more valuable because it can be used in settings beyond the classroom or the training context.

Teachers can look through Elliott and Gresham's (1991) curriculum and simply choose the skills they think are most important for students to know, or they can use a more data-driven approach, as we described previously (see Lane, Kalberg, & Menzies, 2009, for details of how to identify essential skills using the Social Skills Rating System [SSRS; Gresham & Elliott, 1990]). The skills can be taught on a regular basis—for example, introducing one new skill a week or one skill a month. This is particularly effective if implemented at the schoolwide level (see Chapter 1). When all teachers at a school site agree on a common set of skills and then teach them, the entire school climate is improved, not just any one individual class. However, if a single student or small group of students pose a continuing or more intensive challenge, teachers may want to formally assess the student(s) and design a package of social skills that will address their particular needs (see Lane, Wehby, et al., 2003, for an application in a general education context and Miller, Lane, & Wehby, 2005, for an illustration in a self-contained classroom). The Practical Strategies curriculum is designed to be used in conjunction with the SSRS (Gresham & Elliott, 1990). The SSRS is a short questionnaire completed by the teacher (parent and student questionnaires are also available) regarding individual students. Results indicate which social skills the student would benefit from most. The advantage of using the SSRS to pinpoint specific skills for instruction is that it is a standardized measurement tool that can be used to determine whether improvement has occurred. The SSRS can also provide important information for a student study team designing an intervention, for a multidisciplinary team considering eligibility for special education, or for teachers creating an IEP.

Although teaching a social skills curriculum may seem like a great deal of added work, in the end this strategy is likely to save time if a student or students have not responded to any of the positive behavior strategies detailed so far. Disruptive behavior is both time- and energy-consuming, and it is best addressed through preventative, rather than reactive, measures. A teacher who provides a well-managed classroom and engaging instruction and implements low-intensity strategies yet still has students who are truly challenging will need to spend more time up front to positively address behavioral issues.

SUMMARY

This chapter began with information about the importance of fostering intrinsic motivation in students. Schools tend to rely heavily on extrinsic sources of motivation because they are efficient and powerful modes of shaping behavior. However, it is critical to create an environment that supports the development of intrinsic motivation as well. Students who are inwardly motivated to engage in school are more likely to be successful and independent. With the right blend of external support and opportunities for creativity and choice, students can become more intrinsically motivated. Models such as schoolwide positive behavior support address this concern by clarifying desired behaviors and then using applied behavior analytic strategies to reinforce desired behaviors that will ultimately be maintained by intrinsic motivation.

The remainder of the chapter introduced a series of low-intensity strategies that are effective in helping teachers, administrators, and other school-site support staff maintain a proactive approach to behavior management (i.e., active supervision, proximity, overlappingness and with-it-ness, pacing, praise, OTR, instructive feedback, choice and preferred activities, token economies, and the formal teaching of social skills). As we mentioned, these strategies are grounded in research-based and practice-based evidence. The systematic application of these strategies, many of which work in concert with one another, provides a comprehensive and preventative approach to common behavior problems. When these strategies are used in the context of a well-managed classroom with engaging instruction, most behavior problems will be avoided. More intensive interventions for students who still display challenging behaviors despite application of these strategies are addressed in the following chapters. Again, we encourage you to review Table 4.5, which contains other resources that you may find helpful as you develop your skill sets of low-intensity strategies to prevent and respond to low-level behavioral and academic concerns. Also, we invite you to complete the self-assessment in Chapter 8 (Figure 8.7) designed to assist you in evaluating your own knowledge, skills, and confidence in the use of the content presented in this chapter.

In Part II, *Responding to Problem Behaviors*, we focus on more intensive strategies to respond to existing problem behaviors demonstrated by students who have not responded to low-intensity strategies. Specifically, we focus on behavior contracting (Chapter 5), self-monitoring (Chapter 6), and functional assessment-based interventions (Chapter 7). These next chapters in Part II are intended to assist teachers with students who manifest challenging behaviors in spite of a teacher's strong classroom management, effective teaching, and active awareness of how teacher actions can support positive behaviors. Because these strategies are increasingly more intensive, we have provided even more research-based evidence to support the use of these strategies. We want you to be confident that the investment of additional time will be well spent in responding to challenging behaviors that might occur despite your best efforts.

TABLE 4.5. Low-Intensity Strategies Resource Guide

Reference	Description	Target group	Cost/retrieval information
	Books		
Crone, D. A., Horner, R. H., & Hawken, L. S. (2004). *Responding to problem behavior in schools: The Behavior Education Program*. New York: Guilford Press.	Describes the Behavior Education Program (BEP), a targeted system of positive behavior support to reduce the risk that behavior will become worse over time for students who are nonresponsive to primary levels of prevention and display chronic but not dangerous problem behaviors.	Educators of at-risk students in need of secondary intervention for behavior problems	$32.00 *www.guilford.com*
Lane, K. L., & Beebe-Frankenberger, M. (2004). *School-based interventions: The tools you need to succeed*. Boston, MA: Allyn & Bacon.	Addresses primary, secondary, and tertiary levels of intervention designed to provide an effective learning environment in inclusive settings that meet the needs of an increasingly diverse population of students. Emphasis is placed on incorporating essential components for assessing outcomes, intended or unintended (i.e., social validity, treatment integrity, and generalization and maintenance)	K–12 educators	$35.95 *www.mypearsonbookstore.com*
Pianta, R. C., La Paro, K. M., & Hamre, B. K. (2008). *Classroom Assessment Scoring System: Manual K–3*. Baltimore: Brookes.	Assessment tool to help educators assess teacher–student interactions and emotional and instructional environment.	PreK–3 educators	$49.95 *www.brookespublishing.com/store*
Ayllon, T. (1999). *How to use token economy and point systems* (2nd ed.). Austin, TX: Pro-Ed.	A detailed and comprehensive explanation of how to use a token economy.	K–12 educators	$12.00 *www.proedinc.com*
	Websites		
Epstein, M., Atkins, M., Cullinan, D., Kutash, K., & Weaver, R. (2008). *Reducing behavior problems in the elementary school classroom: A practice guide* (NCEE No. 2008-012). Washington, DC: U.S. Department of Education, Institute of Educational Sciences, National Center for Education Evaluation and Regional Assistance.	What Works Clearinghouse practice guide for reducing behavior problems in the elementary classroom, with five recommendations for evidence-based practices. Compiled using stringent criteria for what is considered evidence-based practice by a review board assigned by the Institute of Education Sciences.	Elementary educators	*ies.ed.gov/ncee/wwc/publications/practiceguides.*
IRIS Center	This site is developed by Vanderbilt University and Claremont Graduate University. It has several interactive modules that address a variety of curricular adaptations, modifications, and strategies.	K–12 educators	*iris.peabody.vanderbilt.edu/index.html*

Intervention Central	Offers free tools and resources to help school staff and parents to promote positive classroom behaviors and foster effective learning for all children.	K–12 educators	*interventioncentral.org*
Education World	This site offers a little bit of everything—from free lesson plans to professional development to classroom management strategies. Dr. Fred Jones, a featured columnist for the website, provides multiple articles on classroom management strategies, including the use of proximity and teaching social skills.	K–12 educators	*www.educationworld.com*
	Refereed journal articles		
Pemberton, J., & Borrego, J. (2007). Increasing acceptance of behavioral child management techniques: What do parents say? *Child and Family Behavior Therapy, 29*, 27–45.	This study investigated parents' opinions about six behavioral management techniques. Parents rated their acceptability and indicated whether or not they would use the techniques at home. In order of acceptability were response cost, token economy, time-out, overcorrection, differential attention, and ignoring.	All educators; parents	*Child and Family Behavior Therapy* is published by Routledge. *www.tandf.co.uk/journals/WCFB*
Hutchinson, S., Murdock, J., & Williamson, R. (2000). Self-recording plus encouragement equals improved behavior. *Teaching Exceptional Children, 32*, 54–58.	This article discusses how the combined use of self-monitoring and teacher praise and encouragement decreased disruptive behavior of a student with hyperactivity.	K–12 educators	*Teaching Exceptional Children* is published by the Council for Exceptional Children. *www.cec.sped.org/Content/NavigationMenu/Publications2/TEACHINGExceptionalChildren*
Siegle, D., & McCoach, D. (2005). Making a difference: Motivating gifted students who are not achieving. *Teaching Exceptional Children, 38*, 22–27.	This article offers pointers for teachers and parents on how to motivate gifted students who are not working to their potential. Suggestions include intrinsic motivation tips, as well as how to recognize development, encourage mastery attribution, enhance environmental perceptions, and promote study skills and self-regulation.	Educators and parents of gifted students	
Jolivette, K., Stichter, J., & McCormick, K. (2002). Making choices—improving behavior—engaging in learning. *Teaching Exceptional Children, 34*, 24–29.	The author uses a case study to illustrate how offering choice during mathematics improved the behavior and time on task of a student with behavioral issues.	Math educators	
McIntosh, K., Herman, K., & Sanford, A. (2004). Teaching transitions: Techniques for promoting success between lessons. *Teaching Exceptional Children, 37*, 32–38.	Four techniques that facilitate smooth transitions in the classroom are discussed, including teaching routines, precorrections, positive reinforcement procedures, and active supervision.	K–12 educators	

(cont.)

TABLE 4.5. *(cont.)*

Reference	Description	Target group	Cost/retrieval information
Colvin, G., Sugai, G., Good, R. H., & Lee, Y. (1997). Using active supervision and precorrection to improve transition behavior in an elementary school. *School Psychology Quarterly, 12*, 344–363.	This is a multiple-baseline study in which investigators measured rates of problem behaviors across three different transition settings. The intervention included the use of precorrection and active supervision. Results indicated lower rates of problem behaviors such as running, hitting, and yelling.	K–12 educators	*School Psychology Quarterly* is published by The Guilford Press.
Shogren, A., Fagella-Luby, M., Bae, S. J., & Wehmeyer, M. L. (2004). The effect of choice making as an intervention for problem behavior: A meta-analysis. *Journal of Positive Behavior Interventions, 6*, 228–237.	A meta-analysis of 13 single-case design studies using choice making as an intervention for decreasing problem behavior in students with disabilities was conducted. Choice making interventions included those in which participants selected the order in which to complete tasks, as well as interventions in which they chose between activities. The authors concluded that providing choice-making opportunities resulted in significant decreases in problem behavior.	K–12 educators	*Journal of Positive Behavior Interventions* is published by the Hammill Institute on Disabilities and Sage Publications in association with the Association for Positive Behavior Support.
Sutherland, K., & Wehby, J. H. (2001). Exploring the relationship between increased opportunities to respond to academic requests and the academic and behavioral outcomes of students with EBD. *Remedial and Special Education, 22*, 113–122.	Authors reviewed six studies to examine the effects of opportunities to respond (OTR) on the academic and behavioral outcomes of students with emotional and behavioral disorders (EBD). Authors found increasing OTR resulted in increased academic outcomes and task engagement and decreased inappropriate and disruptive behavior for students with EBD.	K–12 educators	*Remedial and Special Education* is published by Pro-Ed.
Werts, M. G., Wolery, M., Holcombe, A., & Gast, D. L. (1995). Instructive feedback: Review of parameters and effects. *Journal of Behavioral Education, 5*, 55–75.	Authors reviewed the literature base on instructive feedback with the purposes of determining who participated in instructive feedback studies and in what settings it has been used, how instructive feedback has been employed, and what effects result from instructive feedback. Recommendations for using instructive feedback in the classroom and for future studies of instructive feedback are offered.	K–12 educators	*Journal of Behavioral Education* is published by Springer Netherlands.

PART II

RESPONDING TO PROBLEM BEHAVIORS

CHAPTER 5

Behavior Contracts

In the beginning chapters of this book we introduced a range of classwide strategies to prevent problem behaviors from occurring, with recommendations to implement these strategies within the context of a comprehensive three-tiered model of prevention that addresses academic, behavioral, and social components. For example, in Chapter 2 we focused on five essential components of classroom management: classroom climate, physical room arrangement, approach to discipline, procedures and routines, and managing paperwork. By attending to these dimensions, teachers can set the stage for a structured, predictable, safe environment to facilitate teaching and learning.

In Chapter 3, we focused on instructional delivery, addressing such topics as the importance of appropriate curricula, instructional pacing and delivery, choice and preferred activities, and activities that are intrinsically rewarding. A central theme was the importance of developing learning experiences that allow students to engage in work in their zones of proximal development—work that is neither too easy nor too difficult (Gickling & Armstrong, 1978; Umbreit et al., 2004; Vygotsky, 1978).

Collectively, the information regarding classroom management and instructional delivery provides a firm foundation for sound instruction that encourages students to be both engaged and productive. Such an environment not only maximizes academic outcomes for students, but it also prevents problem behaviors from occurring.

To further empower teachers, administrators, and other school-site personnel, we provided several low-intensity, preventative strategies in Chapter 4, beginning with the basics and then addressing additional strategies to increase their repertoire of skills. These included active supervision, proximity, overlappingness and with-it-ness, pacing, praise, OTR, and instructive feedback. Such strategies were introduced to address the needs of students who require additional supports to promote engagement and prevent the occurrence of behaviors that impede instruction for individual students, as well as the class as a whole (Walker et al., 2004). First, we began with a discussion of fostering intrinsic motivation in students so that they become successful, independent learners. We contend that with an appropriate balance between external support and opportunities for creativity and choice, students can become more intrinsically motivated. Second, we introduced a range of low-intensity strategies for scaling up these skills. These topics included choice and preferred activities, token economies, and the formal teaching of social skills. Such tools can provide teachers with a range of strategies to facilitate instruction and prevent subsequent problem behaviors from ensuing. In general, these strategies are efficient and effective, meaning that they take limited time and effort to implement and still yield the desired results.

However, as we mentioned at the onset of this book, there are still going to be students who will need additional supports—academically, behaviorally, and socially—to meet expectations (Lane, Kalberg, & Menzies, 2009). Consequently, it is important that teachers, administrators, and other school-site personnel be equipped with reactive, as well as proactive, strategies for managing challenging behaviors and facilitating instruction.

In this chapter, we present one low-intensity, secondary prevention strategy—behavior contracting—that can be used to increase desired behaviors and decrease undesired behaviors (Cooper et al., 2007). We begin by providing a brief overview of behavior contracts. Then we define the strategy, discussing different types of contracts, such as one-party and two-party contracts. Two-party contracts include quid pro quo and parallel contracts. We include directions on how to conduct behavior contracting in the classroom, followed by a discussion of the benefits and challenges associated with this intervention. Then we provide an overview of the research that supports use of behavior contracts to improve performance with elementary, middle, and high school students in a range of environments. We present a step-by-step set of directions on how to develop, implement, and evaluate behavior contracting interventions in the classroom. We conclude this chapter with one illustration of how behavior contracts can be implemented with elementary students and a second illustration for application in secondary schools.

BEHAVIOR CONTRACTS: AN OVERVIEW

A behavior contract, also referred to as a *contingency contract*, is a written agreement between at least two individuals in which one or both individuals agree to demonstrate certain behaviors. In behavioral terms, a behavior contract is "a document that specifies a contingent relationship between the completion of a specified behavior and access to, or delivery of, a specified reward" (Cooper et al., 2007, p. 551).

Most behavior or contingency contracts include three core components: the behavior, the reward, and the recording sheet. First, let us consider the desired behavior or task. When specifying the behavior, it is important to include four pieces of information: *who, what, when*, and *how well* (Cooper et al., 2007). When specifying the *who*, you indicate the name of each person who is involved in the contract, such as the student, teacher, paraprofessional, and/or the parent. The *what* refers to the specific behavior to be performed. It is very important to clearly define the target behavior so as to eliminate any confusion as to what is required to receive the contingent reward. The *when* refers to temporal components such as the day and time by which the task must be completed. The *how well* refers to the specific levels of performance or standards. This information is often delineated in a list format that includes a series of steps or tasks that can be used by the student to self-monitor his or her performance (a strategy that is discussed in greater detail in Chapter 6). For example, it is not enough to state that Nathan will finish his Algebra II portfolio assignment over the weekend. We need additional information regarding (1) the roles and responsibilities of other involved parties (the *who*); (2) a more comprehensive description of the portfolio assignment (the *what*); (3) the day and time by which the task must be accomplished (the *when*); and (4) the accuracy or quality expectations (the *how well*). In Figure 5.1 you will see a behavior contract that specifies the details of the task.

Second, we need to provide equally specific detail regarding the reward component of the behavior contract. Namely, if Nathan's reward is that he can have his friend Jordon over for a visit, the details of this reward need to be clear. Consequently, it is important that the contract specify the following information: who, what, when, and the amount. For the reward component, the *who* refers to the person who will serve as the contingency manager—the person who evaluates the task completion and makes a determination about whether or not the reward is to be delivered. In the illustration in Figure 5.1, the parent is the contingency manager, as the task focuses on an assignment that will be completed at home. In Figure 5.2, you see another illustration of a behavior contract in which the teacher serves as the contingency manager. The *what* is the reward itself. In the example provided in Figure 5.1, one of the rewards is having Jordon over to play e-rated video games. The *when* specifies the time that the reward will be delivered to the person who met the specified expectations, and *amount* indicates how much time the reward will be available to the person (or dosage). In this example, one of the reward options is to have Jordon come over to Nathan's house from 2 to 4 P.M. on Sunday afternoon provided that Nathan meets all criteria specified (100% completion, with materials submitted online to his teacher by noon on Sunday). It is critical that the reward be delivered *contingent* upon meeting the task demand. In other words, it is "Grandma's rule"—first you eat your vegetables (complete the task

CONTRACT

I, *Nathan*, will complete my Algebra II portfolio by noon on Sunday. This means that it will be 100% complete and submitted online. I understand that meeting this expectation will allow me to choose one of three rewards. The reward choices include:

1. Jordon can come over to my house from 2 to 4 P.M. on Sunday.
2. I can play e-rated video games from 2 to 3 P.M. on Sunday.
3. Mom will take me to the library to check out a book at 2 P.M. on Sunday.

***If I complete my portfolio by 6 P.M. on Saturday, then I can have additional time for my rewards (e.g., Jordon can stay an extra hour).

____________________________ ____________________________
Nathan's signature Date

____________________________ ____________________________
Parent signature Date

FIGURE 5.1. Behavior contract: Assignment completion.

component of the contract) and then you can have your dessert (receive the reward specified in the reward component of the contract; Cooper et al., 2007). We also recommend incorporating choice into the contract. For example, in Nathan's contract, he has the choice of (1) having Jordon come over on Sunday afternoon, (2) playing e-rated electronic games, or (3) checking out a book from the library. This allows Nathan to have some options based on his desired source of reinforcement at the time (Lane, Kalberg, & Menzies, 2009; Umbreit et al., 2007). For example, come Sunday, he might want some social time with his friend (positive reinforcement in the form of peer attention), time to play by himself (positive reinforcement in the form of sensory stimulation—video games), or time to enjoy a good book (positive reinforcement in the form of a preferred activity). Allowing choice addresses the potential challenge of the lack of availability of a specified reinforcer. For example, if time with Jordon were the only reward mentioned and if Jordon were sick or just unable to come over, then the contract would be breached. Such circumstances are disappointing and can undermine the strategy. Another option is to include a bonus clause. For example, we could say that if Nathan completes the assignment ahead of time (e.g., by Saturday evening before 6 P.M.), he could have additional time on any of the three reinforcer options.

The third and final component of the behavior contract is the recording sheet. The recording sheet is designed to serve as (1) a prompt to remind all parties of the agreed-upon components and (2) a method for recording performance in order to make accurate conclusions regarding the delivery of the reward. More specifically, it is possible to design a recording sheet that requires the contingency manager to monitor and record both task completion and reward delivery. Public posting of the contract may also benefit the students in the same way by providing frequent interaction with the contract to remind all parties about the terms of the contract. However, issues related to confidentiality, privacy, and embarrassment need to be weighed. For example, a student might feel embarrassed if his or her contract regarding work completion, work accuracy, or weight loss were publicly displayed. In addition, if the terms of the contract indicate that a number of behaviors must occur (see Figure 5.1) or that the same behavior must occur multiple times (see

CONTRACT

I, *Jameera*, will arrive on time to class each day. Arriving on time is defined as being inside the classroom and seated at my desk prior to the bell ringing. Mr. Valdez will determine if I am on time. If I am on time, I will receive a positive behavior support ticket from Mr. Valdez immediately upon arrival. If I arrive on time for 5 consecutive days, then I can choose 1 of 3 rewards:

1. 30 minutes of computer time on Friday
2. Free homework pass to be used during the following week
3. 30 minutes of reading time with Jake, the golden retriever reading dog

Daily Log: Mr. Valdez will circle "on time" or "late" each day

	Monday	Tuesday	Wednesday	Thursday	Friday
10/7–10/11	On time Late	On time Late	On time Late	On time Late	On time Late
10/14–10/18	On time Late	On time Late	On time Late	On time Late	On time Late
10/21–10/25	On time Late	On time Late	On time Late	On time Late	On time Late
10/28–11/1	On time Late	On time Late	On time Late	On time Late	On time Late

Bonus Clause: If I am on time for all 20 sessions above, I will earn an extra 5 positive behavior support tickets.

______________________ ______________________
Jameera's signature Date

______________________ ______________________
Mr. Valdez's signature Date

FIGURE 5.2. Behavior contract: On-time arrival.

Figure 5.2) before receiving the reward, then the recording sheet is also useful to ensure that the reward is delivered contingent upon completion of all terms specified in the contract.

In sum, most behavior contracts ideally include three core components—the behavior, the reward, and the recording sheet—with the appropriate specifications depending on the type of contract employed. In the next section we review different types of contracts.

Types of Behavior Contracts

As we mentioned, there are one-party and two-party contracts; two-party contracts include with quid pro quo and parallel contracts (Miltenberger, 2004). In this section, we briefly describe each type of contract.

One-Party Contract

The *one-party contract* is also referred to as a unilateral contract (Kirschenbaum & Flanery, 1984) or a self-contract (Cooper et al., 2007). In a one-person contract the individual desires to change his or her own behavior (e.g., writing productivity, exercise, work completion, or time spent on the Internet). To assist in the behavior change process, this individual arranges reinforcement or punishment contingencies with a contingency manager. The contingency manager is responsible for implementing the behavior contract with integrity, meaning that all terms of the contract are honored (Miltenberger, 2004). For example, Figure 5.3 shows a behavior contract for Lulu, who is interested in completing her term paper. During her first semester in college, she realized that she had a tendency to procrastinate on course papers. So this semester she decided to develop a contract. Specifically, she decided to begin her term paper during the third week of the semester, with a goal of completing the paper by the twelfth week of the semester. She anticipated that the paper would be about 30 pages in length, so she decided to write three pages a week. In the contract she specified that a page would be defined as one 8½″ × 11″ inch paper, typed using American Psychological Association (APA) format (12-point font, Times New Roman, double spaced). She met with her advisor, Aiden Crnobori, to specify the terms of the contract. They decided that Lulu would bring three new pages to her weekly meeting with Dr. Crnobori each Friday at 11 A.M. in his office. If Lulu does not bring the three new pages of the term paper to Dr. Crnobori at the weekly meeting, Dr. Crnobori will deduct 5 points from her final grade for the term paper.

Ideally, the contingency manager would be someone (1) with training in applied behavior analysis and (2) who does not stand to benefit personally from the client's (student's) behavioral change. It is possible to have others, such as

CONTRACT

I, *Lulu Menzies*, agree to write three pages of my term paper each week beginning the 3rd week of the semester (9/12/2010) and ending the 12th week of the semester (11/27/2010).

A page is defined as one 8½″ × 11″ paper, typed using APA format (12-point font, Times New Roman, double spaced).

I will bring three new pages each week to my weekly meeting with Aiden Crnobori (my advisor) each Friday at 11 A.M. in his office.

If I do not bring the three new pages of the term paper to Dr. Crnobori at the weekly meeting, Dr. Crnobori will deduct 5 points from my final grade for the term paper.

Lulu Menzies, Student

Aiden Crnobori, Advisor

	Did Lulu show up to the Friday meeting?	How many pages did Lulu have completed?	Additional Comments
9/12/10			
9/19/10			
9/26/10			
10/2/10			
10/9/10			
10/16/10			
10/23/10			
10/30/10			
11/6/10			
11/13/10			
11/20/10			
11/27/10			

FIGURE 5.3 One-party contract.

friends, significant others, or classmates, serve as the contingency managers, but it is important for them to know that it could be awkward to enforce the terms of the contract if the client (student) is emotionally attached to the contingency manager. For example, if a person developed a one-party contract with his or her spouse to increase the amount of time spent exercising, could the spouse really execute the response cost component (taking away a preferred item or activity) if the terms of the contract were not met?

Two-Party Contract

One of the most typical behavior contracts is the *two-party contract*, also referred to as a bilateral contract (Kirschenbaum & Flanery, 1984). The two-party contract is a written contract between two (or more) parties, each of whom is focused on changing a given behavior. Typically there is some level of concern on the part of both parties, which is the reason that the contract is introduced in the first place. We address two types of two-party contracts—quid pro quo contracts and parallel contracts.

QUID PRO QUO CONTRACTS

Quid pro quo contracts are contracts designed so that one person's behavior change is the reinforcer for another person's behavior change. For example, Nathan's mom was concerned that Nathan would not complete the Algebra II portfolio assignment by the end of the weekend. Nathan felt that she was constantly nagging him about it. And he was concerned that he would spend the whole weekend doing homework and not have any time to do things that he wanted. Hence the need for the contract. Nathan's mom felt the portfolio assignment should take precedence over his free time. If Nathan and his mom were to write a quid pro quo two-party contract, they would each agree to change at least one of their behaviors. For example, Nathan's mom would agree to leave Nathan alone about his assignment until Sunday at noon. And Nathan would agree to complete his assignment by Sunday at noon. In this way, Nathan is able to avoid the nagging, and his mom is able to feel confident that Nathan will complete his portfolio. Thus Nathan's behavior is reinforced by avoiding attention from his mom. And his mom's behavior is reinforced by Nathan's portfolio completion. In sum, in a quid pro quo two-party contract, the behavior change of one person reinforces the behavior change of the other (Miltenberger, 2004). This example is illustrated in Figure 5.4.

PARALLEL CONTRACTS

Parallel contracts again involve two or more persons. In this case, each person agrees to implement a behavior change desired by the other person in the contract.

CONTRACT

I, *Nathan Lane*, will:

- Complete my Algebra II portfolio assignment by 12:00 P.M. on Sunday
- Submit my Algebra II portfolio online by 12:00 P.M. on Sunday

Nathan's signature ______________________ Date ______________________

I, *Kathleen Lane*, will:

- Avoid making any comments and asking any questions to Nathan regarding completion of his Algebra II portfolio until 12:00 P.M. on Sunday.

Kathleen's signature ______________________ Date ______________________

FIGURE 5.4. Quid pro quo contract.

However, in contrast to the quid pro quo contract, both parties arrange rewards for their respective behavior changes that are not contingent upon the other party's performance. Using Nathan and his mom again, the contract would involve reinforcers for both parties. For example, if Nathan completes his portfolio assignment by noon on Sunday, he could invite Jordon over for 2 hours. If Nathan's mom refrains from prompting Nathan about his assignment until Sunday at noon, then she might reward herself with something such as having coffee (do you remember the type of latte?) with a friend. It is important to note that his mom's reward is *not* contingent upon Nathan's completion of the portfolio. She can be rewarded when she completes *her* part of the contract. Similarly, if Nathan's mom reminds him about his assignment, thus violating the contract, and Nathan completes the assignment, then Nathan is still able to have Jordon over to his house. This example is illustrated in Figure 5.5.

Contracts can also be written between more than two parties. For example, if the concern is related to work completion, this might involve a contract between teacher, student, and parent. In Figure 5.6, you will see an illustration of such a contract.

In the section that follows, we explain the reasons that behavior contracts are effective in changing behavior. We offer a concise overview of how applied behavioral analytic principles can be used within the context of this strategy.

CONTRACT

I, *Nathan Lane*, will:

- Complete my Algebra II portfolio assignment by 12:00 P.M. on Sunday
- Submit my Algebra II portfolio online by 12:00 P.M. on Sunday

If I complete and submit my portfolio on time, I can choose to (1) invite Jordon over for 2 hours, (2) play e-rated video games for an hour, or (3) go to the library to check out books.

____________________ ____________________

Nathan's signature Date

I, *Kathleen Lane*, will:

- Avoid making any comments and asking any questions to Nathan regarding completion of his Algebra II portfolio until 12:00 P.M. on Sunday.

If I avoid making comments and asking questions to Nathan about his assignment for the said amount of time, I will treat myself to coffee with my friend Terri.

____________________ ____________________

Kathleen's signature Date

FIGURE 5.5. Parallel contract.

Underlying Principles

Before you implement a behavior contract, we would like to offer you some insight as to the science behind behavior contracts. Clearly, the logic behind behavior contracts is grounded in applied behavior analytic procedures. At first glance, it may appear to be a simple illustration of positive reinforcement (introducing a desired stimulus contingent upon performance to increase the probability that the behavior will occur in the future).

However, in actuality, a behavior contract is an intervention package that includes multiple behavioral principles (Cooper et al., 2007). Miltenberger (2004, p. 505) defines a behavior contract as "an antecedent manipulation that makes it more likely that the person will engage in the behavior specified in the contract." It involves the notion of rule-governed behavior (Malott & Garcia, 1987; Skinner, 1969). Essentially, the contract specifies a rule. It indicates the specific behavior that will occur and the specific consequence that will be delivered contingent upon completion of the target behavior. The contract is the antecedent—or prompt—to

CONTRACT

Roles and Responsibilities

Student: Keyshawn will complete one page of his research paper per night for the next 5 nights. He will also check in with his dad when he has completed the page. Finally, he will bring his completed page and signed chart to Mrs. Hernandez each day for the next 5 days. If he completes the page, he will be allowed to watch 1 hour of television. If he does not complete the page, he will not be allowed to watch any television.

Parent: Keyshawn's dad, Mr. Harris, will check in with Keyshawn each night for the next 5 nights to make sure his son has completed one page of his research paper each night. Mr. Harris will read Keyshawn's page and then sign Keyshawn's chart each night indicating they met and Keyshawn completed his work. Mr. Harris will allow Keyshawn to watch 1 hour of television if his page is complete.

Teacher: Mrs. Hernandez will meet with Keyshawn each day for the next 5 days to see if he completed his page and had his chart signed by his dad. Mrs. Hernandez will also sign his chart. If Keyshawn has completed a page and his dad has signed his chart, Mrs. Hernandez will add 1 extra point to his research paper grade for each day Keyshawn meets the objective. Thus Keyshawn has an opportunity to earn 5 extra points on his research paper.

	Number of pages completed by student	Parent signature	Bonus points earned
Monday			
Tuesday			
Wednesday			
Thursday			
Friday			
		TOTAL bonus points earned	

Keyshawn's signature ____________ Date ____________

Mr. Harris's signature ____________ Date ____________

Mrs. Hernandez's signature ____________ Date ____________

FIGURE 5.6. Three-party contract.

elicit the target behavior, which enables consequences (e.g., rewards) to be delivered. Delaying the consequences (e.g., completing *X* activities before earning a reward on Friday evening) can help the contingency manager to control behaviors that occurred earlier in time (e.g., in previous days). Others contend that viewing the contract can actually serve as a negative reinforcing value, meaning that the person can escape guilt associated with not meeting one's goals or expectations by seeing the progress that is being made toward a goal (which can also increase the future probability of behavior occurring). Thus you can think of behavioral contracts as an intervention package that includes features of rule-governed behavior, public commitment, positive reinforcement, and negative reinforcement principles and procedures that operate independently and in conjunction with one another (Cooper et al., 2007; Miltenberger, 2004). In the next section, we highlight some of the benefits and challenges of this multicomponent intervention.

BENEFITS AND CHALLENGES

When determining whether or not to develop a behavior contract with a student, we encourage you to keep the following considerations in mind: (1) the types of deficits for which this strategy is appropriate, (2) the student's developmental phase, (3) the appropriateness of various measurement systems, and (4) what to do if one of the parties does not wish to participate.

First, central to all types of behavior contracts is the necessity that desired behaviors be in the person's skill set or behavioral repertoire. Ideally, the desired behavior should be under stimulus control in the context (environment) in which you would like the behavior to occur. For example, if the goal is to increase a student's time spent writing in a journal, then the behavior (writing in a journal) should be under stimulus control in the classroom. In this case, there needs to be a journal, a prompt on the board, time allotted for writing, and a verbal prompt from the teacher to spend 5–7 minutes working on the journal. Behavior contracts are designed to address performance deficits ("won't do" problems) and fluency deficits (trouble doing problems); they are not appropriate for acquisition deficits ("can't do" problems; Elliott & Gresham, 2007; Lane, Kalberg, & Menzies, 2009). When students have acquisition deficits, the focus of the intervention needs to include skill building by teaching these necessary skill sets using differentiated instruction (see Chapter 3). Once a student has acquired a skill, then the next step is to build fluency or the motivation to perform the new skill or behavior (Cooper et al., 2007).

Second, before designing a contract, we need to consider the student's developmental level. For example, if a student is quite young and is not yet reading, contracts can still be developed. However, they will need to include icons or other graphics to help delineate the terms of the contract (Cooper et al., 2007). The same is true for students who have mild to moderate intellectual disabilities, autism, and similar special needs. It is critical to be certain that the student (or client) is able to be directed by the stimulus control of the visual (or verbal) rules of the contract (Sulzer-Azaroff & Mayer, 1994).

Third, in terms of how to best monitor behavior, the goal is to ensure the highest degree of accuracy possible. Ideally, the behavior would (1) yield a permanent product such as the completed Algebra II portfolio assignment or (2) be directly observed by the contingency manager (e.g., parent, teacher, or paraprofessional watching the student participate in the discussion group). One challenge of behavior contracts is that in some instances the behavior is a covert behavior (e.g., purging after eating or having negative thoughts) that is difficult to measure with a high degree of accuracy (thus having to rely on self-report).

Fourth, another challenge that must be considered is what to do with individuals who do not want to be a part of a contract. It is most advantageous when the parties involved voluntarily collaborate to develop a mutually beneficial contract (Lassman, Jolivette, & Wehby, 1999). Yet some students may still be resistant to this strategy. For instance, consider the high school senior who has been skipping school and is simply not interested in developing a contract to improve attendance. In such cases, it may be better to select a different strategy to elicit a behavior change. For example, you might consider goal-setting, decision-making, or self-monitoring strategies (self-monitoring is discussed in Chapter 6). Fortunately, behavior contracting strategies have been successful in changing a range of behaviors in both adults and children, including increasing athletic skills (Simek, O'Brien, & Figlerski, 1994), improving personal hygiene and grooming behaviors (Allen & Kramer, 1990), and improving academic performance (Wilkinson, 2003).

SUPPORTING RESEARCH FOR BEHAVIOR-CONTRACTING INTERVENTIONS

To date several empirical studies (most of which have used single-case methodology) have examined the impact of behavior contracts. In the following sections, we highlight a few behavior contracting studies conducted in the elementary, middle, and high school settings to improve a range of behaviors.

Elementary School

Contingency contracting has been widely and effectively used with middle school- and high school-age students (e.g., Kelley & Stokes, 1982; McLaughlin & Williams, 1988), and it also holds promise for elementary-age students. For example, Allen, Howard, Sweeney, and McLaughlin (1993) used contingency contracting to increase the academic engagement of three second- or third-grade students who had been wandering around the class, not paying attention to the task, and failing to complete the assigned tasks. In this study, each contract was individualized for each student, identifying (1) the target behavior, (2) the consequences, and (3) the length of the contract. The contracts were reviewed by the teacher and student at the end of each school day. Results revealed that all three students increased on-task behavior when the intervention was in place. Students' behavior changes were immediate and pronounced; furthermore, the intervention required minimal teacher time.

It is also possible to deliver other intervention packages using contingency contracts. For example, De Martini-Scully, Bray, and Kehle (2000) delivered an intervention using a behavior contract to decrease the disruptive behavior of two 8-year-old girls (one African American and one white) who attended a second-grade classroom in an urban public school. The intervention included four components: (1) precision requests, which refers to direct, simple commands (Forehand & McMahon, 1981); (2) antecedent adjustments, such as displaying classroom rules and having the teacher move about the classroom; (3) positive reinforcement of the desired behaviors using a token economy system; and (4) a response-cost component (e.g., taking away a reinforcer, as discussed in Chapter 4) to reduce undesirable behaviors. After the program was explained to the students, they signed a contingency contract indicating that they understood and agreed to participate in the intervention by following the terms of the contract. This multicomponent intervention was effective in decreasing the students' disruptive behavior, and the teacher viewed the procedures to be acceptable.

Miller and Kelley (1994) examined the impact of goal setting and contingency contracting of students' work accuracy and on-task behavior during homework. Participants were four elementary students (two boys and two girls) who had trouble completing their homework. Researchers worked with each parent individually to teach them the rationale and procedures for conducting goal setting and behavior contracting. Results indicated that this combined intervention was effective in improving on-task behavior during homework time and that the accuracy of homework also improved. Furthermore, results of a social validity rating tool indicated that parents were satisfied with the procedures and the outcomes. They indicated that goal setting and contingency contracting were useful and easy to implement. At the end of the study, the parents felt confident in their ability to manage homework.

The literature indicates that behavior contracting is an effective, efficient strategy for shaping a range of behaviors, including attendance, on-task versus disruptive behavior, playground behavior, work accuracy, and goal completion at the elementary level. In addition, behavior contracts are also effective with older students in middle and high school settings.

Middle and High School

The adolescent years are characterized by a number of challenges. For example, students are expected to negotiate the demands of multiple teachers, to master an increasingly differentiated curriculum, and to shift to new methods of demonstrating content knowledge (e.g., long-term assignments; Carter, Lane, Pierson, & Stang, 2008). At the same time, middle and high school students experience a host of developmental changes and the peer group's opinions become increasingly more important—even more reinforcing than teachers' and parents' perceptions or opinions (Carter et al., 2008). Some specific behavioral challenges include academic deficits, poor work completion, and truancy. Fortunately, contingency contracts have also proven efficacious with even the most challenging secondary-level students.

Kelley and Stokes (1982) conducted a study to examine the effects of student–teacher contracts on increasing the academic productivity of 13 high school students (12 males, 1 female) receiving special education services who attended a vocational training program for disadvantaged youths. This contracting procedure was used to reinforce program participation rather than attendance by switching the pay-based structure. In brief, instead of paying students to attend the program (which was part of the regular or baseline practices), the intervention involved shifting the system to pay students for fulfilling their contracts, which focused on workbook assignments. Thus the pay-based structure shifted from reinforcing attendance (baseline) to reinforcing contract fulfillment (workbook assignments, intervention). Results suggested that students and teachers preferred contracting to baseline conditions. In fact, students' productivity more than doubled during the contracting phase relative to baseline.

Behavior contracting also has been used effectively to address work completion, truancy, and disruptive behavior. For example, White-Blackburn, Semb, and Semb (1977) used a behavior contract to change the on-task behavior, disruptive behavior, daily assignment completion, and weekly grades of four 6th-grade students in a general education classroom. Rewards for good conduct and goal completion included access to a variety of classroom privileges and school facilities. Results revealed that on-task behavior and daily assignment completion increased, disruptive behavior decreased, and weekly grades were higher during the contracting period.

Summary

To summarize, behavior contracts have proven effective at the elementary, middle, and high school levels with a variety of students, including those with disabilities, and in a variety of settings (e.g., general education classrooms, self-contained classrooms, playgrounds, alternative schools, parochial schools, etc.). Table 5.1 presents a summary of research on behavior contracting, including brief descriptions of the participants, instructional setting, intervention, dependent variables (i.e., the outcome variables being measured to see whether the intervention effects change), and research design.

TABLE 5.1. Behavior Contracting: Summary of Research

Reference	Students	Instructional setting	Intervention	Dependent variable(s)	Design
			Elementary studies		
De Martini-Scully, Bray, & Kehle (PITS, 2000)	*N* = 3; 3 girls; age: 8; ethnicity: 1 African American, 1 white, 1 Hispanic; school level: elementary (2nd)	General education	Contingency contract: precision requests, antecedent strategies, positive reinforcement, and response cost	Disruptive behaviors	Multiple baseline/ reversal design
Flood & Wilder (ETC, 2002)	*N* = 1; 1 boy; age: 11; school level: elementary (4th)	General education	Functional communication training and contingency contracting	On task	Multiple baseline
Allen, Howard, Sweeney, & McLaughlin (PR, 1993)	*N* = 3; gender: NS; age: NS; school level: elementary (2nd and 3rd)	Not specified	Contingency contracting	On-task behavior: remaining seated, completing assignments, and remaining attentive	ABAB
Kidd & Saudargas (ETC, 1988)	*N* = 2; 1 boy, 1 girl; age: NS; ethnicity: NS; school level: elementary (3rd and 6th)	General education math class	Contingency contracting: (1) positive and negative consequences, (2) positive only, (3) negative only	Arithmetic assignments	Multitreatment
Miller & Kelley (JABA, 1994)	*N* = 3; 2 boys, 2 girls; age: 9–11 years; ethnicity: NS; school level: elementary	General education	Goal setting and contingency contracting	Accuracy of completed homework; on-task behavior	Combination of reversal (ABAB) and multiple-baseline designs
Mruzek, Cohen, & Smith (JDPD, 2007)	*N* = 2; 2 boys; age: 9–10; ethnicity: NS; school level: elementary; disability: ADHD/ASD-Asperger's (1), ASD-Autism(1)	Self-contained special education classroom for children with ASD	Contingency contracting	Rule violations and successful hours	Changing criterion
Murphy (Techniques, 1987)	*N* = 1; 1 boy; age: 11; ethnicity: NS; school level: elementary; disability: LD	General education classroom	Contingency contracting	Attendance	ABCB
Ruth (PITS, 1996)	*N* = 43; 35 boys, 8 girls; age: 7–12; ethnicity: NS; school level: elementary (1st–6th); disability: psychiatric	Self-contained special education classroom	Contingency contracting with goal setting	Goal attainment	Descriptive

	disorders (ADD, 23; ODD, 12; MD, 7; DD, 7; CD, 3, AR, 3; S, 2; ASD, 1)				
Smith (ESGC, 1994)	*N* = 24; 16 boys, 8 girls; age: NS; ethnicity: NS; school level: elementary and middle (K–7th)	General education classroom	Parent–child contingency contracting with teacher evaluation	Goal completion	Group quasi-experimental design
Thomas, Lee, McGee, & Silverman (JRDE, 1987)	*N* = 191; boys and girls (number NS); age: 7–11; school level: elementary (2nd and 5th)	Playground	Contingency contracting and a variety of good-behavior games	Playground misbehavior	Multitreatment
Trice (PR, 1990)	*N* = 96; gender: NS; age: NS; ethnicity: NS; school level: high (11th and 12th)	Not specified	ontingency contracting *or* counseling	Locus of control, truancy, disruptive behavior	Group experimental design
Wilkinson (PSF, 2003)	*N* = 1; 1 girl; age: 7; ethnicity: NS; school level: elementary (1st)	General education classroom	Functional assessment-based intervention using contingency contract	Disruptive behavior	AB
Zimmer, Whitmore, & Eller (JIP, 1981)	*N* = 64; gender: NS; age: NS; ethnicity: NS; school level: elementary (5th and 6th)	General education classroom and after-school sessions	Contingency contracting *or* tutoring	Academic grades	Group experimental design
			Middle/high school studies		
Hess, Rosenberg, & Levy (RASE, 1990)	*N* = 26; 19 boys, 7 girls; ethnicity: 20 white, 6 African American; disability: 24 LD, 1 SLI, 1 EH; school level: middle school (6th–8th)	Comprehensive middle school—setting not specified	Contingency contracting and group counseling	Truancy, grade point average, rates of grade retention	Group experimental design
Kelley & Stokes (JABA, 1982)	*N* = 13; 12 boys, 1 girl; age: 16–21; ethnicity: NS; school level: high	Special education vocational/educational training program for disadvantaged high school dropouts	Contingency contracting	Number of workbook items completed	ABAB withdrawal design

(cont.)

TABLE 5.1. *(cont.)*

Reference	Students	Instructional setting	Intervention	Dependent variable(s)	Design
Newstrom, McLaughlin, & Sweeney (CFBT, 1999)	*N* = 1; 1 boy; age: NS; ethnicity: NS; school level: high (9th); disability: behavior disorder, written communication	Self-contained special education classroom	Contingency contracting	Percent correct capitalization and punctuation	Multiple baseline
Redmon & Farris (JIP, 1985)	*N* = 50; boys and girls; age: NS; ethnicity: NS; school level: high school (9th–12th)	"Guided study center" within the high school	Contingency contracting	Contract completion and letter grades	Group quasi-experimental design
Seabaugh & Schumaker (JBE, 1994)	*N* = 11; 8 boys, 3 girls; ethnicity: 9 white, 1 African American, 1 Hispanic; school level: high school (9th–12th); disability: LD (8)	Private alternative school for high-risk students	Self-regulation intervention including behavior self-contracting, self-instruction, self-recording, self-evaluation, self-reinforcement	Number of lessons completed	Multiple baseline combined with reversal design
White-Blackburn, Semb, & Semb (JABA, 1977)	*N* = 4; gender: NS; ethnicity: NS; school level: middle school (6th)	General education classroom	Contingency contracting	On-task behavior, disruptive behavior, daily assignment completion, weekly grades	Multiple baseline
Williams, Long, & Yoakley (JSP, 1972)	*N* = 4; gender: NS; ethnicity: NS; school level: high (12th)	Academically oriented, parochial school classroom	Contingency contracting (joint student–teacher management of contingencies) and behavior proclamation (teacher-imposed management of contingencies)	Appropriate behavior: task-relevant behaviors, appropriate social interactions Inappropriate behavior: time off task, disruptive behavior	ABAC

Note. NS, not specified; CFBT, *Child and Family Behavior Therapy*; EH, emotionally handicapped. ESGC, *Elementary School Guidance and Counseling*; ETC, *Education and Treatment of Children*; JABA, *Journal of Applied Behavior Analysis*; JDPD, *Journal of Developmental and Physical Disabilities*; JIP, *Journal of Instructional Psychology*; JREC, *Journal for Remedial Education and Counseling*; JSP, *Journal of School Psychology*; PITS, *Psychology in the Schools*; PR, *Psychological Reports*; PSF, *Preventing School Failure*; RASE, *Remedial and Special Education*; LD, learning disability; SLI, speech–language impairment; ED, emotional disturbance; ASD, autism spectrum disorder (American Psychiatric Association, 1987); ADHD, attention-deficit–hyperactivity disorder (American Psychiatric Association, 2000); EBD, emotional and behavioral disorders; ADD, attention deficit disorder (American Psychiatric Association, 1987); ODD, oppositional defiant disorder (American Psychiatric Association, 1987); MD, major depression (American Psychiatric Association, 1987); DD, developmental disorder (American Psychiatric Association, 1987); CD, conduct disorder (American Psychiatric Association, 1987); AR, adjustment reaction (American Psychiatric Association, 1987); S, schizophrenia (American Psychiatric Association, 1987).

IMPLEMENTING BEHAVIOR CONTRACTS IN YOUR CLASSROOM

In this section we provide you with a step-by-step set of procedures for designing, implementing, and evaluating behavior contracts in your classroom. Then, following this guide, we offer you two illustrations of how to apply these procedures: one in an elementary school and one in a middle or high school setting (see Boxes 5.1 , on pages 120–121, and 5.2, on pages 122–123).

Many methods for writing behavior contracts exist (Dardig & Heward, 1981; Downing, 2002). We encourage you to develop a contract that is age-appropriate for the population of students you serve, taking into account variables such as the students' age and your own philosophy about reinforcement. In this section, we synthesize the various existing methods and guidelines for writing behavior contracts into a simple step-by-step process. Additionally, we offer practical suggestions for making each step manageable, feasible, and effective.

Step 1: Identify the Target Behavior(s)

Similar to functional assessment procedures (see Chapter 7), the first step in writing a behavior contract is to identify the target behavior—or, in other words, the student's behavior of greatest concern that the teacher would like to change. The teacher should choose a behavior that will have the greatest positive impact on the student's success in the classroom (Downing, 2002). Namely, the target behavior should be a socially valid behavior (Kazdin, 1977; Wolf, 1978). If the student exhibits multiple undesirable or concerning behaviors, the teacher may want to make a list of all possible target behaviors, prioritize them, and then select the one he or she would most like to replace with an appropriate behavior. This is not to say that only one behavior should be identified in the contract, but more than two or three behaviors may be difficult for both teacher and student to monitor.

Once you have identified the target behavior, you will collect and summarize data on this behavior. You will collect data using direct observation procedures. Specifically, you will take notes, as well as quantify the behavior through some type of recording system (i.e., frequency counts, duration, latency, etc.; Downing, 2002). Also, during each observation session, you will need to be aware of antecedent events that prompt the behavior to occur, as well as the consequences of the behavior. This is also referred to as A–B–C data collection (i.e., antecedent–behavior–consequences). Upon completing your direct observations, all notes and data should be summarized in a logical, easy-to-understand way in preparation for meeting with the student and other possible stakeholders. By collecting and summarizing data on the target behavior, you will be able to provide evidence that speaks to the nature of the problem and the need for a behavior contract.

BOX 5.1. Behavior Contracting: Elementary Illustration

Ms. Moeaki ran a structured, well-organized classroom, such as those described in previous chapters. Students were well-versed in the schoolwide rules and classroom procedures, as Ms. Moeaki consistently modeled and reinforced the expectations. Despite her efforts, Ms. Moeaki still had one particular student who consistently did not meet the behavioral expectations for the class. Hayden had a horrible habit of blurting out during inopportune times, which more often than not tended to interrupt the flow of instruction by distracting other students. He rarely followed the procedure for speaking in class, which was to raise his hand and wait to be called on. When Ms. Moeaki reprimanded Hayden for not raising his hand, he huffed and puffed and then refused to participate the rest of the day. At her wits' end, Ms. Moeaki decided it was time for a new strategy—behavior contracting!

Step 1: Identify the target behavior(s). Although Hayden exhibited multiple problem behaviors, Ms. Moeaki knew that if she could just get him to raise his hand and curb his outbursts, then he would be more successful in class—not to mention that the overall classroom climate and flow of instruction would improve, thus benefitting everyone. Ms. Moeaki defined Hayden's behavior as *out-of-turn comments*, which were comments blurted out without teacher permission (i.e., he didn't raise his hand and wait to be called on). To verify that *out-of-turn comments* were actually a problem, Ms. Moeaki recorded the frequency of his *out-of-turn comments* during math, reading, social studies, and science for 3 consecutive days. It turned out that the vast majority of Hayden's problem behavior occurred during math (n = 19) and reading (n = 22)—the two periods with the most whole-class instruction. Science and social studies, on the other hand, usually involved small-group activities with peers, which may have been the reason that Hayden had far fewer (n = 8 total) *out-of-turn comments*.

Step 2: Meet with stakeholders. After Ms. Moeaki wrote a brief summary of her observations, she called a meeting with Hayden and his father. At the meeting, Ms. Moeaki explained that the purpose of the meeting was to discuss behavior contracts and the possibility of creating one between herself and Hayden. Hayden especially liked the idea that he could contribute ideas to the contract. His father, not surprised by Ms. Moeaki's observational data, agreed that the contract might be a positive way to help Hayden.

Step 3: Discuss the student's good and bad behavior. Because Ms. Moeaki didn't want Hayden to feel that she didn't want him to participate in class, she explained to him that he often has positive things to contribute. She simply wanted him to follow the procedures like everyone else in the class. Hayden said he liked to participate, but sometimes he just couldn't wait to be called on. He said he got frustrated by constantly being told to raise his hand, which was the reason he refused to participate after being reprimanded. When Ms. Moeaki asked him the procedure for speaking in class, he acknowledged that he should be raising his hand. Ms. Moeaki praised him for his honesty and being so willing to talk about his behavior.

Step 4: Write behavior objectives/tasks. Because she had seen Hayden raise his hand in class before (although not very often) and because he clearly knew the procedure for speaking in class, Ms. Moeaki determined that hand raising was, in fact, in his behavioral repertoire. So they were able to write a behavioral objective to be included in the contract. The behavioral objective read: "During math class, Hayden will make a total of one or fewer *out-of-turn comments* as determined by Ms. Moeaki, who will tally the number of out-of-turn comments throughout math class." The same objective was written for reading class.

Step 5: Identify rewards and consequences. Each day during independent reading time, students were required to read at their desks. Hayden mentioned that he would like to read on the floor rather than at his desk. He also stated that he was saving up positive behavior support tickets to buy a skateboard from the positive behavior support store and that he liked hard candy. So Ms. Moeaki and Hayden agreed that at the end of each period (i.e., math and reading), if he had one or fewer out-of-turn comments, he could choose from the reward menu: a positive behavior support ticket, reading time spent on the floor, or

(cont.)

a piece of candy. Ms. Moeaki even offered a bonus clause: If Hayden met the objectives for math and reading on Monday through Friday, then on Friday she would give him 5 extra positive behavior support tickets.

Step 6: Determine the evaluation process. In addition to the behavioral objective and rewards, the behavior contract also included a chart to record Hayden's *out-of-turn comments*. Hayden decided he wanted to keep the contract taped to his desk. Ms. Moeaki said that she would keep a tally on a notepad and then discuss it with Hayden so he could fill in his chart. Because they were planning to meet each day to fill in his chart, these "meetings" served as a logical checkpoint to see how the contract was being fulfilled. They decided the contract would be open-ended in that they would continue with the contract as long as both Hayden and Ms. Moeaki were meeting the terms. They also decided to meet with Hayden's dad in a month to review Hayden's progress.

Step 7: Sign on the dotted line! Ms. Moeaki, Hayden, and Hayden's dad read over the contract and agreed that the contingency and procedures were fair and feasible. Each person signed and agreed to meet again in 1 month.

CONTRACT

Behavioral Objectives:

1. During math class, Hayden will make a total of one or fewer *out-of-turn comments* as determined by Ms. Moeaki, who will tally the number of out-of-turn comments throughout math class.
2. During reading class, Hayden will make a total of one or fewer *out-of-turn comments* as determined by Ms. Moeaki, who will tally the number of out-of-turn comments throughout reading class.

Rewards:

1. If Hayden meets the objective for math class, he will choose one of the three rewards from the reward menu at the end of math class.
2. If Hayden meets the objective for reading class, he will choose one of the three rewards from the reward menu at the end of reading class.

Reward Menu:

1. Positive behavior support ticket
2. Independent reading time on the floor
3. 1 piece of hard candy

Bonus Clause:

1. If Hayden meets the objective for math and reading on Monday through Friday, then on Friday, Ms. Moeaki will give him 5 extra positive behavior support tickets.

Chart: to be filled in daily at the end of each class period

	Monday	*Tuesday*	*Wednesday*	*Thursday*	*Friday*
Math (# of out-of-turn comments)					
Reading (# of out-of-turn comments)					

______________________________ ______________________________
Teacher signature Student signature

____
Parent signature

BOX 5.2. Behavior Contracting: High School Illustration

Gunnar and Ingrid, both outgoing and likeable students, were not the most reliable when it came to completing homework. Each day, Ms. Nelson assigned homework to be turned in the following day. And each day, at the beginning of class, she collected the homework. Since the beginning of the school year (about 1 month ago), Gunnar and Ingrid had turned in just 5 out of 20 and 6 out of 20 homework assignments, respectively. At this rate, Ms. Nelson worried that Gunnar and Ingrid were at serious risk for failing her English class. To prevent them from failing, Ms. Nelson decided she needed to try something immediately. Her principal wisely suggested a behavior contract.

Step 1: Identify the target behavior(s). Ms. Nelson had few, if any, complaints about Gunnar and Ingrid's in-class behavior. Her biggest concern was their homework completion, or lack thereof. Given that she already had a record of their homework completion, direct observation of their behavior was unnecessary. So she simply defined their target behavior as *homework completion*. On every previous assignment that had been turned in, the work was completed. But the assignments not turned in were assumed to be incomplete. She suspected that they were simply not doing their homework, because the assignments that they actually turned in were both complete and accurate, showing that they understood the work. To verify this, Ms. Nelson needed to meet with Gunnar and Ingrid.

Step 2: Meet with stakeholders. She called individual meetings with each student during their study halls. She asked both of them why they hadn't turned in numerous assignments. Was it a matter of not understanding the content? Or was it because they had done their homework but had just forgotten to bring it back to school? Or had they just chosen not to do it? As she suspected, Gunnar and Ingrid both admitted to not doing the assignments—not because they didn't understand, but because they just didn't want to spend the time. Ms. Nelson suggested that a way to rectify this lack of homework completion might be to use a behavior contract. Both students were open to the idea, but expressed concern that their friends might make fun of them if they found out. Ms. Nelson assured them that the contract was completely confidential and that the only way their friends would find out would be if they told them.

Step 3: Discuss the student's good and bad behavior. Ms. Nelson praised Gunnar and Ingrid for the assignments they had turned in, citing that they had both done great work. However, she contended, completing only 25% of the assignments would likely lead to failing the class.

Step 4: Write behavior objectives/tasks. Because she knew Gunnar and Ingrid were capable of completing their homework as evidenced by prior work completion, as well as by their class participation, work completion was most definitely in their respective behavioral repertoires. Clearly, they were exhibiting a *performance deficit*—they could do the work but were refusing to do so. Next, they wrote a behavioral objective to be included in the contract. The behavioral objective read: "Gunnar/Ingrid will turn in completed and accurate homework to Ms. Nelson at least 4 out of 5 days per week. Although she obviously would have preferred 100% of assignments to be turned in, Ms. Nelson wasn't sure it was reasonable to jump from 25% to 100% work completion. Her idea was to address 100% completion as part of the bonus clause.

Step 5: Identify rewards and consequences. Going into the meeting, Ms. Nelson didn't know what would be reinforcing to high school students. Surprisingly, Gunnar and Ingrid came up with quite a list: parking passes, movie tickets, mp3s, getting out of class and assignments, hanging out with friends, and, of course, money. Ms. Nelson deemed some of these items to be excessive rewards for the task required. So they came to a reasonable compromise that matched

(cont.)

the task value to the reward value. The school was having a drawing in 1 month for a big Homecoming package—dinner for two, tickets to the dance, and a limo ride for a group of friends. Ms. Nelson agreed to give them one raffle ticket for each assignment turned in up until the drawing. Additionally, if they turned in their homework for 5 consecutive days, the bonus clause stated that they could complete only the odd-numbered problems on an assignment of their choice in the following week. Given their past history, Ms. Nelson worried that Gunnar and Ingrid might not comply, so she also suggested some consequences. Although the possibility of failing the class served as a natural consequence, she of course did not want them to fail. Thus they added a clause to the contract stating that if the students did not meet the goal in any given week, then they would have to spend their study hall of the following week in Ms. Nelson's classroom at an individual study carrel completing their homework.

Step 6: Determine the evaluation process. At the end of each week, Ms. Nelson decided she would meet with each student to discuss how the contract was going. Because the school drawing was 1 month away and raffle tickets would no longer be valid after the drawing, they also decided to meet after the drawing to renegotiate the terms of the contract.

Step 7: Sign on the dotted line! Ms. Nelson, Ingrid, and Gunnar each read over their individual contracts and agreed that the contingency and procedures were reasonable. Each person signed and agreed to meet at the end of each week, as well as in 1 month for contract renegotiation.

CONTRACT

Behavioral Objectives:

1. The student will turn in completed and accurate homework to Ms. Nelson at least 4 out of 5 days per week.

Rewards:

1. One raffle ticket per homework assignment

Consequences:

1. If the student does not meet the goal in any given week, then he/she will spend his/her study hall of the following week in Ms. Nelson's classroom at an individual study carrel completing English homework.

Bonus Clause:

1. If the student turns in completed and accurate homework for 5 consecutive days, then he/she will complete only the odd-numbered problems on an assignment of his/her choice the following week.

______________________	______________________
Teacher signature	Student signature
______________________	______________________
Date	Date

Step 2: Meet with the Stakeholders

Once data on the target behavior have been collected and summarized, the teacher or other school-site personnel establishing the contract (e.g., guidance counselor or behavior specialist) should hold a meeting with those stakeholders in the behavior contract. These may include only the teacher and student but could also include parents, administrators, or counselors. At the meeting several things should be discussed, including the purpose of the meeting, how a behavior contract works, how a contract may facilitate a better relationship between teacher and student, and how the contract may help the student to meet both academic and behavioral goals (Cooper et al., 2007). Further, the teacher should facilitate an open and honest dialogue so that all members of the group feel that they are equal participants. Students, especially, must view this as a reciprocal process and not just another set of rules that the teacher has imposed (Cooper et al., 2007). We admit this could be difficult when the teacher discusses her or his observations of the student's target behavior, as it is not easy for students to hear about their own undesirable behavior. However, the teacher or the person leading the meeting can emphasize that the contract will provide ways for the student to have his or her needs met and will allow him or her to be rewarded for positive, appropriate behavior. Once the purpose of the meeting and the way a behavior contract works are understood by all parties, discussion of the specifics of the behavior contract can begin.

Step 3: Discuss the Student's Strengths and Areas of Concern

You will begin by discussing your observations of the target behavior, but it is also wise to point out some of the students' strengths. For example, the teacher may acknowledge ways in which the student contributes to class or tasks the student can perform well. In this way the student receives positive attention for appropriate behaviors that he or she has displayed (Cooper et al., 2007). After discussing the target behavior and positive performance, the group should examine ways in which the student could improve by listing specific tasks that will help him or her be more successful at school. This list can then be used to generate potential tasks to be included in the behavior contract.

Step 4: Write Behavioral Objectives and/or Tasks

Using the created task list, the group will identify tasks to be included in the contract. Additionally, the group must write down *who* will perform the task, *what* the task is, *how well* and *when* the task must be completed, and any possible exceptions (Cooper et al., 2007). These tasks can be written in the form of a behavioral objective. Like curricular objectives, behavioral objectives should be specific, measurable, and observable (Downing, 2002). The behavioral objective must include the specifically desired behavior, the setting and task demands, the criteria for determining success, the time allotted for completion, and the data collection method

(Downing, 2002). An example of a behavioral objective might read: *Paige will arrive on time to math class and be seated before the bell rings for 4 out of 5 days as determined by her math teacher, who will listen for the bell and observe Paige's location.*

It is critical to determine whether the behavior included in the objective is in the student's repertoire. If the student is not capable of performing the appropriate replacement behavior in lieu of the target behavior (an acquisition deficit), then contracting will be ineffective. Instead, the behavior should be taught rather than placed on a contingency. During the earlier data collection (Step 1), the teacher may have observed the student periodically performing the replacement behavior. This indicates a performance deficit in that the student can perform the replacement behavior but is simply choosing not to. Given that the student can perform the replacement behavior, the contract may be an appropriate intervention.

Step 5: Identify Rewards and Consequences

Once the behavioral objectives have been agreed upon and written, the group can identify potential rewards for the student when he or she meets the objective. This is a great opportunity for the student to tell the group what is reinforcing to him or her, which may be beneficial beyond the behavior contract meeting. Potential reinforcers include not only tangible items such as candy, CDs, and movie tickets but also activities such as an extra recess, a teacher's attention, and avoidance of nonpreferred activities (e.g., homework). It is important to choose a reward that fits the task so that it is neither excessive nor insignificant but fair for the selected objective (Cooper et al., 2007). Ideally, your school will have an SWPBS program that can be written into the contract. For example, Paige might receive a certain number of positive behavior support tickets for completing the said behavior. If such a program is not established, then you will need to determine meaningful yet manageable rewards.

Downing (2002) suggested considering these questions when selecting rewards: (1) What is the student willing to work for? (2) How often does the student need to be reinforced? and (3) How quickly does he or she become bored with the reinforcer? Rather than selecting one reward per task, another option is to offer a menu from which the student can choose one of a variety of rewards upon meeting the objective (see our previous discussion regarding the importance of choice in contracts). For contracts expected to last for a longer duration, a reward menu may prevent the student from becoming bored with the rewards. Additionally, the group might consider building in a bonus clause to increase motivation. Using the previous example of Paige being on time to class, the bonus clause might specify that if she is on time 5 (rather than 4) consecutive days, then she can choose two rewards from the menu or double the amount of positive behavior support tickets. Failure to meet the behavioral objectives serves as a natural consequence such that the student will not receive the associated reward. It is also important to think about when to modify the contract to address new or increasing expectations, perhaps with the use of more meaningful rewards (but delivered less frequently than in the initial reward structure).

Most important, the rewards must be reinforcing enough to the student so that he or she will perform the appropriate behavior. This is achieved not only by letting the student be a part of the reward selection process but also through the way the reward is delivered. Namely, the reward must be delivered a timely manner and in the amount specified when the task is completed as agreed upon in the contract (Cooper et al., 2007).

Step 6: Determine the Evaluation Process

After the behavioral objectives and contingent rewards have been written, the next step is to determine the evaluation process. To aid the student, a record of task completion may be included on the contract (Cooper et al., 2007). For example, the contract might include a chart that allows the student to check off tasks that have been completed, as well as whether or not a reward was received. This provides a visual cue to help the student remain focused until the objective is met or task completed (Cooper et al., 2007).

In addition, the group should set a time line for contract implementation and termination. Some contracts may be completed in a week, whereas others may be open ended or in effect until all objectives are met (Downing, 2002). The contract may be terminated for one of two reasons: either (1) the student performs at a level that meets the objectives, or (2) one or both signed parties consistently fails to meet the terms of the contract (Cooper et al., 2007). Checkpoints should also be included in the implementation time line, especially for lengthy contracts (Downing, 2002). These checkpoints will both allow evaluation of progress toward meeting the contractual objectives and allow any necessary adjustments to be made to the objectives or rewards.

Step 7: Sign the Contract

Finally, once all parties have read, reviewed, and agreed on the objectives, rewards, and evaluation, each person can sign the contract. This will draw the meeting to a close and signify that the contract is in effect.

To assist you in your planning, we have included two illustrations. In Boxes 5.1 and 5.2 you will see applications for use at the elementary level and the middle or high school levels, respectively.

SUMMARY

In this chapter we introduced one low-intensity, secondary prevention strategy—behavior contracting—that is effective in shaping behaviors. We provided an overview of behavior contracting, defining the strategy and delineating different types of contracts (e.g., one-party, two-party quid pro quo, and two-party parallel contracts). Next, we included information on how to conduct behavior contracts in the classroom followed by a discussion of the benefits and challenges associated with this intervention. Then we provided an overview of the research that supports use of behavior contracts to improve performance with elementary, middle, and high school students within a range of environments. Finally, we concluded the chapter with (1) information on how to develop, implement, and evaluate behavior contracting interventions in your classroom and (2) two illustrations, one demonstrating how behavior contracts can be implemented with elementary students and a second illustration for application in middle and high schools. We also would like to direct your attention to the resource guide provided in Table 5.2. This guide contains information on other books, websites, and refereed journal articles that also may be useful to you as you develop behavior contracts for use at your school site. You may also want to look at Chapter 8, which contains (1) a template for developing a behavioral contract, (2) a quick guide to determining student eligibility for behavior contracts, and (3) a sample treatment integrity form to help inform you planning as your take steps to make sure that the contract is implemented as originally designed.

In the next chapter, we introduce another strategy that can be used to shape behavior: self-monitoring. We begin the chapter by providing a brief overview of five common self-management interventions, one of which is self-monitoring. Then the remainder of the chapter focuses on self-monitoring: defining the strategy, providing guidance on how to implement such strategies in the classroom, reviewing the associated benefits and challenges, and reviewing relevant research of self-monitoring interventions conducted in elementary, middle, and high school settings. We conclude by providing direction on how to implement self-monitoring interventions in your classroom, including an illustration of the strategy, as well as related resources.

TABLE 5.2. Behavior Contracting Resource Guide

Reference	Description	Target group	Cost/retrieval information
	Books		
Cooper, J. O., Heron, T. E., & Heward, W. L. (2007). *Applied behavior analysis* (2nd ed.). Upper Saddle River, NJ: Pearson Education.	This is a comprehensive textbook on the principles, applications, and research methods associated with applied behavior analysis. An entire chapter is devoted to behavior change procedures that include both contingency contracting and group contingencies.	K–12 educators	List price: $101.33 *www.amazon.com*
Walker, H. M., Colvin, G., & Ramsey, E. (1994). *Antisocial behavior in school: Strategies and best practices.* Pacific Grove, CA: Brooks/Cole.	This book takes a comprehensive approach to preventing and remediating antisocial behavior problems. The book offers practitioner-friendly suggestions for identifying students who need support, methods for designing an effective classroom, and practical applications of interventions. The text includes guidelines for setting up behavior contracts, as well as sample contracts for use at home and in the classroom.	K–12 educators	List price: $70.61 *www.amazon.com*
Miltenberger, R. G. (2007). *Behavior modification: Principles and procedures* (4th ed.). Belmont, CA: Wadsworth/ Thomson Learning.	To help the reader learn the principles and procedures of behavior modification, the book includes precise descriptions, self-assessments, quizzes at the end of each chapter, and application exercises. The chapter on behavior contracts addresses what a behavior contract is, the components of a behavior contract, the difference between one- and two-party contracts, how to negotiate a contract, and how these contracts influence behavior.	K–12 educators	List price: $141.95 *www.amazon.com*
	Websites		
Behavior Contracts	Jim Wright, a school psychologist and administrator, designed a website devoted to offering free resources that promote positive classroom behavior to school personnel and parents. The behavior contracts page describes the simple steps in creating a behavior contract, addresses common problems associated with behavior contracts, and offers a free download of a behavior contract template.	K–12 educators; parents	*www.interventioncentral.org/htmdocs/interventions/behavior/behcontr.php*
Free Behavior Contracts	Although this website was intended for parents, the free materials can also be used in school settings. For example, users can download free behavior contracts and charts.	K–12 educators; parents	*www.freebehaviorcontracts.com/index.php*

Behavior Contracts: How to Write Them	The National Education Agency provides a brief overview of how to write effective behavior contracts. An easy-to-follow example is presented.	K–12 educators	*www.nea.org/tools/19617.htm*
Special Connections: An Introduction to Classroom/Group Support.	Special Connections is a website dedicated to providing teachers and other educational stakeholders with resources to help students with special needs access the general education curriculum. The behavior plan module offers specific guidance on positive classroom and group supports. Further, there is an extensive section on different types of group contingency plans with an emphasis on positive reinforcement.	K–12 educators	*www.specialconnections.ku.edu/cgi-bin/cgiwrap/specconn/main.php?cat=behavior§ion=main&subsection=classroom/positive*
Behavior Advisor	Behavior Advisor is a website designed by Dr. Tom McIntyre, a professor of special education. This website offers thousands of strategies and lesson plans, including podcasts and templates, for managing behavior. The section on behavior contracts offers a short description, provides examples of contracts, describes how to use contracting, and provides activities and discussion questions.	K–12 educators	*www.behavioradvisor.com/Contracts.html*
	Refereed journal articles		
Cook, M. N. (2005). The disruptive or ADHD child: What to do when kids won't sit still and be quiet. *Focus on Exceptional Children, 37*, 1–9.	In this article, the author offers a variety of interventions for disruptive behavior disorders, including: anger management training; problem-solving skills training; strategies for improving attention compliance, organization, and productivity; and behavior contracts. The advantages (e.g., to make a situation more positive, build self-esteem, and teach child how to get positive attention) of using contracts are explained, as well as practical advice for how to create them.	K–12 educators with disruptive students	*Focus on Exceptional Children* is published by Love Publishing Company. *www.lovepublishing.com/journals.html*
Downing, J. A. (2002). Individualized behavior contracts. *Intervention in School and Clinic, 37*, 168–172.	In this article the author discusses potential uses of behavior contracts, including introducing and teaching new behaviors, increasing rate of desired behaviors, maintaining and supporting application or generalization of skills, decreasing or extinguishing undesirable behaviors, monitoring completion of academic tasks or objectives, and documenting results of problem-solving or crisis-intervention sessions. Also described is one step-by-step strategy for developing a contract.	K–12 educators	*Intervention in School and Clinic* is published by Pro-Ed, Inc. *isc.sagepub.com/cgi/pdf_extract/37/3/168*

(cont.)

TABLE 5.2. *(cont.)*

Reference	Description	Target group	Cost/retrieval information
Murphy, J. J. (1988). Contingency contracting in schools: A review. *Education and Treatment of Children, 11*, 257–269.	This is a review of empirical studies using contingency contracts to improve behavior. It begins by defining contingency contracting and its theoretical basis. Also included is a review of the literature in which contracts are used to increase academic productivity, performance accuracy, study skills, school attendance, and social behavior. Advantages and disadvantages of using contracts are described. Also included are recommendations on how to effectively use contingency contracts, as well as suggestions for future research.	K–12 educators	*Education and Treatment of Children* is published by the West Virginia University Press. *eric.ed.gov/ERICWebPortal/custom/portlets/recordDetails/detailmini.jsp?_nfpb=true&_&ERICExtSearch_SearchValue_0=EJ403951&ERICExtSearch_SearchType_0=no&accno=EJ403951*
Simonsen, B., Fairbanks, S., Briesch, A., Myers, D., & Sugai, G. (2008). Evidence-based practices in classroom management: Considerations for research to practice. *Education and Treatment of Children, 31*, 351–380.	This review describes outcomes of a systematic literature search to identify evidence-based classroom management practices. Five suggestions for incorporating these into practice are described, with one being to use a continuum of strategies to acknowledge appropriate behavior, including behavioral contracting, specific and/or contingent praise, classwide group contingencies, and token economies	K–12 educators	*Education and Treatment of Children* is published by the West Virginia University Press. *museweb02-pub.mse.jhu.edu/login?uri=/journals/education_and_treatment_of_children/v031/31.3.simonsen.pdf*

Note. See Table 5.1 for a summary of peer-reviewed articles on behavior contracting.

CHAPTER 6

Self-Monitoring

The vast majority of students—80–90%—are likely to respond to primary prevention efforts, particularly when they are in classrooms in which teachers have strong proactive management skills (e.g., managing transition and routines, implementing schoolwide expectations consistently, effectively using low-intensity strategies, and providing engaging instruction; Kauffman & Brigham, 2009; Walker & Severson, 2002). Yet the three-tiered model of prevention is predicated on the notion that not all students will respond to primary prevention efforts. It is expected that 10–15% of students may require secondary prevention efforts and that between 3 and 5% will require additional, more individualized and intensive supports. These supports should be targeted to address students' particular skill, fluency, or performance deficits. This level of response aims to match the intervention to the specific academic, social, or behavioral difficulties the student is experiencing (Gresham, 2002c; Lane, Kalberg, & Menzies, 2009). For school personnel who do not work at a site that uses a schoolwide approach, the concept of using more intensive interventions for the most challenging behaviors is the same. It just may not be applied as systematically as in school systems in which three-tiered models are in place.

In addition to behavior contracting, which we introduced in Chapter 5, another low-intensity, secondary prevention strategy is self-monitoring (Mace, Belfiore, & Hutchinson, 2001). We begin this chapter with an introduction to self-management strategies and then provide an in-depth discussion of self-monitoring—one self-management strategy. Self-monitoring is a versatile intervention that can be used to address behavioral, social, or academic needs. In addition, it is relatively simple to implement. We provide direction as to how to conduct self-monitoring in the classroom and offer an overview of the benefits and challenges associated with its use. We also provide an overview of the supporting research on improving academic outcomes for elementary, middle, and high school students with challenging behaviors in a range of environments.

SELF-MANAGEMENT: AN OVERVIEW

Over the course of the regular school day, all students—including those who have or are at risk for EBD—need to meet certain expectations. These expectations, which are designed to help teachers and students with the business of teaching and learning, include skills in social, behavioral, and academic domains. All are equally important in helping students become well-rounded, lifelong learners. For example, students are expected to attend to and participate in instruction, to produce quality work in a timely manner, to work cooperatively with others, and to manage conflict situations with peers and adults (Hersh & Walker, 1983; Kerr & Zigmond, 1986; Lane, Wehby, & Cooley, 2006). In addition, students are expected to engage in a wide range of self-determined behaviors that enable them to live a high-quality life and assume responsibility for a variety of life activities (Carter et al., 2008; Houchins, 2002). Self-determined behaviors encompass a range of skills: (1) choice making, (2) decision making, (3) problem solving, (4) goal setting and attainment, (5) self-management and self-regulation, (6) self-advocacy and leadership, (7) self-awareness (8) self-knowledge, and (9) self-evaluation (Wehmeyer & Field, 2007). Unfortunately, many students with and at risk for EBD struggle in these exact areas, lacking the skill sets to act strategically to successfully negotiate teacher and student relationships and ultimately experience academic success (Cameto, Levine, Wagner, & Marder, 2003; Carter, Lane, Pierson, & Glaeser, 2006; Levendoski & Cartledge, 2000).

Self-Management Strategies

To date, a number of self-management strategies to help students become more successful learners have been studied. These strategies may also be referred to as *self-regulation strategies* (Harris & Graham, 1996a; Mooney et al., 2005). In this section we discuss self-evaluation, self-instruction, goal setting, and self-monitoring, as well as combinations of the strategies (e.g., self-monitoring and goal setting combined). Students who are able to effectively use self-management strategies such as these are more likely to experience greater academic and social success in the school setting (Mooney et al., 2005).

Self-Evaluation

This strategy, also referred to as self-assessment, helps a student compare his or her performance to a benchmark or standard. This standard could be determined by either the teacher or the student, or the two could work together to decide on a standard acceptable to both of them. It is also possible to involve the parents in establishing goals. For example, let us use a work completion and accuracy illustration with a parent and child. Perhaps Nathan and his mom are concerned about his test scores in science. In looking over the last two tests, they notice that he has inadvertently skipped a couple of questions and has made several errors while solving multiple-step problems. As a result, they decide to implement a self-monitoring and self-evaluation intervention. First, they define the desired behavior (completing the test with accuracy) and design a brief checklist that includes the following steps to be completed before turning in the test:

1. Did I answer all of the questions? ☐ *yes* or ☐ *no.*
2. Did I double-check (rework) each of the problems? ☐ *yes* or ☐ *no.*
3. Did I get the same answer both times? ☐ *yes* or ☐ *no.*
   a. If yes, turn in the test.
   b. If no, rework these problems for a third time, then turn in the test.

Similarly, if the focus is on engagement or participation, the student might self-evaluate his or her performance by determining whether engagement occurred for 80% of the time—a standard determined by the teacher and the student. In this illustration, Step 3 is also a method for promoting self-evaluation.

There are other types of self-evaluation strategies, such as teacher-mediated and peer-mediated approaches (DuPaul, McGoey, & Yugar, 1997). In teacher-mediated approaches, the teacher trains the student on behavioral expectations and assists the student in self-evaluation or also records behavior to compare it with accuracy of student self-evaluation. In peer-mediated approaches, peers are included as intervention participants with the target student. For example, a designated peer may share responsibility for discussing and completing the self-monitoring form with the target student or may independently rate the target student's behavior to serve as a comparison with the student's self-evaluation reports. This allows the target student to obtain more attention, allows the teacher to focus on classroom instruction, and promotes generalization and maintenance of the skill. As demonstrated by DuPaul and colleagues (1997), teacher-mediated approaches can be faded effectively through the use of peer mediation as the student gains competence in self-evaluating behavior.

In each case, the student receives a predetermined reinforcer (e.g., positive behavior support ticket, a free homework pass, or extra points on the next quiz) when he or she meets criteria. Again, it is important that the reinforcer be sufficiently motivating to the student. Avoid assuming that what is reinforcing to one student is reinforcing to all students (Cooper et al., 2007; Umbreit et al., 2007).

Self-Instruction

Another self-management strategy is the use of self-instruction, or self-talk, to improve performance. For example, in reading this text right now, you might be considering a break. But because you have so much reading to do tonight, you would like to have a certain amount completed before you stop. If you use a self-instruction strategy to direct your behavior, you might say something like:

> "I have a lot to do tonight, so I am going to finish this by dividing the chapter into sections. Right now I am going to read until I get to the section titled 'Self-Monitoring.' Then I am going to take a quick break and get a soda and some chips before I continue with the chapter."

The same strategy has been used with school-age students to teach them how to direct their own behavior (e.g., "This is a long assignment, but I can finish this work by breaking it into smaller chunks"; Graham, Harris, & Reid, 1992). In brief, students are taught statements (academic, behavioral, or social) to think or whisper to themselves that encourage engagement, work completion, or solving a conflict (see Harris & Graham, 1996a). Fish and Mendola (1986) taught three elementary-age students with emotional disturbances to increase their rate of homework completion using a self-instruction strategy. In this study, the three students with the lowest homework completion rate in the class participated in eight self-instruction training sessions over 2 weeks, based on a specific self-instruction strategy (Meichenbaum & Goodman, 1971). Results indicated that when students used the self-instruction strategy, homework completion rates improved. This approach can also work with older students. For example, Miller, Miller, Wheeler, and Selinger (1989) used a combination of self-monitoring and self-instruction strategies to support two middle and high school students with severe behavior disorders. Each student was taught a step-by-step sequential self-instruction strategy for solving problems (Touch Math for the first participant and decoding words for the second) using modeling and individualized teaching procedures with scaffolded support as students demonstrated competency. Both students demonstrated improved academic performance (math and reading scores, respectively). Also, the intervention was associated with a reduction in inappropriate classroom behaviors for both participants.

Goal Setting

Goal setting is a strategy in which students are taught to set a behavioral target. This target could be an academic goal that results in a product, such as writing a story or completing a work sheet. Or the target could be an academic goal that does not yield a product, such as reading a book, participating in a class discussion, or being engaged during an independent work assignment. Goals can also target behaviors that facilitate instruction but are not academic in nature (e.g., using positive social initiations with peers). The intent of establishing a goal is to structure the students' effort, motivate the student to move toward goal completion, and provide progress monitoring information to the student (Menzies et al., 2009; Schunk, 2001). Goal-setting strategies can be used in conjunction with other metacognitive strategies. For example, Smith, Nelson, Young, and West (1992) used goal setting, along with self-evaluation, to increase the quality and quantity of academic tasks, as well as task engagement across special and general education settings for eight students who had either learning disabilities or behavior disorders and were receiving special education services. The intervention included teacher-mediated self-evaluation in which participants compared self-monitoring checklist reports with reports of the teacher paired with academic goal setting. This component was followed by fading procedures involving peer-mediated self-instruction and academic goal-setting components. Results indicated that self-evaluation and goal-setting interventions can help students with high-incidence disabilities evaluate and monitor classroom behavior and academic work in regular and special education classroom settings. Furthermore, results also showed reduced disruptive classroom behavior and improved academic performance.

Self-Monitoring

When teaching a student to improve self-monitoring, two processes must occur: observing and recording. The observation component requires that a student be able to determine whether a given behavior (e.g., engagement) occurred. This requires that the student be very clear as to the exact definition of the required behavior. In the behavioral literature, this is referred to as an *operational definition* (Cooper et al., 2007). For example, in a classroom the expectation for engagement may be to pay attention to the teacher and complete assigned tasks. The operational definition of engagement refers to the amount of time spent actively attending to group instruction, assigned academic tasks and group activities, or relevant materials. Examples include looking at the teacher or the person who has permission to talk while he or she is talking, working on the assigned task, requesting assistance appropriately (e.g., raising one's hand), and following directions. Non-examples include any activity other than attending to the teacher-assigned task, such as disruptive (e.g., audible vocalizations inappropriate to the assigned task, stomping feet) and off-task (e.g., walking around the classroom, looking around the room away from work) behaviors.

At the end of a given interval (e.g., 3 minutes), the student must make a determination as to whether or not he or she was engaged during that entire period (e.g., "Was I working on my teacher's task for the last 3 minutes?") Then the student needs to record his or her behavior—the second process of self-monitoring.

The recording component requires students to take note of and mark off whether or not they performed the desired behavior (Mace et al., 2001). For example, in answering the question "Was I working on my teacher's task for the last 3 minutes?" the student could indicate "yes" or "no." In addition to coming to consensus on the definition of the behavior to be monitored, it is also important for the teacher and student to (1) develop a self-monitoring form, (2) set a goal for the criteria to be met, and (3) establish the reinforcement for meeting such a goal. Figure 6.1 shows an example of a self-monitoring checklist to address work completion and accuracy for math instruction. Using this self-monitoring form, the

Name: ______		Date: ______	
Subject	Task	Did I complete my assignment?	% Accuracy
	1.		
	2.		
	3.		
	4.		
	Homework		
	Percentage of Assignments Completed	%	
	Accuracy of Assignments	%	

FIGURE 6.1. Daily self-monitoring checklist.

student, Nathan, would evaluate his performance on a specific task (e.g., a systems of equations math worksheet). At the end of the time allotted for the task or after Nathan determined he was done, he would take out this self-monitoring checklist and ask himself the designated questions, marking the appropriate response. If class procedures included regularly scoring assignments, Nathan would also be able to record his accuracy.

Some students may require an external reinforcer that meets the function of the behavior. This concept is discussed in greater detail in Chapter 7. In brief, people engage in behaviors to either obtain (positive reinforcement) or avoid (negative reinforcement) attention, activity, or sensory experiences (Umbreit et al., 2007). However, for other students the act of monitoring and recording their behavior is reinforcing enough to increase the future probability of the target behavior occurring (e.g., accurate completion of the math worksheet).

Prerequisite Components for Using Self-Management Strategies in the Classroom

Before developing and using self-management strategies in the classroom, we recommend consideration of the following issues. First, it is necessary to determine whether the desired replacement behavior is part of the student's repertoire. To this end, we must determine whether the students understands and is capable of performing the desired behavior. For example, if we are asking a student to be engaged during silent reading, then we begin by checking whether the student is capable of reading. If the student (1) can perform the behavior but does not do so fluently (fluency deficit; student is a slow reader) or (2) is not motivated to perform (performance deficit; student does not wish to read the assigned book), self-management strategies are appropriate for both types of deficits. However, if the student has an acquisition deficit, meaning that he or she simply does not have the skills necessary to perform the task (the book is beyond the student's reading level), then intervention efforts will need to first focus on instruction in the desired behavior (Elliott & Gresham, 1991).

Second, once you have determined that self-management or metacognitive strategies are appropriate, the next step is to make certain that the behavior is clearly defined, readily observable, and reasonable for the students to record. For example, if you are asking the students to be academically engaged, you would provide clear direction that includes examples and non-examples of engagement and disengagement for the context and task of interest (see Figure 6.2 for a definition of academic engagement during silent reading). Also, it is important for the recording procedures to be reliable and feasible so that accurate information is recorded and interpreted. If the measure suffers from poor reliability, then it is possible that changes in data patterns as graphed may be due to measurement error rather than to true changes in student behavior (Cooper et al., 2007). In Figure 6.3 we present see an illustration of a data collection form that can be used for a duration or *real-*

Academic engagement refers to the amount of time spent actively engaged in silently reading appropriate material. Examples include looking at the book or other reading materials, looking away to think about material for a duration of less than 10 seconds, appropriately asking the teacher about a word. Non-examples include any activity other than reading the appropriate material, such as disruptive (e.g., audible vocalizations inappropriate to the assigned task, stomping feet) and off-task (e.g., walking around the classroom, looking away from the book for more than 15 seconds, reading an unapproved video game manual).

FIGURE 6.2. Academic engagement during silent reading: An operational definition.

Student: ____________________

Observer: ____________________

Date: ____________________

Session 1

Time Start: __________ Time Stop: __________

__________ / __________ = __________ × 100 = ______%
seconds on stopwatch — length of session — AET

Session 2

Time Start: __________ Time Stop: __________

__________ / __________ = __________ × 100 = ______%
seconds on stopwatch — length of session — AET

Session 3

Time Start: __________ Time Stop: __________

__________ / __________ = __________ × 100 = ______%
seconds on stopwatch — length of session — AET

Interobserver Agreement: Session __________

__________ / __________ = __________ × 100 = ______%
seconds on stopwatch — length of session — IOA — %IOA (>90%)

FIGURE 6.3. Academic engagement data collection form (duration recording).

time recording system. Figure 6.4 presents a graph depicting student performance, with data collected using the form provided in Figure 6.3.

Third, the behavior must occur at a sufficiently high frequency to allow it to be monitored. For example, if the behavior is completion of long-term assignments, then it may not be appropriate to self-monitor that specific behavior because the occurrences are too far apart to see meaningful changes. Instead, it might be wise to self-monitor a more incremental target behavior that—if performed over a sufficient period of time—leads to the longer term goal.

Fourth, if you elect to have a student self-monitor an undesirable behavior (e.g., tantrums or episodes of extreme verbal aggression) that have a low rate of occurrence (hopefully!), then other behavioral interventions such as differential reinforcement schedules or functional assessment-based interventions may need to be employed before beginning with metacognitive strategies (e.g., self-evaluation). This is especially true if the problem behavior poses safety issues for the student of interest or his or her classmates. In this case, one option is to begin by designing, implementing, and evaluating a functional assessment-based intervention (see Chapter 7). In this way, the motive (or function) of the target behavior can be determined first. Then the corresponding intervention is linked to the maintaining function, and the student is taught more reliable, efficient methods (which may include metacognitive strategies) of meeting his or her needs. Then, once interfering behavior problems (which could include externalizing [aggression] and/or internalizing [anxiety or depression] behaviors) are better controlled, one can shift efforts toward self-management interventions.

Should you decide you want to implement self-monitoring or other self-management procedures with selected students in your classroom, we encourage

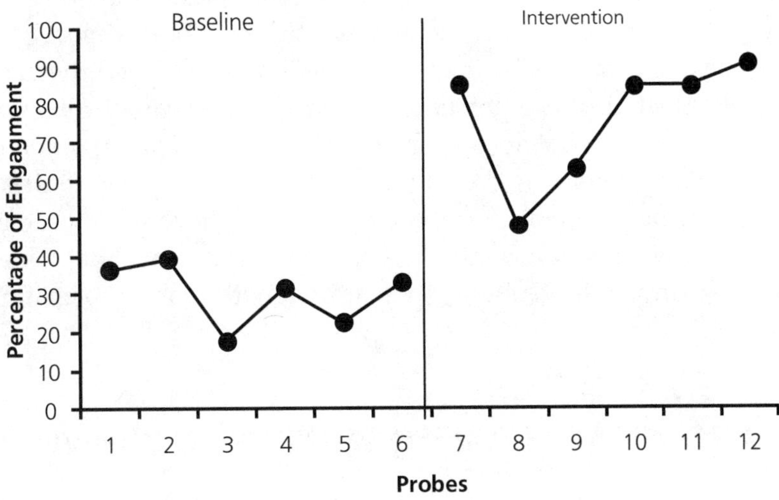

FIGURE 6.4. Academic engagement over time: Performance during silent reading.

you to weigh the following benefits and challenges associated with these procedures.

BENEFITS AND CHALLENGES

When we think about self-management skills, we are generally talking about being able to plan and carry out a task (e.g., writing a book report), to monitor one's behavior (e.g., how many words one wrote), to analyze a problem ("I'm not blocking out enough time to write"), to apply a strategy ("I'll work on my report as soon as I get home from school"), to maintain attention ("I'll turn off my music and eat a healthy snack before I start working"), and to evaluate or monitor completion of an activity ("I'll look at my work carefully before I turn it in to my teacher"; Butler, 1998). Collectively, these skills and steps help students be active participants in their learning experiences. They learn and apply techniques that can help them in a variety of situations.

One particular benefit of conducting self-management interventions is that these strategies, when learned and applied, can positively affect behavior (e.g., engagement), productivity (e.g., work completion), and accuracy, which collectively lead to improved academic performance (Nelson, Smith, Young, & Dodd, 1991). A second benefit is that such strategies empower students to become more independent and self-sufficient in their ability to regulate their environment. In comparison with teacher-directed interventions, self-directed strategies empower students and shift responsibilities from the teachers to the students. However, as we mentioned previously, it is important to recognize that these strategies are not appropriate for all behaviors. They are not recommended for use with acquisition deficits. Furthermore, they are not appropriate for potentially self-injurious or aggressive behaviors that require more immediate behavior changes.

Once you have (1) considered prerequisite skills, (2) weighed the benefits and challenges of conducting these procedures, and (3) determined the appropriateness of self-management strategies to facilitate improvements in students' metacognitive abilities and behavior, we encourage you to consider the different self-management strategies available for use. Because we believe self-monitoring to be easy to implement, effective for a variety of students, and easily adaptable to either behavioral or academic interventions, we continue with more information on this strategy.

SUPPORTING RESEARCH FOR SELF-MONITORING INTERVENTIONS

Before launching into any intervention, it is important to determine whether the practice is supported as either an evidence-based or a promising practice. Mooney and colleagues (2005) conducted an extensive, systematic review of self-management interventions that focused on academic outcomes for students with EBD. Their intent was to provide practitioners and researchers with information regarding the effectiveness and focus of self-management interventions for this often difficult-to-teach population.

In this review, they identified a total of 22 studies published in 20 articles. These studies involve a total of 78 students across the K–12 continuum. In terms of the overall body of literature, Mooney et al. (2005) indicated that (1) self-monitoring interventions were the most commonly used self-management strategy and (2) self-management strategies were generally favorable in improving academic outcomes in the areas of math, writing, reading, and social studies. Relative to baseline conditions, students with EBD showed improvements in specific, targeted academic skills when the self-management strategies were introduced. It should be noted that the interventions targeted math computation skills more than any other content area. Also, evidence suggested that the improved outcomes generalized beyond the training setting and were maintained over time.

Findings of this review are particularly encouraging given that students with and at risk for EBD struggle in their ability to attend to instruction and to act strategically to foster productive work environments (Walker, Ramsey, & Gresham, 2004). In short, they struggle to manage their own academic behavior. Fortunately, self-management procedures such as self-monitoring strategies implemented in isolation or with other self-management strategies (e.g., self-evaluation) have met with success.

In this section, we provide information on a few of the studies included in the Mooney et al. (2005) review to illustrate how these strategies can be applied across the K–12 grade span. We encourage you to see Table 6.1 for a summary of the eight studies identified by Mooney as involving self-monitoring as a core intervention component.

Elementary School

As you can see in Table 6.1, the majority of self-monitoring interventions among students with or at risk for EBD were conducted with elementary-age students. One particularly noteworthy study was conducted by Levendoski and Cartledge (2000). Whereas most of the early studies examining self-monitoring of academic behaviors focused on drill and practice, this study focused on students' self-monitoring their behavior while practicing newly taught skills. Also, this study was quite feasible in the sense that students monitored their behavior with the use of minimal auditory (two tones) and visual (one card) cues.

The students were four boys (three Caucasian, one African American) attending a self-contained class located in a general education elementary school. The students were between 9 and 11 years of age, and all received free or reduced-price lunches. There were five other students in the self-contained class, but the intervention was focused on just the four students mentioned, as they had very low

TABLE 6.1. Self-Monitoring Interventions Focused on Academic Outcomes for Students with Emotional and Behavioral Disorders

Reference	Students	Instructional setting	Intervention	Academic focus	Design
McLaughlin, Burgess, & Sackville-West (CBT, 1981)	*N* = 6; 3 girls, 3 boys; age: 10–12; school level: NS	Self-contained special education classroom	Self-monitoring + self-evaluation	Reading	Counterbalanced multiple baseline
McLaughlin & Truhlicka (BE; 1983)	*N* = 12; 8 boys, 4 girls; age: 9–11; school level: NS	Self-contained special education classroom	Self-monitoring + self-evaluation	Reading	Pretest–posttest between-groups design
McLaughlin (CEP, 1984)	*N* = 12; 3 girls, 9 boys; age: NS; school level: NS	Self-contained special education classroom	Self-monitoring + self-evaluation	Reading	Pretest–posttest experimental design with repeated measures
Osborne, Kosiewicz, Crumley, & Lee (TEC, 1987)	*N* = 5; 3 boys, 2 girls; age: 10–16; school level: elementary	Self-contained resource special education classroom	Self-monitoring	Oral reading Math calculation	Withdrawal: ABAB
Lloyd, Bateman, Landrum, & Hallahan (JABA, 1989)	*N* = 5; 2 girls, 3 boys; age: 10–11; school level: elementary	Special education resource classroom	Self-monitoring	Math calculation	Alternating treatment
Carr & Punzo (BD, 1993)	N = 3; boys; age: 13–15 years; school level: middle	Self-contained classroom in an inner-city public middle school	Self-monitoring	Reading, math, and spelling	Multiple baseline
McDougall & Brady (JER, 1995)	*N* = 3 boys; age: 5–8; school level: elementary	Special education summer school adaptive behavior program	Self-monitoring	Spelling	Multiple baseline
Levendoski & Cartledge (BD, 2000)	*N* = 4; boys; age: 9–11; school level: elementary	Self-contained class within a general education elementary school	Self-monitoring	Math calculation	Withdrawal: ABABC

Note. CBT, *Child Behavior Therapy*; CEP, *Contemporary Educational Psychology*; BD, *Behavior Disorders*; BE, *Behavior Engineering*; ETC, *Education and Treatment of Children*; JEBD, *Journal of Emotional and Behavioral Disorders*; JEIBI, *Journal of Early and Intensive Behavior Intervention*; JPBI, *Journal of Positive Behavior Interventions*; TEC, *Teaching Exceptional Children*. From Mooney, Ryan, Uhing, Reid, and Epstein (2005).

levels of on-task behavior. The study took place from 10:00 to 11:20 A.M. each day, during math period.

Each student had his own self-monitoring card (5″ × 8″ index card) that contained one question: "At this exact second am I doing my work?" Also, the card contained the words *yes* (with a happy face) and *no* (with a sad face). The instructional tasks were math worksheets designed for each student's instructional level. Two behaviors were monitored: percentage of time on task during independent math practice and percentage of math problems completed. In brief, the study contained five phases: baseline, intervention, return to baseline, return to intervention, and fading. Results suggested that for three of the four students, on-task behavior increased, as did academic productivity. Furthermore, the students indicated that they liked using the self-monitoring procedure and that it helped them to stay on task and finish their math. One limitation of this study was that academic accuracy was not addressed; however, this outcome has been addressed in other studies, such as the one highlighted in the next section.

Middle and High School

Self-monitoring procedures have also been successful with older students. For example, Carr and Punzo (1993) examined the effects of self-monitoring on (1) both productivity and accuracy of academic performance and (2) engagement of three middle school boys who were identified as behaviorally disordered/emotionally disturbed. All three students were African American, ranging in age from 13 to 15 years. They were placed in a self-contained classroom in an inner-city public middle school.

In this study, self-monitoring procedures were introduced in three content areas—reading (12 minutes), math (20 minutes), and spelling (15 minutes)—which were evaluated using a multiple-baseline-across-content-area design. In this design, the intervention is staggered, beginning first in one content area, and later beginning in the second or third area once the desired behavior has improved in the previous content area. Three behaviors were monitored: academic accuracy, academic productivity, and on-task behavior. During baseline, students worked individually and were allowed to ask questions. After collecting baseline data, the teacher taught each student how to self-monitor his behaviors (accuracy and productivity) in reading. Students used one self-monitoring sheet each week and recorded academic accuracy and academic productivity each day. To make sure that the students were accurate in their self-monitoring, the teacher calculated interrater reliability, which indicated that students were quite accurate in their self-monitoring. During this time, baseline data continued to be collected during math and spelling until students increased their performance a minimum of 15% in reading. Once this criterion was achieved and maintained, students were taught how to self-monitor in math. Baseline data collection continued in spelling until the 15% improvement criterion was reached in math. At that time, self-monitoring was implemented in spelling. Students' on-task behavior was measured by the teacher for 10 minutes of each independent work period using a 5-second time-sampling procedure.

Results indicated that students' performance improved. During baseline, students' accuracy was generally low and variable. Then, when the self-monitoring procedures were implemented successively across reading, math, and spelling, performance patterns shifted. Specifically, students' accuracy increased, as did productivity and engagement. Anecdotal information from the teacher indicated that students were eager to record their daily scores and appeared to be aware of and pleased with their improvement.

Summary

Several different methods exist for designing, implementing, and evaluating self-monitoring interventions in elementary, middle, and high school settings. We encourage you to find an approach that works best for you and your student. If you want to consult the research literature for examples of different procedural applications of self-monitoring interventions with different populations, see Table 6.2 at the end of the chapter for information on related readings and resources (books, websites, and refereed articles). In addition, the next section provides detailed instructions on how to create a self-monitoring intervention.

IMPLEMENTING SELF-MONITORING INTERVENTIONS IN YOUR CLASSROOM

As you can see, self-monitoring is a feasible and potentially highly effective practice to support the academic and behavioral performance of students, including those with and at risk for EBD. Self-monitoring interventions can be structured and implemented in a variety of ways. In this section, we offer one research-based approach to conducting a self-monitoring intervention within the classroom context (Menzies et al., 2009; Vanderbilt, 2005) and provide you with a step-by-step set of procedures for designing, implementing, and evaluating self-monitoring procedures in your classroom. We also include an illustration of how to apply these procedures in the high school setting.

Step 1: Establish Prerequisite Conditions

As discussed earlier, before implementing any self-management strategy, the teacher should identify whether the student is capable of replacing the target behavior with a more appropriate one. If a student knows how to perform acceptable classroom behavior but does not do so, this is considered a *performance deficit*, which can be remediated through self-monitoring. In contrast, if the problem behavior is due to an *acquisition deficit*, meaning that the replacement behavior is not in his or her repertoire, the student must first become proficient in the skill before a self-monitoring strategy will be successful. In this case, the teacher must provide the student with explicit instruction in the new skill (Elliott & Gresham, 1991).

The teacher must also determine whether the student can control the problem behavior. It is unlikely that a self-monitoring intervention will be sufficiently intense to remediate student behavior that has advanced to out-of-control levels (e.g., extreme aggression or expressions of anger). If it is determined that the student cannot control the problem behavior, a higher intensity intervention must first be implemented to bring the problem behavior under control (e.g., functional assessment-based interventions, discussed in Chapter 7). Once behaviors are under more control, a self-monitoring strategy can be employed.

Another prerequisite condition for a self-monitoring intervention to be successful is that the problem behavior must occur frequently. Though high-intensity, low-frequency behaviors can be detrimental to classroom activities, these behaviors may be better addressed through alternative intervention strategies (e.g., adjusting rates of reinforcement using differential reinforcement schedules; Cooper et al., 2007). Self-monitoring strategies are unlikely to be sensitive enough to address and reinforce infrequent behavior problems sufficiently to produce meaningful, immediate behavior change and are better used for behaviors that occur frequently.

Finally, the problem behavior and the preferred replacement behaviors should be readily observable and easy for the student to record. Likewise, the recording system chosen should be reliable and feasible for student use. Before starting the intervention, a baseline estimate of the student's level of performance should be collected using this recording system. This baseline objectively illustrates the magnitude of the problem and allows later comparison to evaluate the success of the self-monitoring system and modify it if necessary. When given the option of monitoring the preferred replacement behavior (e.g., on task) or the problem behavior (e.g., off task), we encourage you to focus on the former—focus on the positive!

Once these prerequisite conditions are established, a teacher can feel confident that self-monitoring is an appropriate strategy. The next five steps can be used to implement a self-monitoring procedure with an optimum likelihood for success.

Step 2: Identify and Operationally Define the Behaviors

To initiate a self-monitoring intervention, the problem behavior must first be identified and operationally defined. The teacher should explicitly communicate the target behavior and operational definition to the student through discussion and role play. Examples of the problem behavior should be made clear so that both the teacher and the student agree on exactly what the problem behavior looks like. Accordingly, examples of the replacement behavior should be discussed or role-played by the teacher and student. This is especially important, because the focus of self-monitoring should not be exclusively on reducing problem behaviors but also on improving academic and behavioral performance by ensuring that the student exhibits more appropriate behaviors. The more proficient and successful a student becomes at demonstrating appropriate behavior, the less likely he or she will be to engage in problem behavior. With continued appropriate behavior, the student will have increased access to the curriculum, will learn more meaningful skills, and in turn will be less likely to engage in undesirable behaviors to escape too easy or too difficult tasks (Umbreit et al., 2004). This is particularly the case for self-monitoring interventions that focus on academic engagement or work completion, which can also result in improved quality and quantity of students' work in addition to classroom behavior (Smith et al., 1992).

Step 3: Design the Self-Monitoring Procedures, Including a Monitoring Form

After operationally defining the behaviors, the teacher should create a simple data monitoring sheet for the student. The day should be broken down into segments appropriate for the situation and the student. Specifically, the periods should be of an appropriate length to encompass times when problem behavior is likely to occur, should allow the student the opportunity to attain success or reinforcement for at least one segment, and should be age appropriate and in accordance with the daily schedule. The data monitoring sheet should also be age appropriate in other ways. For example, it should reflect the students' reading level, using some symbols and simple sentences for a very young student and more complex text for an older, proficient reader. Also, the form may be more discreet for an older student who might be embarrassed using a self-monitoring technique in front of his or her peers. Goal behaviors or items on the self-monitoring sheet should be clear and explicit, as well as easy to identify and record.

Consider using a reinforcement contingency in conjunction with self-monitoring. One such example is to design the self-monitoring intervention so that the student earns breaks from nonpreferred activities (negative reinforcement) or access to preferred activities (positive reinforcement) contingent upon meeting the predetermined goals that he or she monitors (e.g., Umbreit et al., 2007). Be sure to set realistic goals that allow the student to be successful, and carefully select the type of reinforcement in collaboration with the student. For the reinforcer to be most likely to have the maximum effect, consider the function of the problem behavior to be decreased or the reason that it is occurring. After determining what the student receives or avoids (such as attention, an activity or task, or a sensory experience) by engaging in the problem behavior, a reinforcer that meets that same function can be identified and used as a part of the self-monitoring system. Contingencies should then be adjusted so that reinforcement can be obtained only when the student meets predetermined goals for performing the appropriate replacement behavior, as determined by the self-monitoring data (Umbreit et al., 2007).

Step 4: Teach the Student the Self-Monitoring Procedures

Just as the student should be explicitly taught the desirable and undesirable behaviors that are the focus of self-monitoring, he or she should be taught how to use the self-monitoring form. It is important to convey to the student that self-monitoring is not a punishment. Instead, it is a tool that the student can use to become more aware of his or her actions and be more successful in learning and behavioral outcomes (e.g., obtaining rewards, increasing learning). Teachers should use discussion, modeling, coaching, and role play when explaining how to use the form (e.g., Lane, Eisner, et al., 2009; Lane, Weisenbach, Little, Phillips, & Wehby, 2006). As the student completes the form independently, the teacher should remind him or her at the beginning of each time period to be aware of the target behavior and should gradually fade the frequency of this support. When redirecting a behavior to be decreased, be explicit in reminding the student to instead demonstrate appropriate behavior and avoid engaging in an argument. Also, reinforcers may be used to teach the procedures and increase the likelihood that the student will complete the self-monitoring forms.

Step 5: Monitor Student Progress

Compare the data collected during the self-monitoring process with the student's previously established baseline level of performance to track student progress. This allows the teacher to objectively evaluate whether the intervention is working, to assess student progress, and to determine whether modifications should be made (Vanderbilt, 2005).

The teacher can also monitor (and reward) accuracy of the student's self-recording by completing the form during the same intervals and comparing teacher and student results (matching; McLaughlin, Burgess, & Sackville-West, 1981). If this comparison reveals that the student is not being truthful when collecting his or her own data, the teacher may need to remediate this by (1) discussing the discrepancy with the student, (2) modifying the contingencies so that the student is more likely to achieve success or obtain reinforcement, and/ or (3) simply continue monitoring the accuracy of the student's self-recording.

Students can be taught to graph their self-monitoring data in order to illustrate their behavior over time. Graphing may increase intrinsic reinforcement by providing concrete evidence of changes in behavior (Carr & Punzo, 1993). Graphs can also be used to share outcomes with other stakeholders such as parents or other teachers, or to demonstrate progress on IEP goals.

Step 6: Consider Maintenance and Follow-Up

The self-monitoring system should be gradually faded once the student has successfully and consistently used it and demonstrated improved and acceptable academic or behavioral performance (Vanderbilt, 2005). The ultimate goal is for the student to demonstrate and maintain appropriate behavior independently. Successful fading can occur by lengthening the intervals the student is monitoring, by fading teacher support (e.g., decreased matching; McLaughlin et al., 1981), or by having the student self-monitor for a shorter duration or during fewer activities during the day. Fading should gradually decrease until self-monitoring is no longer occurring at all and behavior is maintained across settings. However, intermittent behavior-specific praise or reinforcement should continue as necessary to support appropriate behavior, particularly when the self-monitoring system is completely faded.

To assist you in implementing self-monitoring interventions, we provide a detailed illustration that begins with defining the target behavior and moves you through the process, ending with evaluation (see Box 6.1). As you read this illustration, we encourage you to look at how this process moved through the following steps:

- Step 1: Establish prerequisite conditions.
- Step 2: Identify and operationally define the behaviors.
- Step 3: Design the self-monitoring procedures, including a monitoring form.
- Step 4: Teach the student the self-monitoring procedures.
- Step 5: Monitor student progress.
- Step 6: Consider maintenance and follow-up.

We hope that you find this illustration helpful. To further support you in your planning efforts, we would also like to refer you to an article by Menzies, Lane, and Lee (2009) that appears in *Beyond Behavior.* This article contains many of the key concepts presented in this chapter and offers teachers, administrators, and other school-site personnel another step-by-step approach to designing, implementing, and evaluating self-monitoring procedures for students who require more than primary prevention efforts.

SUMMARY

This chapter provided an overview of five common self-management interventions: self-evaluation, self-instruction, goal setting, strategy instruction, and self-monitoring, as well as combinations of these strategies (e.g., self-monitoring and goal setting). Then we provided additional information on self-monitoring, one of the most commonly used strategies. We offered an overview of the benefits and challenges associated with self-monitoring, as well as information on the research that supports its use as an effective technique. We concluded this chapter with (1) directions on how to design, implement, and evaluate self-monitoring interventions in your classroom, (2) an illustration to use as a guide, and (3) resources to assist teachers, administrators, and other school-site personnel in using this strategy.

BOX 6.1. Self-Monitoring Illustration

Mrs. Wheeler was a fourth-grade teacher in a general education classroom that included students with high-incidence disabilities alongside typically developing students. She consistently implemented and reinforced her SWPBS plan and maintained a structured daily schedule. She had many years of successful classroom experience, and her teaching style and classroom organization strategies had always allowed her to maintain a well-behaved inclusion class. This year the majority of the class responded well to her management style as always, but she was concerned about three students who frequently engaged in off-task and disruptive behaviors. They continued to have problems with academic engagement and work completion despite her best efforts at correction using her primary classroom management strategies. One student received special education services for emotional disturbance, and two students received no extra services but were clearly in need of additional behavioral support.

Mrs. Wheeler asked the special education teacher to help her identify some strategies for her students that would improve their classroom behavior and performance. After discussing the situation, observing the classroom, and considering how busy Mrs. Wheeler's days already were in meeting the varying needs of all 25 students in her inclusionary class, the special education teacher knew that she needed a strategy that was effective but required minimum teacher effort. She recommended a self-monitoring intervention to Mrs. Wheeler.

Step 1: Establish Prerequisite Conditions

The two teachers worked together to determine whether a self-monitoring intervention was likely to be effective for the problem behaviors Mrs. Wheeler was seeing. The special education teacher asked Mrs. Wheeler whether each of the three target students was able to perform appropriate on-task behavior during some activities. She wanted to make sure that behavior problems were not due to a skill deficit. Because all three had demonstrated on-task behavior and adequate work completion at times, had tested within grade-level limits in both mathematics and reading, and were able to complete the work they were assigned, the teachers determined that the behavior was a performance deficit. Thus this condition was met. Next, the special education teacher wanted to make sure that the problem behaviors occurred frequently for all the students. Mrs. Wheeler assured her that they did and that silent reading or other independent work was the most problematic activity. The special education teacher decided to observe the class for several days during silent reading and confirmed that all three students displayed below-average levels of academic engagement time (in fact, below 50%). For each student, the special education teacher took several observational probes to establish a baseline level of performance. This would allow Mrs. Wheeler to evaluate whether the intervention improved student behavior. Because academic engagement is a readily observable behavior that the students and teachers could easily identify and record, along with the other established prerequisite conditions, both teachers felt confident that a self-monitoring intervention was an appropriate strategy and had an optimum probability for success.

(cont.)

BOX 6.1 *(cont.)*

Step 2: Identify and Operationally Define the Behaviors

Because the primary behavior of concern for all three students was off-task behavior, sometimes disruptive in nature and sometimes just off task, the teachers identified the problem behavior as off-task behavior, to include both. They agreed that appropriate behavior would be academic engagement. After the teachers discussed their classroom experiences and observations, they operationally defined the problem and replacement behaviors (as shown in Figure 6.2).

Step 3: Design the Self-Monitoring Procedures, Including a Monitoring Form

Next, the teachers designed a self-monitoring sheet for the students to use. They decided to begin the intervention during silent reading, a problematic time during the day for all three students, and then generalize the behavior to other activities as behavior improvements were observed. Because the silent reading block lasted for 20 minutes each day, they decided to break the period into four 5-minute segments at first. Later, other activities could be added, or the segments could be lengthened as the students mastered the skill. The teachers considered appropriate reading level, kept the form simple, and added icons for novelty and interest. They also kept it short so that it could be printed on a small sheet of paper (3" × 5") that would be inconspicuous to other students to prevent embarrassment or jealousy and also to be unobtrusive in the student's work space. The daily self-monitoring form looked like this:

Name: ______________________		Date: ____________
At this exact second, am I reading on task?	Yes ☺	No ☹
Bell 1		
Bell 2		
Bell 3		
Bell 4		

The teachers also decided to provide reinforcement opportunities in conjunction with the self-monitoring procedures to enhance their effectiveness. Their school had an SWPBS plan in which students could earn tickets for achieving specific behavioral expectations and then use those tickets to earn privileges or prizes. Because they had worked successfully as reinforcers for each of the three students in the past, tickets were chosen as the reinforcer. Both teachers agreed that, to start, students would have the opportunity to earn a ticket each day by accurately checking three of four "yes" options on their self-monitoring forms.

(cont.)

Step 4: Teach the Student the Self-Monitoring Procedures

Mrs. Wheeler met with the three students in a small group after arrival one day to explain the self-monitoring procedures to them. First, she informed them that they were going to try something that might help them stay on task and do better in school, as well as avoid getting into trouble. She introduced the problem and the off-task behaviors that she had identified and gave them examples of what not to do. She then explained the behavior that was expected, academic engagement, and provided an example of what that looks like. To ensure that the students understood the definitions, she first modeled examples and non-examples of academic engagement. Then she had students' role-play each behavior. Next, she explained the self-monitoring form and procedures to the students and showed them all the materials, including the form and the kitchen timer that she would set to ring every 5 minutes to cue them to complete the form. She modeled how to fill out the form and then had each student practice completing it, using the kitchen timer. Finally, she explained to students that they would have the opportunity to earn a ticket each day for checking three "yes" options. She informed them that she would be making sure that the data they kept was accurate by also taking periodic data herself. She asked the students if they had any questions about what was expected and discussed their concerns with them.

Step 5: Monitor Student Progress

In order to help Mrs. Wheeler to objectively determine whether the intervention was improving student behavior, the special education teacher agreed to record and graph academic engagement data for each student. She decided that she would use duration, or "real-time," recording of each student for three 2-minute sessions, twice per week, and designed a simple data collection sheet (see Figure 6.3). After the intervention had been in place for 3 weeks, the two teachers met to review the data for each student. See Figure 6.4 for an example of one of the graphs that the special education teacher made, which allowed them to determine that the intervention was working. Data were similar for the other two students, and Mrs. Wheeler was excited to share the visual display of behavioral progress with each of them. This helped them maintain behavioral improvement and momentum for generalizing their new skills.

Step 6: Consider Maintenance and Follow-Up

After showing the students their data, Mrs. Wheeler told them that they would be trying these procedures for more activities throughout the day. She introduced the self-monitoring form for independent math work and independent science/social studies, and she increased the intervals to 10 minutes. Now students would have the opportunity to earn one ticket for achieving behavioral criteria across all three activities each day (or six of eight sessions now in each day). As time went on, Mrs. Wheeler continued to extend the intervention to new activities (e.g., whole-group instruction). By spring, she was able to start to gradually fade the intervention, eventually taking only random probes throughout the school day. Around the end of the year, the special education teacher commented to Mrs. Wheeler that she was most pleased with the outcomes.

In Table 6.2 you will find other resources that you may find helpful as you develop self-monitoring interventions. We also invite to you turn to Chapter 8, which contains (1) a self-monitoring procedures guide, (2) a quick guide to determining student eligibility for self-management interventions, and (3) a sample treatment integrity form to help inform your planning as you take steps to make sure that the self-monitoring strategy is implemented as originally designed.

In the next chapter, we provide information on an even more intensive support: functional assessment-based interventions. Chapter 7 introduces one team-based approach to designing and implementing functional assessment-based interventions for use with individual students to address academic and behavior issues. First, we provide an overview of functional assessment-based interventions, defining the intervention; we describe one systematic approach to conducting these highly individualized interventions; and we provide an overview of the benefits and challenges associated with this intervention approach. Next, we review the supporting research on functional assessment-based interventions using the process developed by Umbreit and colleagues (2007), noting the limited investigations in secondary-level schools. Finally, we offer direction on how to implement functional assessment-based interventions in the classroom, providing an illustration from peer-reviewed studies, as well as other resources, to assist with this intensive intervention process.

TABLE 6.2. Self-Monitoring Resource Guide

Reference	Description	Target group	Cost/retrieval information
	Books		
Knapczyk, D. (2004). *Teaching self-discipline: A self-monitoring program*. Verona, WI: Attainment.	Instilling self-discipline in students promotes a comfortable and productive instructional atmosphere for all involved. In this book, classroom discipline is a curricular concern, comparable to teaching reading and math. The author outlines how to incorporate discipline training into the general curriculum and how to teach students to set goals for their behavior, apply themselves to their work, direct their own behavior, make decisions about their actions, and moderate their actions in accordance with those of peers.	K–12 educators	$39.00 for book and CD; National Professional Resources, Inc. *www.nprinc.com/classmgt/tsdi.htm*
	Websites		
Mulkey, S. L. (2009). *Self-monitoring and management for behavior: Online module*. Indiana Designs Equitable Access for Learning, Mulkey Educational Consulting & Training.	This site is funded by the Indiana Department of Education and the Office of Special Education Programs (OSEP). This module provides an overview of effective self-monitoring and management across both general and special education settings, with individual students or entire groups and a focus on increasing on-task behavior and reducing passive or active off-task behavior. Describes a five-step process for use in general or special education settings. Key topics include benefits of self-monitoring, different types of self-management, steps for setting up and implementing a program, tips and other supports for strengthening self-monitoring programs, and specific ideas for teaching students to monitor and keep track of their behavior.	K–12 educators	*www.idealindiana.com/ideal/modules/19*
Lesson Planet	Provides over 500 lesson plans to directly teach self-monitoring strategies or that incorporate self-monitoring into specific content. Excellent resource for teachers to gain a comprehensive understanding of how to directly teach self-monitoring to students.	K–12 educators	*www.lessonplanet.com/search?grade=all&keywords=self-monitoring&media=lesson&page=2&rating=3&search_type=related*

(cont.)

TABLE 6.2. *(cont.)*

Reference	Description	Target group	Cost/retrieval information
Tip sheet for self-monitoring.	This site is maintained by the University of Minnesota Center for Early Education and Development. Provides an overview of self-monitoring and its benefits, how it can be used in the classroom for students to monitor themselves, how to begin using self-monitoring in the classroom, and how to improve outcomes. Includes a tip sheet for self-monitoring.	Preschool and early elementary educators	*slhslinux.cla.umn.edu/Tip%20Sheets/Other%20Tip%20Sheets/selfmon.pdf*
Gusinger, P. (2009). *Self-monitoring.* Ohio Resource Center for Mathematics, Science, and Reading.	Defines self-monitoring and how it relates to reading instruction, how skilled readers self-monitor, activities to promote self-monitoring when reading, and additional resources pertaining to this topic.	Educators of struggling adolescent readers	*ohiorc.org/adlit/strategy/strategy_each.aspx?id=000010#top*
	Refereed journal articles		
Amato-Zech, N. A., Hoff, K. E., & Doepke, K. J. (2006). Increasing on-task behavior in the classroom: Extension of self-monitoring strategies. *Psychology in the Schools, 43*, 211–221.	This study presents a tactile self-monitoring intervention involving teaching elementary students to use an electronic beeper to remind them to self-monitor their attention. On-task behavior improved to above-average rates for participants, and teachers and students evaluated the intervention favorably.	Elementary and middle school educators	*Psychology in the Schools* is published by John Wiley & Sons, Inc. *www3.interscience.wiley.com/journal/112252198/abstract?CRETRY=1&SRETRY=0*
Gunter, P. L., Miller, K. A., & Venn, M. L. (2003). A case study of the effects of self-graphing reading performance data for a girl identified with emotional/behavioral disorders. *Preventing School Failure, 48*, 28–31.	In this study an elementary student with severe EBD was taught to graph her own performance as a rate of correct words read per minute using a computer. Her reading rate improved, ultimately to levels on target for her grade level, concurrent with implementation of the intervention.	Elementary educators	*Preventing School Failure* is published by Heldref Publications. *eric.ed.gov/ERICWebPortal/custom/portlets/recordDetails/detailmini.jsp?_nfpb=true&_&ERICExtSearch_SearchValue_0=EJ770007&ERICExtSearch_SearchType_0=no&accno=EJ770007*

Menzies, H. M., Lane, K. L., & Lee, J. M. (2009). Self-monitoring strategies for use in the classroom: A promising practice to support productive behavior for students with emotional or behavioral disorders. *Beyond Behavior, 18*, 27–35.	This article describes how self-monitoring strategies can be used in the classroom to address a variety of behaviors exhibited by students with EBD. Academic outcomes are emphasized given that students with EBD struggle in all content areas. The concept of metacognition is introduced, a range of metacognitive strategies are presented, and step-by-step procedures for designing and implementing self-monitoring procedures in your classroom are provided.	K–12 educators of students with EBD	*Beyond Behavior* is published by the Council for Children with Behavior Disorders of the Council for Exceptional Children *www.ccbd.net/beyondbehavior*
Pelco, L. E., & Reed-Victor, E. (2007). Self-regulation and learning-related social skills: Intervention ideas for elementary school students. *Preventing School Failure, 51*, 36–42.	This article explores the literature on individual differences in self-regulation and related social skills. An inability to learn to self-regulate emotions, attention, and behavior can result in decreased academic achievement and later social and academic problems. Strategies for interventions to address these deficits at the elementary level are discussed, including primary, secondary, and tertiary prevention; changing the nature of instructional strategies; changing the organization of classroom time; and changing interaction patterns between individuals.	Elementary educators of students who have difficulty learning to self-regulate	*Preventing School Failure* is published by Heldref Publications. *heldref-publications.metapress.com/app/home/contribution.asp?referrer=parent&backto=issue,-5,7;journal,11,24;linkingpublicationresults,1:119942,1*
Rock, M. L. (2005). Use of strategic self-monitoring to enhance academic engagement, productivity, and accuracy of students with and without exceptionalities. *Journal of Positive Behavior Interventions, 7*, 3–17.	In this study a strategy designed to help disengaged students take control of their learning by teaching students to self-monitor attention and performance was evaluated. Improved outcomes related to task engagement, problem behavior, productivity, and accuracy were observed, indicating that this was an effective intervention for fostering self-monitoring and enhancing academic performance for students with and without disabilities in inclusive settings.	Elementary educators	The *Journal of Positive Behavior Interventions* is published by Pro-Ed, Inc. *pbi.sagepub.com/cgi/content/abstract/7/1/3*
Vanderbilt, A. (2005). Designed for teachers: How to implement self-monitoring in the classroom. *Beyond Behavior, 15*, 21–24.	The authors outline 10 key steps for using self-monitoring strategies in the classroom to improve the on-task behavior of students by encouraging them to monitor their own behavior. Includes frequently asked questions about self-monitoring.	Elementary educators; also relevant to K–12 educators	*Beyond Behavior* is published by the Council for Children with Behavior Disorders of the Council for Exceptional Children *www.ccbd.net/beyondbehavior*

Note. See Table 6.1 for a summary of journal articles from a systematic literature review of self-monitoring interventions (Mooney et al., 2005).

CHAPTER 7

Functional Assessment-Based Interventions

When students do not respond to primary prevention efforts (e.g., schoolwide PBS programs) or to more targeted supports, such as behavioral contracting or self-monitoring interventions, the next step is tertiary prevention (Lane, 2007; Walker & Severson, 2002). Tertiary supports are the most intensive type of supports. They are typically reserved for students who are exposed to multiple risk factors (e.g., high mobility, poverty, harsh and inconsistent parenting practices; Eber, Sugai, Smith, & Scott, 2002; Reid & Patterson, 1991) and those most resistant to other intervention efforts (Kazdin, 1987). Functional assessment-based interventions are a type of tertiary prevention that considers the communicative intent of behavior, a respectful approach to addressing challenging behaviors that looks at the reasons that problem behaviors occur (Umbreit et al., 2007).

In this chapter, we introduce one approach to designing and implementing functional assessment-based interventions for use with individual students (including those who do and do not have specific disabilities) to address academic and behavior issues. We begin by providing an overview of the intervention and describe one systematic approach to conducting these highly individualized treatments. Next, we examine the associated benefits and challenges and then provide an overview of the supporting research, including information on studies conducted at the elementary, middle, and high school levels to support students with challenging behaviors in a range of environments. We conclude this chapter with a discussion of how to implement functional assessment-based interventions in your classroom, providing direction on how to design, implement, and evaluate this tertiary support. To this end, we provide an illustration from peer-reviewed studies and offer resources to assist you in the classroom.

FUNCTIONAL ASSESSMENT-BASED INTERVENTIONS: AN OVERVIEW

Whereas many interventions focus on the *form* of behavior (what the behavior looks like), functional assessment-based interventions focus on the *function*—the reason that a problem behavior occurs (Umbreit et al., 2007). These types of interventions originated in clinical settings with individuals with developmental disabilities (Iwata, Dorsey, Slifer, Bauman, & Richman, 1982). Today, functional assessment procedures are used with a wide range of students, including those with severe disabilities, attention-deficit disorders, learning disabilities, EBDs, and those at risk for behavior problems (Ervin, DuPaul, Kern, & Friman, 1998; Kern, Delaney, et al., 2001; Lane, Rogers, et al., 2007; Sasso, Reimers, Cooper, & Wacker, 1992). In addition to their use with a wide range of students, functional assessment-based interventions have been used to shape a range of behaviors by decreasing undesirable behaviors (e.g., aggression and disruption) and increasing more desirable behaviors (e.g., academic engagement and participation) in a variety of school settings, including self-contained schools, self-contained classrooms, resource settings, and general education classrooms (see Lane, Bruhn, Crnobori, & Sewell, 2009). These procedures have been applied across the educational continuum, with interventions being conducted successfully with preschool, elementary, middle, and high school students (albeit the majority of interventions conducted to date have been implemented with elementary-age students). There have been fewer applications with adolescent students in middle and high school settings (Conroy, Dunlap, Clarke, & Alter, 2005; Kern, Hilt, & Gresham, 2004; Lane, Kalberg, & Shepcaro, 2009).

A Description of the Process

There are many different approaches to conducting functional assessment-based interventions. In this section, we provide a brief description of the overall process. We then focus on one systematic approach to conducting functional assessment-based interventions, developed by John Umbreit and colleagues (2007).

A Brief Introduction

As we previously stated, functional assessment-based interventions are designed on the basis of the reasons that specific behavior problems occur. Rather than simply eliminating problem behaviors through reductive procedures, such as differential reinforcement of lower rates of behavior (Cooper et al., 2007), functional assessment-based interventions take a more instructional approach to problem behavior. Using this approach, a teacher, service provider, behavior specialist, or university researcher begins working with a student's teacher to identify a socially significant behavior that—if changed—could result in socially important improvements in the student's life (Baer, Wolf, & Risley, 1968; Wolf, 1978). The primary goal of all interventions is to produce meaningful, lasting change that is in the student's best interest (Baer et al., 1968). In other words, the focus is on teaching students new, socially valid behaviors that help to improve the quality of their lives both within and beyond the school setting.

The process begins by determining what *exactly* needs to be changed. Examples of such target behaviors (the behaviors we want to eliminate or minimize) may include aggression, disruption, off-task behavior, negative social interactions, or inappropriate physical contact. Again, the goal is to teach the student new, more desirable replacement behaviors that will allow him or her to engage more successfully with his or her peers, teachers, and parents.

The next step is to determine *why* the student engages in the target behavior in the first place. We know that behavior as a means of either seeking (positive reinforcement) or avoiding (negative reinforcement) (1) attention; (2) tasks, activities, or tangibles; or (3) sensory experiences. It is important to note that both positive *and* negative reinforcement serve to increase or maintain behavior. In terms of positive reinforcement, a student may demonstrate a certain behavior to obtain (1) a teacher's attention; (2) tasks, activities, or tangibles; or (3) sensory experiences. For example, when asked by the teacher to begin a less than exciting activity, a student (Jake) may argue with the teacher, saying "This is boring! I am not going to do this!" If the teacher comes over to Jake and engages in a lengthy discussion of why this task is important, Jake has obtained positive reinforcement in the form of teacher attention. Specifically, Jake's arguing or noncompliant behavior helped him get something (in this case, positive attention in the form of accessing teacher attention) that he wanted. And you might also recognize that negative reinforcement has occurred as well: Specifically, Jake's arguing or noncompliant behavior also helped him avoid the task that he did not want to do (in this case, negative reinforcement in the form of escaping a nonpreferred task). Again, both positive and negative reinforcement are behavioral principles that serve to increase the future probability of a behavior occurring—one by obtaining a stimulus (positive reinforcement) and one by avoiding a stimulus (negative reinforcement; Umbreit et al., 2007).

When a functional behavior assessment is conducted, a range of descriptive and experimental tools are used to determine the antecedent conditions (A) that prompt a given target behavior (B; e.g., verbal aggression), as well as the consequences (C; i.e., positive or negative reinforcement) that maintain the target behavior. Descriptive procedures may include interviews with teachers, parents, and/or students; use of rating scales, such as the Social Skills Improvement System (SSIS; Elliott & Gresham, 2007), to see whether the behavior is an acquisition or performance deficit; and direct observations in the classroom to collect A–B–C data (Bijou, Peterson, & Ault, 1968). Experimental procedures (also referred to as *functional analysis*) involve manipulating conditions such as teacher attention that are suspected to be maintaining the undesirable behavior. Information collected from these tools and procedures are examined, and a hypothesis is developed as to *why* the behavior occurs. For example, the hypothesis may be: When transitioning to language arts class following lunch, Landon engages in verbal and physical aggression with his peers to escape participating in the assigned reading tasks.

Once the hypothesis is developed, an intervention *linked to the function of the behavior* is created. The goal is to teach the student a new behavior (referred to as the replacement behavior) that serves as a new way to meet his or her goals. Because response rate matches reinforcement (matching law), it is important that the replacement behavior work better than the target behavior (Cooper et al., 2007). Namely, the replacement behavior has to work more reliably (work almost every time) and more efficiently (take less energy and/or resources), thus taking less effort than the target behavior.

Rather than just putting an intervention in place and hoping for the best, one needs to use an experimental design (e.g., an ABAB withdrawal or multiple-baseline design) so that accurate conclusions can be drawn regarding how well the intervention worked. Gone are the days when we could simply put an intervention in place, observe the changes in student behavior, and say, "it's working!" In order to have legally defensible plans that meet minimum requirements with respect to due-process hearings and the requirements established in the Individuals with Disabilities Education Improvement Act (IDEA, 2004), it is important to use an experimental design that allows one to determine whether a functional relation is established between the introduction of the intervention (putting the plan in place) and changes in student behavior (increases in compliance and/or decreases in disruption).

In addition to having a strong design, it is also important to accurately measure the target and replacement behaviors (interobserver agreement), the extent to which the intervention is put in place as planned (treatment integrity), and consumers' opinions about the intervention goals, procedures, and outcomes (social validity). Fortunately, special education teachers, school psychologists, and behavior specialists all have training in how to design, implement, and evaluate functional assessment-based interventions. This is not a process that a general education teacher is expected to do in isolation; this is a team-based process. There are resources available at your building or district level to assist with this most intensive level of support. The key for the general education teacher, as well as other school-site personnel, is to be aware of this process with a sufficient level of understanding to support the design, implementation, and evaluation of these interventions. In our work, many general education teachers have become well versed in this process to the point that they are able to (1) assist in analyzing functional assessment data collected, (2) assist in designing the intervention, (3) collect data on student performance during baseline and intervention conditions, and (4) monitor the extent to which the plan is put in place (see Lane, Weisenbach, Phillips, & Wehby, 2007). But again, this is a team-based process and should not be the sole responsibility of any one individual at the school site.

As you might imagine, there have been a number of approaches to conducting functional assessment-based interventions, some offering a five-step approach and others a seven-step approach. Several approaches provide very clear directions on how to collect direct and indirect functional assessment measures (e.g., interviews and direct observation). However, oftentimes the processes for analyzing functional assessment data to determine the hypothesized function for the target behavior and then developing an intervention linked to the function of the target behavior are unclear (Lane, Bruhn, et al., 2009). Next we describe one systematic approach to designing, implementing, and evaluating functional assessment-based interventions, developed by Umbreit et al. (2007), that provides explicit guidelines for these tasks. In Figure 7.1, you will see a description of this approach. Before we introduce this systematic approach, we want to direct your attention to the functional assessment-based intervention resource guide (Table 7.2). This guide contains specific books, websites, and refereed journal articles that may be of use to you should you decide to work with a school-site or district-level team to design, implement, and evaluate functional assessment-based interventions using this process.

A Systematic Approach

The approach developed by Umbreit and colleagues (2007) begins, as most approaches do, by operationally defining the target behavior (i.e., the problem behavior you want to change). Next, descriptive and experimental functional assessment tools are used to describe the antecedent conditions that set the stage for the

Part I. Conduct the Functional Behavioral Assessment.

- 1.1 Identify and operationally define the target and replacement behaviors.
- 1.2 Functional behavioral assessment—Interviews.
- 1.3 Functional behavioral assessment—Direct observations.
- 1.4 Determine the function of the target behavior—Function matrix.

Part II. Develop and Test the Intervention.

- 2.1 Intervention Method 1: Teach the replacement behavior.
- 2.2 Intervention Method 2: Improve the environment.
- 2.3 Intervention Method 3: Adjust the contingencies.
- 2.4 Identify the measurement system.
- 2.5 Test the intervention.
- 2.6 Write the behavior intervention plan.

Part III. Implement the Intervention.

- 3.1 Assess social validity.
- 3.2 Monitor treatment integrity.
- 3.3 Program for generalization and maintenance.
- 3.4 Monitor the intervention and analyze outcomes.

FIGURE 7.1. Overview of the steps to conducting a functional behavioral assessment and a functional assessment-based intervention. Adapted from Umbreit, Ferro, Liaupsin, and Lane (2007). Copyright 2007 by Pearson Education, Inc. Adapted by permission.

target behavior to occur and the consequences that maintain the target behavior. A hypothesis statement is generated, based on results from the functional assessment, to explain the conditions that are maintaining the target behavior. Then a desired replacement behavior (i.e., the behavior the student will perform in lieu of the target behavior) is operationally defined. Finally, an intervention is developed based on the results of the functional assessment data. In general, the intervention should have three components: (1) adjustments to the antecedent conditions that prompt the target behavior, (2) increases in reinforcement rates for the replacement behavior, and (3) extinction of the target behavior (Umbreit et al., 2007).

To assist in analyzing the functional assessment data and intervention construction, Umbreit and colleagues developed two tools: the *function matrix* and the *function-based intervention decision model*. The function matrix (see Figure 7.2) is a six-celled (2 × 3) grid that is used to analyze data collected from the functional assessment tools. The team analyzing the functional assessment data begins with the teacher interview. They read results of the interview and then place quotes that indicate a given function in the respective cell of the function matrix. For example, in the teacher interview, the teacher said, "If he becomes disruptive when he leaves the classroom, like when he goes to music, then I will pull him out and bring him back to the classroom. I will spend that time talking with him about what was wrong. Then, he'll usually finish up the period helping me do work in the classroom." This statement suggests that the student is engaging in disruptive behavior (the target behavior) to access teacher attention. Therefore, this information is placed in the box that corresponds to accessing attention. This process is repeated with the parent interview and the student interview, with representative comments placed into the appropriate cell. If the parents are not available (or are unwilling) to complete the intervention or if the student is not able to complete the interview (e.g., the student is too young or his or her cognitive abilities prohibit participation), simply focus on the teacher interview. If there is another individual who spends a significant amount of the school day with the student (e.g., paraprofessional, reading specialist), then you might consider interviewing this person as well.

Then the next step is to analyze direct observation data. As part of this model, up to 3 hours of direct observation data (or 8–10 occurrences of the target behavior—whichever comes first) are collected. Then each instance of the target behavior is numbered (e.g., the number 1 is assigned to the first instance of the target behavior, the number 2 is assigned to the second instance of the target behavior, and so on). The team reads the sequence for each instance and states the outcome of that behavioral sequence. For example, let us say that one sequence was as depicted in Figure 7.3.

In reading this sequence, the team determines that the behavior (disruption) was maintained by escape from task (negative reinforcement) and access to teacher attention (positive reinforcement). In this case, both observations #3 and #4 would be placed in two cells (in Figure 7.2), as disruption served a dual function, maintained by negative and positive reinforcement.

EXPLANATION

Type of Reinforcer	**Type of Reinforcement**	
	Positive (Access)	Negative (Avoid)
Attention	Access attention	Avoid attention
Tangibles/Activities	Access a tangible or an activity	Avoid a tangible or an activity
Sensory	Access sensory stimulus	Avoid sensory stimulus

APPLICATION

Type of Reinforcer	**Type of Reinforcement**	
	Positive (Access)	Negative (Avoid)
Attention	Teacher Interview: *If he becomes disruptive when he leaves the classroom, like when he goes to music, then I will pull him out and bring him back to the classroom. I will spend that time talking with him about what was wrong. Then, he'll usually finish up the period helping me do work in the classroom.* Parent Interview: *When he's out of line at home, we try to figure out why he's acting that way. We usually talk with him.* Student Interview: *I hate going to music and art. They are really boring. I'd rather just stay in the class with Miss McD or go to the principal's office. Our principal is really cool. And, when you go to the office you can see a whole bunch of stuff—like who's in trouble, who forgot their lunch money, and who got a bloody nose on the playground.* Direct Observation: 1, 2, 3, 4, 6, 8, 9, 10, 11, 12, 13, 14, 15, 16, 17, 18, 19, 21	
Tangibles/ Activities		Teacher Interview: *3e—If he becomes disruptive when he leaves the classroom, like when he goes to music, then I will pull him out and bring him back to the classroom. 3h—He likes to go to Dr. Davis's office, our principal. I sometimes send him there when he acts up.* Direct Observation: 1, 2, 3, 4, 5, 7, 9, 10, 12, 13, 14, 17, 18, 19, 20, 21
Sensory		

FIGURE 7.2. Function Matrix. "Explanation" section adapted from Umbreit, Ferro, Liaupsin, and Lane (2007, p. 85). Copyright 2007 by Pearson Education, Inc. Adapted by permission.

Observation: #3	Date: September 5, 2011	Time: 9:45 am
Setting: Art Class	Context: Whole-class instruction	
A: Art teacher gives a direction		
B: Student refuses to do the task, shoving the papers off of his desk		
C: Art teacher engages student in a discussion (7 minutes) of why it is important to follow directions.		
Maintaining function: Teacher attention and escape from activity		
Observation: #4	Date: September 5, 2011	Time: 9:52 am
Setting: Art Class	Context: Whole-class instruction	
A: Art teacher concludes the conversation and tells Jimmy to start on the project.		
B: Jimmy responds by saying, "You can't make me! I can't stand you!"		
C: Art teacher sends another student to get Miss McDonald to take Jimmy back to homeroom. Then, the art teacher again revisits the importance of following directions		
Maintaining function: Teacher attention and escape from activity		

FIGURE 7.3. A–B–C data collection cards. Based on Carr et al. (1994).

This process is repeated with data collected from rating scales and functional analysis results. Then the team inspects all data placed into the function matrix and writes a hypothesis statement that describes the data patterns. For example, if the team were to summarize the function of the target behavior described in Figure 7.2, the hypothesis statement might read as follows: "During art class, Jimmy's disruption is maintained by teacher attention and escape from nonpreferred tasks."

Next, the function-based intervention decision model is a tool used to guide intervention planning. The model is composed of two key questions: (1) Is the replacement behavior in the student's repertoire? and (2) Does the classroom environment represent effective practices? (see Figure 7.4). The team answers these two questions to determine which of the following three intervention methods is most appropriate. Next we provide a brief overview of each method. Those interested in learning more about each method may refer to the first book in the resource guide (Table 7.2) and to the studies listed in Table 7.1 (on pages 166–167).

Method 1: Teach the Replacement Behavior is used when (1) the student is not able to perform the replacement behavior (an acquisition deficit) or when he or she is unable to perform the behavior fluently and (2) the classroom represents effective practices. In this situation, although the classroom has clear routines, procedures, and practices, no amount of M&Ms is going to motivate the student to perform the replacement behavior because it is not yet in his or her repertoire. Consequently, this method requires that the students be taught the replacement behavior. For example, if the replacement behavior is to participate in the assigned reading task and if you determine that the student is not capable of reading the

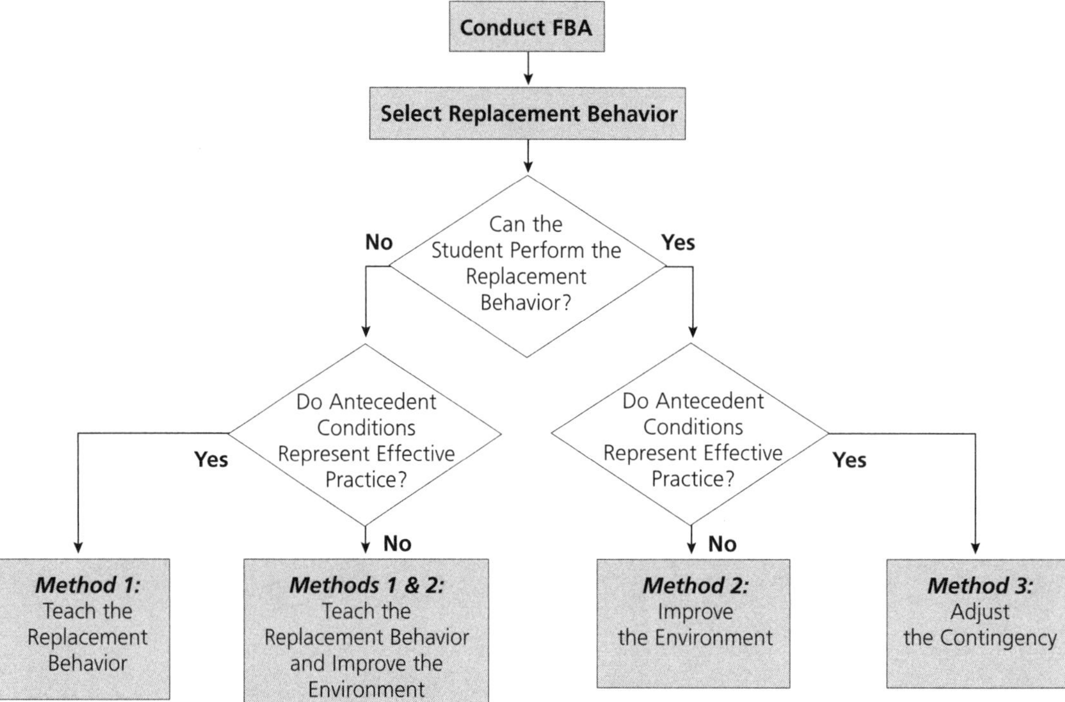

FIGURE 7.4. Function-Based Intervention Decision Model. From Umbreit, Ferro, Liaupsin, and Lane (2007). Copyright 2007 by Pearson Education, Inc. Reprinted by permission.

material because it is too difficult, then the appropriate intervention would be to provide targeted reading instruction so that the student *is* able to complete the desired reading task.

Method 2: Improve the Environment is used when (1) the student is capable of performing the desired replacement behavior (not an acquisition deficit but a performance deficit) and (2) the antecedent conditions in the classroom may need improvement to support the replacement behavior and promote learning for the given students. Therefore, the main focus of this intervention is on improving the environment by removing aversive conditions and developing a positive, predictable context that prompts the desired behavior. For example, the classroom rules and routines may not be clear, or instructions may not be given explicitly. The main focus of this method is to improve the environment to make it more consistent and predictable. Sometimes an intervention may need to be a combination of Methods 1 and 2. For example, this combined approach would be used in circumstances in which the student does not have the desired replacement behavior in his or her repertoire (e.g., does not have the skills to do what the teacher is asking) and in which the classroom environment could benefit from modification or the teacher could make some general modifications to the environment (see Chapter 2) or instructional delivery (see Chapter 3).

Method 3: Adjust the Contingencies is used when (1) the student is able to perform the replacement behavior (not an acquisition deficit) and (2) the antecedent conditions represent effective practices (e.g., clear expectations and routines are in place). The main emphasis is on adjusting the rate of reinforcements so that the student receives a high rate of reinforcement for the replacement behavior and a low rate of reinforcement (or even no reinforcement) for the target behavior.

Once the appropriate method is selected using the answers to the preceding two key questions, then the intervention plan tactics are designed by the team and the teacher. For each of the intervention methods mentioned, the final behavior intervention plan will include three core components: (1) teaching the desired replacement behavior and/or modifying antecedent conditions; (2) reinforcing the occurrence of the replacement behavior; and (3) gradually extinguishing the target behavior by withholding reinforcement (extinction). Again, for a more detailed description of this systematic approach, we encourage you to read the book by Umbreit, Ferro, Liaupsin, and Lane (2007) and look over the studies conducted using this model (see Table 7.1).

BENEFITS AND CHALLENGES

One of the main reasons we support functional assessment-based interventions is that they are a highly respectful approach to problem behavior. Namely, this approach subscribes to an instructional, data-driven approach that focuses on the communicative intent of the behavior and explores why the behavior occurs. Then, rather than just suppressing undesirable behaviors, students are taught new, more socially valid behaviors that will serve them better in the future.

Yet, as you can see from what you have learned already, functional assessment-based interventions are not a quick fix. This type of intervention takes time, which can be frustrating for those seeking immediate change. However, if the goal is meaningful lasting change (Baer et al., 1968) and if less intensive approaches have been unsuccessful, this approach may be worth the investment.

We also want to mention that it is possible to focus the intervention on more than one target behavior; however, for simplicity's sake we have focused our examples on one main target behavior. From a behavioral perspective, it is wise to identify a target behavior that contains a variety of behaviors that are part of the same functional response class (meaning that they are all occurring for the same reasons in terms of the reinforcement they are obtaining [positive reinforcement] or avoiding [negative reinforcement]; Cooper et al., 2007). In this way, you will see decreases in a range of undesirable behaviors (e.g., hitting, biting, and kicking) and increases in replacement behaviors such as help seeking (e.g., verbally asking for assistance or signing a request for help) because the new skill (help seeking) works better than any of these other undesirable behaviors in getting assistance immediately.

TABLE 7.1. Functional Assessment-Based Intervention Studies Conducted Using the Function-Based Intervention Decision Model of Umbreit et al. (2007)

Reference	Students	Instructional setting	Target behavior	Function	Method	Design
Umbreit, Lane, & Dejud (JPBI, 2004)	Jason: 10 years; fourth grade; typically developing	General education classroom at a public elementary school; Arizona	Off task	Access to activities (helping peers with their work)	Method 2	ABAB reversal
Lane, Weisenbach, Little, Phillips, & Wehby (ETC, 2006)	Marcus: second grade; typically developing Julie: second grade; typically developing	General education classrooms at one elementary school in middle Tennessee	Marcus: nonengagement Julie: task avoidance	Marcus: access attention from teachers and peers Julie: access attention and avoid instructional tasks	Marcus: Method 3 Julie: Method 2	Marcus: ABAB withdrawal Julie: ABAB withdrawal
Liaupsin, Umbreit, Ferro, Urso, & Upreti (ETC, 2006)	Fiona: 14 years; seventh grade; typically developing, with mild, unilateral hearing loss	Charter school	Off task	Escape too-difficult activities	Math: method 1 and 2; social studies: Method 1	Multiple baseline across settings; science, social studies, and math
Stahr, Cushing, Lane, & Fox (JPBI, 2006)	Shawn: 9 years; fourth grade; ADHD, internalizing behavior problems, and a speech and language impairment	Self-contained school that served students with EBD; large metropolitan city in middle Tennessee	Off task	Access to teacher attention and escape from independent tasks	Method 2	Multiple baseline across two settings (language arts and math) with a withdrawal component (ABAB)
Lane, Rogers, Parks, Weisenbach, Mau, Merwin, et al. (JEBD, 2007)	Claire: 7 years; first grade; typically developing	Claire: general education classroom in an inclusive school district in middle Tennessee	Claire: nonparticipation	Claire: escape attention from teacher and peers	Claire: Method 3 Aaron: Method 2	Claire: changing criterion

	Aaron: 14 years; eighth grade; learning disability in written expression	Aaron: general education classroom in an inclusive school district in middle Tennessee	Aaron: noncompliance	Aaron: access teacher attention and escape assigned task		Aaron: ABAB withdrawal
Lane, Smither, Huseman, Guffey, & Fox (JEIBI; 2007)	Harry: 6 years; kindergarten; typically developing	General education classroom in an inclusive public school district in middle Tennessee	Total disruptive behavior	Access teacher and peer attention	Method 2	Multiple baseline across settings
Lane, Weisenbach, Phillips, & Wehby (ETC; 2007)	Margaret: 7 years; first grade; typically developing; identified at risk for EBD Charlie: 7 years; first grade; typically developing; identified at risk for EBD	Two inclusive, general education public schools; middle Tennessee	Margaret: negative social interactions Charlie: off task	Margaret: access peer attention Charlie: access adult and peer attention; participate in activities with peers; escape nonpreferred activities	Margaret: Methods 1 and 2 Charlie: Method 3	Margaret: ABAB withdrawal Charlie: ABB′AB′
Turton, Umbreit, Liaupsin, & Bartley (BD, 2007)	Saida: 16 years; high school; behavior problems	Special alternative high school program for students with serious behavior problems; Bermuda	Profanity/ inappropriate responses	Access attention from staff and escape class assignments	Methods 1 and 2	ABAB reversal
Wood, Umbreit, Liaupsin, & Gresham (ETC, 2007)	Josh: 8 years; third grade; performing at or above level of his peers	Not stated; teacher certified in elementary education; geographic location not specified	Off task	Access attention and escape certain assignments	Method 3	ABAB brief reversal

Note. BD, *Behavior Disorders*; ETC, *Education and Treatment of Children*; JEBD, *Journal of Emotional and Behavioral Disorders*; JEIBI, *Journal of Early and Intensive Behavior Intervention*; JPBI, *Journal of Positive Behavior Interventions*; ADHD, attention-deficit/hyperactivity disorder (American Psychiatric Association, 2000); EBD, emotional and behavioral disorders; Method 1, Teach the Replacement Behavior; Method 2, Improve the Environment; Method 3, Adjust the Contingencies (Umbreit et al., 2007).

Functional behavioral assessments have been endorsed by a number of highly reputable entities. For example, they have been endorsed by the National Association of State Directors of Education (NASDE), National Institutes of Health (NIH), and the National Association of School Psychologists (NASP). The Individuals with Disabilities Education Act Amendments of 1997 and then The Individuals with Disabilities Education Improvement Act (2004) required that school-based teams conduct functional behavioral assessments when students in special education commit specific disciplinary infractions (Kern & Manz, 2004). Specifically, a functional behavioral assessment *must* be conducted and a behavioral intervention plan *must* be implemented when school-based teams conduct a manifestation determination (i.e., a review of the relationship between a student's misbehavior that led to a disciplinary action and the student's disability) and conclude that the student's misbehavior that led to a school's disciplinary sanction was related to his or her disability. A functional behavioral assessment must also be conducted when a student in special education is (a) removed from school for more than 10 consecutive days for a disciplinary infraction *if* the student's misbehavior was a manifestation of his or her disability and (b) removed to a interim alternative educational placement for drug or weapons violations or the infliction of serious bodily injury, *regardless of whether the misbehavior was a manifestation of the student's disability* (Drasgow & Yell, 2001).

Yet, despite these endorsements and mandates, not all researchers are convinced that they are actually warranted (e.g., Gresham, 2004; Kern et al., 2004; Quinn et al., 2001; Sasso, Conroy, Stichter, & Fox, 2001). For a practice to be considered evidence based for a given group of students (e.g., middle school students) or in a given setting (e.g., inclusive classrooms), it must have been sufficiently tested, with each test or study meeting scientifically rigorous standards. As you may recall, we mentioned at the beginning of this chapter that functional behavioral assessments were originally conducted with individuals with developmental disabilities. Some researchers contend that there is not sufficient evidence to support functional assessment-based interventions as an evidence-based practice for use with students with and at risk for EBD in school settings (see Lane, Kalberg, & Shepcaro, 2009, for a detailed review). In short, some feel that a generalization error may have occurred: Practices may have been recommended prematurely without the necessary scientific support (e.g., Sasso et al., 2001). However, we view functional assessment-based interventions conducted using the model we described to be a highly promising practice for students with and at risk for EBD.

In the next section, we review the supporting research for functional assessment-based interventions conducted with school-age students. Specifically, we present studies using the systematic approach from Umbreit and colleagues (2007) that have been conducted in elementary, middle, and high schools.

SUPPORTING RESEARCH FOR FUNCTIONAL ASSESSMENT-BASED INTERVENTIONS

Before mandating wide-scale implementation of a practice, it is important to know whether that practice is indeed evidence based (Horner et al., 2005). Specifically, have a sufficient number of studies been conducted with sufficient scientific rigor to collectively determine that the practices "work" to improve the behavior of school-age youths with or at risk for high-incidence disabilities (e.g., learning disabilities, emotional disturbances)? In terms of the supporting research for functional assessment-based interventions conducted using this systematic approach developed by Umbreit and colleagues (2007), we ask the question: Is this an evidence-based approach for supporting school-age students? Fortunately, Horner and colleagues (2005) have provided recommended guidelines to help answer this question. In their article, they offered two sets of guidelines: one for evaluating the quality of an individual study to determine whether it meets specific standards and a second for evaluating the body of literature meeting these specific standards to determine whether the practice is actually evidence-based.

Lane, Bruhn, et al. (2009) conducted a review of the literature to determine whether the systematic approach to functional assessment-based interventions developed by Umbreit et al. (2007) meets the recommended quality indicators to be considered an evidence-based practice. If this practice is actually evidence based, then it may be one scientifically valid approach to conducting these tertiary interventions, which are recommended by NASDE, NIH, and NASP and mandated in IDEA (Lane, Bruhn, et al., 2009).

As part of this review, the authors identified nine studies that used Umbreit et al.'s (2007) systematic approach to functional assessment-based interventions with school-age students with or at risk for high-incidence disabilities. Of these studies, six met 80% of the seven core quality indicators (see Figure 7.5). Findings suggested that the majority of studies used scientifically rigorous methodological standards. In terms of the overall body of literature, Lane and colleagues (2009) found that (1) practices were defined explicitly; (2) contexts (e.g., where the interventions took place) and student outcomes associated with the practice were defined; (3) interventions were implemented as initially planned; (4) functional relations were present between the practice and changes in student outcome measures (dependent variables; i.e., the interventions yielded the desired changes in students' behaviors), and (5) effects were replicated across at least five peer-reviewed studies that were conducted in three different locations by three different first authors (Horner et al., 2005; Lane, Bruhn, et al., 2009). The only criterion for establishing this systematic approach as an evidence-based practice that was not met was that the total body of literature reviewed focused on only 9 students, falling short of the 20 participants required to establish the practice as evidence based. However, since that time, one additional study has been published by another research team (Renshaw, Christensen, Marchant, & Anderson, 2008). In this study, general education elementary teachers were taught how to use this model to design, implement, and evaluate functional assessment-based interventions as part of their prereferral intervention team process. Hopefully, additional studies will be published that will allow this model to move from a promising practice to an evidence-based practice. Given that this model was only introduced to the research community in 2004, we are hopeful that it will soon become validated (Lane, Rogers, et al., 2007). Nonetheless, we do view functional assessment-based interventions as a promising practice that is well worth the investment when other, less intensive interventions have failed to yield the desired behavior changes.

In the sections that follow, we provide information on the nine studies conducted to date in schools with students with or at risk for high-incidence disabilities. The following content is technical in nature, presented with a goal of providing all members of the school-site and district-level teams (particularly the behavior specialists and school psychologists) with sufficient information to develop their team's skill sets as they move forward with this process. In addition, we believe it is important that general education teachers, too, have access to information about functional assessment-based interventions so that they are conversant with the topic. We encourage you to see Table 7.1 for a summary of the studies mentioned.

Elementary School

As you see in Table 7.1, the vast majority of studies of functional assessment-based interventions have been conducted with elementary-age students. Of the 12 students supported in the 9 studies reviewed by Lane and colleagues, 9 (75%) students were of elementary age (kindergarten through fourth grades). The interventions were conducted mostly in inclusive general education classrooms; however, one was conducted in a self-contained school for students with EBD (Stahr et al., 2006). Students presented with a range of target behaviors, including off-task behavior, nonparticipation, disruption, and negative social interactions. In terms of motives (or function) for behavior, four students' target behaviors were maintained by access to attention (positive reinforcement; Jason, Marcus, Harry, Margaret); one student's target behavior was maintained by escape from attention (negative attention; Claire); and four students' target behaviors served a dual function—access to attention (positive reinforcement) and escape from tasks (negative reinforcement; Julie, Shawn, Charlie, Josh).

When it came to type of intervention method, four students (Jason, Julie, Shawn, and Harry) were able to perform the desired replacement behaviors. However, the environment did not represent best practices for those students. Consequently, according to the intervention decision model, Method 2: Improve the Environment was selected, designed, implemented, and evaluated for these students. One student, Margaret, demonstrated an acquisition deficit, meaning that

Indicator	Topic
1	Describing Participants and Setting
2	Dependent Variables
3	Independent Variable
4	Baseline
5	Experimental Control/Internal Validity
6	External Validity
7	Social Validity

FIGURE 7.5. Quality indicators for single-case design studies (Horner et al., 2005).

she could not perform the replacement behavior. Furthermore, the classroom was identified as needing some environmental improvements. Therefore, a combination of Method 1: Teach the Behavior and Method 2: Improve the Environment was selected for Margaret. Four students (Marcus, Claire, Charlie, and Josh) were capable of performing the desired replacement behaviors and educated in classrooms that employed effective classroom procedures. Therefore, Method 3: Adjust the Contingencies was conducted for these students. In all three methods, the interventions included three core components: (1) antecedent adjustments to prompt the desired behavior, (2) adjustments to the reinforcement conditions to ensure high rates of reinforcement for the replacement behavior, and (3) extinction of the target behavior (Umbreit et al., 2007). Although it is beyond the scope of this chapter to detail each of the interventions reported in this review of the literature, we encourage you to read the specific intervention designed so that you and your school-site or district-level team can gather ideas for each of these three intervention components.

In terms of the experimental designs used to evaluate how well the intervention produced changes in the target behaviors, the majority of studies used ABAB withdrawal designs or some variation of this design (e.g., Charlie). Two studies (Liaupsin, Umbreit, Ferro, Urso, & Upreti, 2006; Stahr et al., 2006) used a multiple-baseline-across-settings design (meaning that the intervention was introduced first in one setting; then, once the students' behavior showed improvement, the intervention was put in place in the next setting), one of which also included a withdrawal component (see Stahr et al., 2006), and one study used a changing criterion design (Lane, Rogers, et al., 2007). As we mentioned previously, in this age of accountability, it is important to employ rigorous designs so that experimental control can be established. In other words, it is necessary to use experimental designs to determine that changes in the students' behavior are actually due to the intervention and not to other changes that may be occurring either within the environment (e.g., the presence of a student teacher) or within the student (e.g., taking medication).

Middle and High School

Umbreit and colleagues' (2007) systematic approach to designing, implementing, and evaluating functional assessment-based interventions has also been conducted with two middle school students: one seventh-grade student (Fiona) attending a charter school due to extreme behavioral issues (Liaupsin et al., 2006) and one eighth-grade student (Aaron) with a learning disability attending an inclusive middle school (Lane, Rogers, et al., 2007). Fiona's target, off-task behavior, was maintained by escape from too difficult tasks (negative reinforcement). Aaron's target behavior, noncompliance, was maintained by access to teacher attention (positive reinforcement) and escape from assigned tasks (negative reinforcement).

In Fiona's case, she had acquisition deficits that required Method 1: Teach the Replacement Behavior in both math and social studies. However, the math classroom context did not represent effective practices. Therefore, a combination of Method 1 and Method 2: Improve the Environment was implemented in the math class. A multiple-baseline-across-settings design was used to evaluate these supports.

In Aaron's case, he was able to perform the replacement behavior, but the environment was in need of improvement. Thus a Method 2: Improve the Environment intervention was designed, implemented, and evaluated using an ABAB design.

Only one published study has been conducted with a high school student, Saida, a 16-year-old student who was in a special alternative high school program in Bermuda for students with serious behavior problems (Turton, Umbreit, Liaupsin, & Bartley, 2007). The target behavior was use of profanity, which was maintained by attention from staff and escape from assignments. Results of the intervention decision model led to a combined intervention using Method 1: Teach the Replacement Behavior and Method 2: Improve the Environment, as Saida was not able to perform the replacement behavior and the classroom did not represent effective practice for her. Results of an ABAB design revealed changes in student behavior that were contingent upon the introduction of the intervention.

Summary

If you are considering using this systematic approach to conducting functional assessment-based interventions in your school, we encourage your school-site and district-level teams to read the book written by John Umbreit and colleagues (Umbreit et al., 2007) as well one or more of the studies previously mentioned. We also encourage you to look at Chapter 8 in this volume, which contains (1) a quick guide to determining student eligibility for functional assessment-based interventions, (2) a planning form to guide you through the systematic process developed by Umbreit and colleagues (2007), (3) a report form to use for reporting functional assessment outcomes and constructing the behavior intervention plan, and (4) a sample treatment integrity form to help inform your planning as you take steps to make sure that the functional assessment-based intervention is implemented as originally designed.

Clearly, this is an involved process, and we recommend that you read beyond the introductory information provided in this chapter to learn more about the procedures involved in moving from identifying a behavior you would like to change to determining *why* the behavior is occurring and then designing an intervention linked to the function of the behavior. We want to emphasize that this is but one approach to conducting functional assessment-based interventions. There are other approaches you might consider as well. To this end, we have included information on related resources that might be of interest as you move forward with this tertiary level of support (see Table 7.2).

IMPLEMENTING FUNCTIONAL ASSESSMENT-BASED INTERVENTIONS IN YOUR CLASSROOM

As this introductory chapter on functional assessment-based intervention comes to a close, we would like to provide you with a detailed illustration of this systematic approach conducted as part of a research project in conjunction with Vanderbilt University. This article is published in the *Journal of Emotional and Behavioral Disorders* (Lane, Rogers, et al., 2007), including all relevant details that might appeal to researchers, practitioners, and teams interested in attempting this type of tertiary prevention effort.

In the included illustration (see Box 7.1 on pages 178–179), we provide a view from the teacher's perspective. As you read this illustration, we encourage you to look at how this process moved step by step.

1. Obtaining permission to support the student.
2. Determining and operationally defining the main behavior of concern.
3. Identifying a recording system and making sure the data were collected accurately.
4. Conducting a functional assessment (including interviews and direct observations).
5. Using the function matrix to analyze the data and determine the function of the behavior.
6. Using the function-based intervention decision model to determine which method of intervention would be most appropriate.
7. Designing the intervention to include antecedent adjustments, reinforcement, and extinction components.
8. Assessing social validity before and after implementing the intervention to determine stakeholders' perceptions of the intervention goals, procedures, and outcomes.

TABLE 7.2. Functional Assessment-Based Intervention Resource Guide

Reference	Description	Target group	Cost/retrieval information
	Books		
Umbreit, J., Ferro, J., Liaupsin, C., & Lane, K. (2007). *Functional behavioral assessment and function-based intervention: An effective, practical approach.* Upper Saddle River, NJ: Pearson Education.	This book describes a systematic, step-by-step approach to conducting functional behavior assessments, designing function-based interventions, and implementing and monitoring the interventions.	K–12 educators	List price: $50.33 *www.amazon.com*
O'Neill, R. E., Horner, R. H., Albin, R. W., Sprague, J. R., Storey, K., & Newton, J. S. (1997). *Functional assessment and program development for problem behavior: A practical handbook.* Pacific Grove, CA: Brooks/Cole.	This guide to functional assessment procedures teaches professionals and students strategies for assessing problem behavior and, subsequently, how to use those assessments in designing behavioral support programs.	K–12 educators; students	List price: $90.95 *www.amazon.com*
Crone, D., & Horner, R. H. (2003). *Building positive behavior support systems in schools: Functional behavioral assessment.* New York: Guilford Press.	A practical approach for school personnel to use in assessing problem behavior and creating interventions to solve these problems	K–12 educators	List price: $32.00 *www.amazon.com*
	Websites		
Epstein, M., Atkins, M., Cullinan, D., Kutash, K., & Weaver, R. (2008). *Reducing behavior problems in the elementary school classroom: A practice guide* (NCEE #2008-012). U.S. Department of Education, Institute of Education Sciences, National Center for Education Evaluation and Regional Assistance.	What Works Clearinghouse practice guide for reducing behavior problems in the elementary classroom, with five recommendations for evidence-based practices; compiled using stringent criteria for what is considered evidence-based practice by a review board assigned by the Institute of Educational Sciences.	Elementary educators	*ies.ed.gov/ncee/wwc/publications/practiceguides*

Hansen, B. D., Kamps, D. M., Wills, H. P., & Greenwood, C. R. (2008). *Effects of the class-wide function-based intervention team "CW-FIT" group contingency program*. Juniper Gardens Children's Project, University of Kansas.	The CW-FIT is a group contingency program that includes four elements on the assessment and treatment of problem behavior: teaching socially appropriate communicative skills to access attention or brief escape; extinction or eliminating potential reinforcement (attention, escape) for problem behavior; strengthening alternative or replacement behaviors (i.e., differential reinforcement) at individual levels within the context of peer groups with shared group contingencies; and self-management for program maintenance.	K–12 educators	*www.jgcp.ku.edu/~jgcp/projects/Grants_Present/Class-Wide_Function-Based_Intervention_Teams.shtml* or *soe.ku.edu/uploads/specialedu/temp-docs/50th-Anniversary/PDD%20 Sessions/C-Hansen.ppt-2008-11-17*
Center for Effective Collaboration and Practice. (2001). *Functional behavior assessment*.	A four-part Web miniseries on functional behavior assessment (FBA) (part of a larger website dedicated to fostering the development and adjustment of children with or at risk for emotional disturbance) Part 1: An IEP Team's Introduction to Functional Behavior Assessment and Behavior Intervention Plans Part 2: Conducting a Functional Behavior Assessment Part 3: Creating Positive Behavioral Intervention Plans and Supports Part 4: A Trainer of Trainers Guide	K–12 educators	*cecp.air.org/fba*
Technical Assistance Center on Positive Behavioral Interventions and Supports: Effective Schoolwide Interventions.	A website designed to provide information and technical assistance on effective positive behavioral interventions and supports. For functional assessment information, see the tertiary level of schoolwide positive behavior support.	K–12 educators	*www.pbis.org*

(cont.)

TABLE 7.2. *(cont.)*

Reference	Description	Target group	Cost/retrieval information
	Refereed journal articles		
Arter, P. (2007). The Positive Alternative Learning Supports Program: Collaborating to improve student success. *Teaching Exceptional Children, 40*, 38–46.	This article discusses the Positive Alternative Learning Supports (PALS) program, including critical features, implementation, and evaluation results. PALS was developed to address the targeted needs of the 10% of students most in need of behavioral intervention. Results of a study are presented indicating positive outcomes for using this collaborative school-based approach to conducting functional behavioral assessments (FBAs) to implement a multicomponent intervention in an urban middle school.	K–12 educators of students with chronic behavior problems	*Teaching Exceptional Children* is published by the Council for Exceptional Children. *www.cec.sped.org/Content/NavigationMenu/Publications2/TEACHINGExceptionalChildren*
Ryan, A. L., Halsey, H. N., & Matthews, W. J. (2003). Using functional assessment to promote desirable student behavior in schools. *Teaching Exceptional Children, 35*, 8–15.	In this article, the authors present a rationale for using functional behavioral assessment (FBA) to solve student behavior problems. Components and various applications of FBA are presented, as well as advantages of FBA as compared with traditional approaches to dealing with problem behavior and the legal and ethical reasons for using FBA. Finally, a case study is used to illustrate a four-stage decision-making framework or problem-solving model approach to FBA (Bergan & Kratochwill, 1990).	K–12 educators of students with behavior problems	

Note. See Table 7.1 for a summary of functional assessment-based intervention studies conducted using the function-based intervention decision model (Umbreit et al., 2007).

9. Monitoring treatment integrity to make sure that the intervention was implemented as intended.
10. Using a design (e.g., withdrawal or multiple baseline) that allows accurate conclusions to be drawn about intervention outcomes (whether or not it worked).

SUMMARY

In this chapter we provided information on one approach to designing and implementing functional assessment-based interventions with individual students to address academic and behavior issues. First, we offered an overview of functional assessment-based interventions and provided an overview of the benefits and challenges associated with this intervention approach. Next, we reviewed the supporting research of functional assessment-based interventions using the process developed by Umbreit and colleagues (2007), noting the limited number of studies conducted with middle and high school students. Finally, we provided direction on how to implement functional assessment-based interventions at your school site, offering an illustration from peer-reviewed studies, as well as other resources, to assist your school-site and district-level teams with this intensive intervention process.

In the final chapter, we provide guidelines for teachers, administrators, and other school-site personnel on how to get started. We include a self-assessment, practical suggestions for determining which procedures to employ, and feasible guidelines for monitoring outcomes. We emphasize the importance of addressing schoolwide components and offer suggestions for how to help start schoolwide programs, as well as these more individualized supports.

BOX 7.1. Functional Assessment-Based Intervention Illustration

Ms. Stewart, a second-year middle school science teacher, ran a fairly orderly classroom. She implemented the SWPBS plan by handing out positive behavior support tickets to students for displays of positive behavior, such as arriving on time with appropriate materials, holding the door, or voicing frustrations in a respectful way (which isn't always easy for middle schoolers, who are experts at eye rolling and loud sighing). To add further structure to her class, she used the same type of *entrance activity* each day. When students came into class, they took out their *boardwork* notebooks, wrote down the boardwork question Ms. Stewart had written on the board prior to class, and wrote down the answer. Students were free to consult with other students, use the textbook, or look at their notes to answer the question. The incentive for students was that all boardwork questions would appear on the unit exam. Essentially, students created a study guide for themselves.

One student, Aaron, rarely completed the boardwork. Aaron, an eighth grader with a learning disability in written expression, was a very sweet and social teenager. Unfortunately, he was notorious for being off task, failing to comply with directions, and talking to his friends (not about assignments, as you probably guessed). Ms. Stewart constantly prodded Aaron to get his work done. She noticed that the way he started class typically dictated his behavior for the rest of the class time. Consequently, if he could focus and complete his boardwork, he was relatively compliant and productive the rest of the period. Sadly, this didn't happen very often. Afraid that Aaron was going to fail her class, Ms. Stewart solicited help from a local university whose graduate students were training to be behavior specialists.

A team of three university students who were enrolled in the Board Certified Behavior Analyst certification program *obtained consent* from Ms. Stewart, Aaron's parent, and Aaron himself to *conduct a functional assessment* of Aaron and design a subsequent intervention. This included a school records search, an interview with Ms. Stewart, an interview with Aaron, and direct observation of Aaron's behavior during science class. This information was used to *identify and operationally define the target (or problem) behavior*, noncompliance, and to *determine the function of the behavior*, or, in other words, why Aaron was not complying with the boardwork activity.

After entering data into the *function matrix*, it was clear that Aaron engaged in noncompliance to gain Ms. Stewart's attention and to escape the assigned activity (in this case, the boardwork). Using the *function-based intervention decision model*, the team determined that Aaron was, in fact, able to perform the *replacement behavior*—completion of the boardwork activity. Ms. Stewart confirmed that she, too, had seen Aaron complete boardwork activities. The team decided that despite the rules and procedures currently in place, the classroom environment and methods did not represent the most effective practices for Aaron (although they may have been sufficient for most other students in the class). For example, Aaron rarely recorded his answers to the boardwork question in the allotted time, and, as a result, he was not able to refer to them later. While Ms. Stewart discussed the answers with the class, the answers were not written on the board. Once the answer was discussed and recorded (theoretically), Ms. Stewart expected students to quickly transition to the next activity, leaving Aaron unable to catch up. Thus the team selected *Method 2: Improve the environment* to guide intervention planning. Using this information, the team worked with Ms. Stewart to design and implement an intervention tied to the function of Aaron's behavior. The intervention consisted of three components: (1) *antecedent adjustments*, (2) *reinforcement of the replacement behavior*, and (3) *extinction of the target behavior*.

For the *antecedent adjustments*, Ms. Stewart agreed to include both the boardwork question *and* the answer on the board until Aaron had copied both into his notebook. In addition, Aaron was provided with a checklist of steps to follow when completing the boardwork. For example, the first step reminded him to take out his boardwork notebook. The next step reminded him to write down the question. Other steps included writing down the answer, asking Ms. Stewart for help if needed, and checking in with Ms. Stewart upon completion.

(cont.)

To *reinforce the replacement behavior,* Ms. Stewart provided positive attention (behavior-specific praise) to Aaron when he successfully completed the boardwork and the checklist. Once Aaron completed five checklists (which could be accomplished in 1 week), Aaron was allowed to choose a friend to sit by. Finally, Ms. Stewart gave Aaron bonus points on the unit test for completing the boardwork and checklists.

The last component entailed *extinguishing the target behavior.* If Aaron was noncompliant, then Ms. Stewart would give him a brief, verbal redirection. All other attention was withheld until he completed his boardwork and checklist. The team also asked the students sitting at his table to refrain from talking to Aaron until he was done. Aaron was required to raise his hand to let Ms. Stewart know he had finished. With this cue, she would immediately attend to Aaron by inspecting his checklist, giving praise, and initialing the checklist. For some teachers, including Ms. Stewart, this component is the most difficult. She had spent most of the early fall constantly pleading with him to do his work. She had to break that habit by providing only one prompt and walking away until he complied.

The university team consulted with Ms. Stewart to make sure she was on board with the intervention, and she enthusiastically agreed to implement it. *To monitor how well the intervention was implemented,* Aaron, Ms. Stewart, and the team completed checklists about the intervention components. These checklists showed the intervention components to be in place from 72 to 92% of the time. While the team monitored implementation, they also took data on Aaron's compliance (i.e., the replacement behavior) using a *whole-interval recording system* (meaning that each interval was marked as "yes" only if Aaron was compliant for the entire interval; see Lane, Rogers, et al., 2007, for complete description). This step was important, as it provided visual evidence of Aaron's behavior. In examining the graph below, it is clear the intervention worked. Aaron showed much higher levels of compliance during the intervention phases than during baseline conditions when the intervention was not in place. Although maintenance levels that were recorded a month later were not quite as high, this may be attributed to the fact that Ms. Stewart agreed to let Aaron discontinue the checklist. As indicated on *social validity rating scales,* Aaron and Ms. Stewart found this intervention to be practical, feasible, and more than acceptable. Perhaps the most rewarding aspect of this process for both Ms. Stewart and Aaron was that his science grade went from 55% in the first quarter to 78% in the second quarter to 82% in the third quarter. To top it off, Aaron received Ms. Stewart's "Most Improved Student" award at the eighth-grade graduation ceremony, an impressive accomplishment for a student who was on the verge of failure.

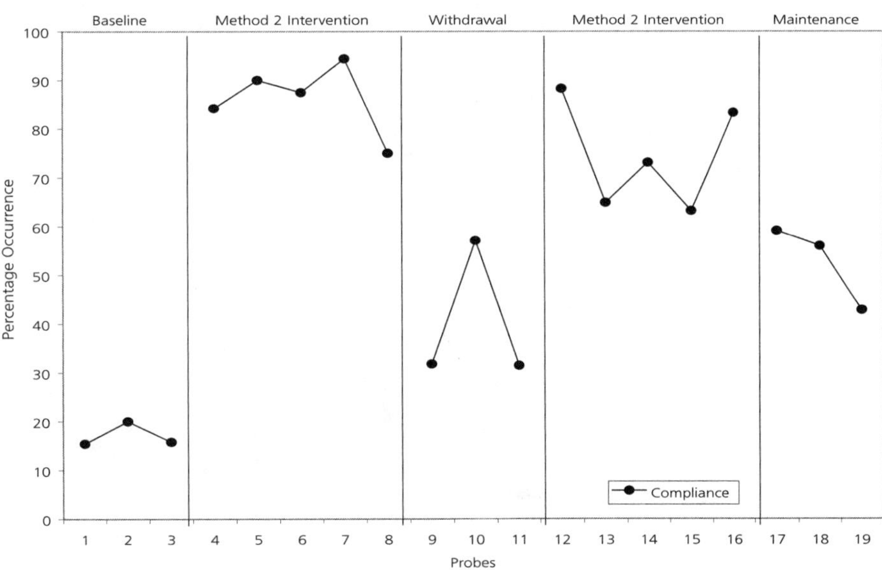

Aaron's compliance. From Lane, Rogers, et al. (2007). Copyright 2007 by Sage Publications, Inc. Reprinted by permission.

PART III

GETTING STARTED

CHAPTER 8

Getting Started in Your Classroom

As we mentioned in Chapter 1, many teachers, administrators, and other school-site personnel enter the field of education with a goal of providing students with a well-planned, meaningful instructional experience. Yet too often teachers report that they do not have the requisite skill sets to prevent problem behaviors from occurring and to respond effectively when problem behaviors do occur (Harris, 1991; Schumm & Vaughn, 1995). Furthermore, this lack of confidence with respect to classroom management skills not only negatively impacts students' learning experiences but is also associated with teachers' leaving the profession (Brouwers & Tomic, 2000; Martin, Linfoot, & Stephenson, 1999).

The intent of this book is to provide teachers, administrators, and other school-site personnel with a reader-friendly resource to empower them to acquire the knowledge, skills, and confidence to use a range of strategies to prevent problem behaviors from occurring (Chapters 2–4) and to respond effectively and efficiently to problems that do occur (Chapters 5–7). This continuum of supports begins with proactive strategies that focus on general classroom management and instructional delivery, as well as low-intensity strategies that focus on establishing a well-run, predictable environment. Then additional, more intensive strategies, such as behavioral contracting (Downing, 2002), self-monitoring (Mooney et al., 2005), and functional assessment-based interventions (Umbreit et al., 2007), are introduced for students who do not respond to primary prevention efforts (Lane, Kalberg, & Menzies, 2009).

In brief, this extensive repertoire of knowledge and skills allows teachers and other school-site personnel to deliver instruction that better meets the academic, social, and behavioral needs of the increasingly diverse students they serve—particularly the needs of those with and at risk for EBD (Walker et al., 2004). Rather than beginning with reactive strategies (e.g., consequence-based interventions), teachers can begin by invoking preventative measures that involve an instructional approach to academic, behavioral, and social skill sets (Lane, Kalberg, & Menzies, 2009).

Ideally, all teachers and support staff would be able to work at school sites that have developed comprehensive, three-tiered models of support that include the full continuum of behavior support, that is, primary (Tier 1), secondary (Tier 2), and tertiary (Tier 3) levels of prevention (Sugai et al., 2002). However, if such a structure is not in place at the school site, the information in this book is even more critical to helping school-site personnel promote desired outcomes for both themselves and their students, particularly given the relation between instruction and behavior—namely, that *how* we teach influences how students behave, and how students behave influences how we teach (Lane & Wehby, 2002).

In this chapter we offer you some direction on how to get started in your classroom. First, we introduce a series of assessments that can be used by teachers, administrators, and other school-site personnel who deliver instruction to examine their knowledge, skills, and confidence in using the strategies offered in each chapter. Second, we offer an overview of how to use (a) behavior and behavior screening tools to identify accurately students who may benefit from secondary or tertiary supports and (b) more precise measures to design interventions and monitor student outcomes. Third, we provide guidelines for making determinations about the quality and efficacy of potential secondary and tertiary interventions.

ASSESSMENTS: TEACHER PERSPECTIVE

In this chapter, we have included a series of assessments and checklists to assist you in learning, retaining, and enriching the information on practices addressed in this book. For Chapter 1, we include a self-assessment to help you to think deliberately about the structures in place at your school and within your classroom and thus about your readiness to implement the strategies provided in this chapter. For Chapters 2, 3, and 4 we provide knowledge, confidence, and use (KCU) surveys, which are assessment tools you can use to evaluate and reflect on the strategies introduced in the chapter and to identify strategies that you might want to develop in your own skill set.

These surveys can also be used by those involved in teacher preparation and staff development activities as pre–postmeasures. Specifically, before teaching the content in Chapters 2, 3, or 4, you can have preservice and inservice teachers and other individuals who deliver instruction complete these surveys as a preassessment (pretest) to determine whether the content in each of these chapters may be useful to you (meaning, that they can be used to determine a person's current knowledge base). After reading each chapter, these KCU surveys can be completed a second time as a postassessment (posttest) measure to examine changes in people's knowledge, confidence, and/or use of the strategies mentioned in each chapter. You can also use the information to identify those strategies (e.g., increasing OTR, increasing choice) that might need to be addressed in greater detail to develop people's skill sets. This type of assessment tool has been used in teacher–staff development studies to determine changes in teachers' knowledge, confidence, and ability to use various strategies (e.g., social skills instruction; Barton-Arwood, Morrow, Lane, & Jolivette, 2005). The reliability of the instrument was found to be psychometrically sound (e.g., coefficient alphas ≈ .80).

For Chapters 5, 6, and 7, we provide a brief set of procedures (a process guide) for conducting the interventions presented in the chapters from start to finish. These include behavior contracting (Chapter 5), self-monitoring (Chapter 6), and functional assessment-based interventions (Chapter 7). In addition, for these chapters we provide a quick checklist of questions to determine for which students these individualized interventions are appropriate. Finally, we include a sample treatment fidelity checklist that can be used to evaluate and document to what degree each intervention is being implemented as originally planned (treatment integrity; Gresham, 1989; Lane & Beebe-Frankenberger, 2004). We have included these additional surveys and supports in Chapter 8 for your ease of access. Rather than flipping between chapters to identify these measures, you can find these implementation aids and instructional features in the current chapter.

Chapter 1

We have written the **self-assessment** to guide you in your planning and learning (to find a jumping-off point), as well as to make you more aware of the structures in place at your school and within your classroom (see Figure 8.1). By helping you to think deliberately about these things, we hope to increase your self-awareness and thus your readiness to implement the helpful strategies provided in this book. For example, you may realize that your school or your class is in desperate need of an extreme makeover. Or perhaps your classroom just needs a few touch-ups. Either way, we want this assessment to help guide your thinking (and your reading). So, please begin by taking a few minutes to reflect on the questions in Figure 8.1.

Chapter 2

In Chapter 2, *Classroom Management*, we discussed the five essential components of classroom management: classroom climate, physical room arrangement, approach

Personal

1. Why do you teach (or administer)?

2. How much of your time is consumed with behavior management rather than instruction?

3. Do you ever feel burnout setting in?

4. If you answered "yes" to number 3, how much of this burnout is related to dealing with problem behaviors?

5. What are you hoping to achieve from reading this book?

(cont.)

FIGURE 8.1. Self-asssessment.

Schoolwide

1. Does your school have a schoolwide three-tiered model of prevention to address academic, behavioral, and social skills?

2. If you answered "yes" to number 1, think about how the model works. Describe how students move from one tier to another to obtain extra supports. If you answered "no," describe what you know about three-tiered models of prevention.

3. How does your school manage behavior? Specifically, what are the proactive and reactive components of the behavior management plan?

4. In terms of academics and behavior, how does your school use data to drive decision making?

5. What services or supports does your school provide for students who may need extra help with academics, behavior, and/or social skills? And how do students become eligible for those supports?

(cont.)

FIGURE 8.1. *(page 2 of 3)*

Classroom

1. How do you teach and reinforce behavioral expectations in your classroom?

2. Describe the types of behavior problems you encounter. Also, do you have a class full of behavior issues or just a couple of students who constantly demand your attention?

3. How do you handle these behavior problems (see #2)? In other words, what sort of preventative strategies do you use? If those don't work, what do you do when the behaviors occur?

4. How do you, personally, foster a safe, organized, and productive learning environment (hint: think about the physical arrangement of the classroom, transitions, supervision, etc.)?

5. How do you, personally, create an engaging learning environment in which students are driven to reach or exceed their potential?

FIGURE 8.1. *(page 3 of 3)*

to discipline, routines and procedures, and managing paperwork. We would like you to consider how each of these classroom dimensions creates an optimum environment for teaching and learning and prevents behavior problems. If you have not read Chapter 2, complete the classroom management self-assessment: knowledge, confidence, and use survey in Figure 8.2 to evaluate and reflect on your current classroom management strategies or as a preassessment to determine whether the content may be useful to you. If you have already read Chapter 2, we encourage you to complete the KCU survey to review the classroom management strategies presented to identify your strengths and areas for potential improvement.

To provide you with a guide for further inquiry into more specific skill sets, we have also constructed three additional self-assessments. In Figure 8.3 we offer you a **classroom climate checklist** to help you evaluate student-level (e.g., "Am I aware of students' individual interests, likes, and dislikes?"), teacher-level (e.g., "Do I use descriptive rather than judgmental language?"), and school-level (e.g., "Have I identified resources available to me, such as a teacher mentor or specialized personnel at the school or district level?") variables that affect the climate or feel of your classroom. The **physical space checklist** in Figure 8.4 can be used to assess the physical space in your classroom (e.g., "Are materials and supplies strategically placed around the room to minimize traffic?"). In Figure 8.5 on page 192, **classroom management: teacher behavior checklist**, we provide you with a few statements for you to consider in examining your own behavior as it relates to classroom management skill sets (e.g., "I have taught and reinforced all necessary procedures to establish routines for common classroom transitions and events"). As you collect this information, we encourage you to consider areas of strength, as well as those areas that you might target for improvement or additional supports.

Chapter 3

In Chapter 3, *Instructional Delivery*, we examined how to make curricular decisions, utilize powerful instructional methods, and employ effective teaching strategies. Engaging curriculum and instruction, coupled with a well-managed classroom, will prevent the majority of behavior problems. Chapter 3 discusses how to choose appropriate curricula, as well as how to differentiate instruction to best meet students' needs. Topics include: choosing appropriate curricula, differentiating the curriculum, engaging instructional delivery. If you have not read Chapter 3, complete the **instructional delivery self-assessment: knowledge, confidence, and use survey** in Figure 8.6 (on page 193) to evaluate and reflect on your current instructional practices or as a preassessment to determine whether the content may be useful to you. If you have already read Chapter 3, we encourage you to complete the KCU survey to review the instructional delivery strategies and tactics presented to identify your strengths and areas for potential improvement.

Directions: Using the criteria provided, rate the concepts or strategies in terms of how knowledgeable you are about them, how confident you are in your ability to implement them in your classroom, and how useful each concept or strategy is for you.

Knowledge:

0—I have no knowledge of this concept or strategy.
1—I have some, but not much, knowledge of this concept or strategy.
2—I have more than average knowledge of this concept or strategy.
3—I have a substantial amount of knowledge about this concept or strategy.

Confidence:

0—I am not confident in my ability to use or implement this concept or strategy.
1—I am a little confident in my ability to use or implement this concept or strategy, but I definitely need to know more.
2—I am confident in my ability to use or implement this concept or strategy.
3—I am very confident in my ability to use or implement this concept or strategy.

Useful:

0—This concept or strategy is neither useful nor relevant to my teaching.
1—This concept or strategy may be useful and/or relevant to my teaching.
2—This concept or strategy is useful and/or relevant to my teaching.
3—This concept or strategy is very useful and/or relevant to my teaching.

Concept/Strategy	Knowledge	Confidence	Use
1. Academic learning time	0 1 2 3	0 1 2 3	0 1 2 3
2. Classroom climate	0 1 2 3	0 1 2 3	0 1 2 3
3. Managing student behavior	0 1 2 3	0 1 2 3	0 1 2 3
4. Classroom routines	0 1 2 3	0 1 2 3	0 1 2 3
5. Seating arrangements	0 1 2 3	0 1 2 3	0 1 2 3
6. Classroom procedures	0 1 2 3	0 1 2 3	0 1 2 3
7. Managing paperwork	0 1 2 3	0 1 2 3	0 1 2 3
8. Classroom transitions	0 1 2 3	0 1 2 3	0 1 2 3
9. Approach to discipline	0 1 2 3	0 1 2 3	0 1 2 3
10. Classroom rules/expectations	0 1 2 3	0 1 2 3	0 1 2 3
11. Responding to disruptive behaviors	0 1 2 3	0 1 2 3	0 1 2 3
12. Contextual and cultural variables of classroom climate (student, teacher, school)	0 1 2 3	0 1 2 3	0 1 2 3
13. Building a rapport with students	0 1 2 3	0 1 2 3	0 1 2 3
14. Room decorating	0 1 2 3	0 1 2 3	0 1 2 3
15. Classroom flow	0 1 2 3	0 1 2 3	0 1 2 3
16. Nonverbal and verbal interactions	0 1 2 3	0 1 2 3	0 1 2 3

FIGURE 8.2. Classroom management self-assessment: Knowledge, confidence, and use survey.

Students

1. Am I familiar with my students' background? ☐
2. Do I know about particular challenges or difficulties they may encounter outside of school? ☐
3. Have I identified any needed academic supports or enrichment for my students? ☐
4. Am I aware of students' individual interests, likes, and dislikes? ☐

Teacher

1. Have I made my students feel welcome and safe in our classroom? ☐
2. Do I treat my students respectfully? ☐
3. Do I communicate that I am interested in my students and concerned with their welfare? ☐
4. Do I maintain a calm, patient demeanor even when I am upset with a student? ☐
5. Do I use descriptive rather than judgmental language? ☐
6. Do I provide a good model of how to work with and treat others? ☐

School

1. Is there a schoolwide plan in place that I need to implement and support? ☐
2. Have I identified resources available to me, such as a teacher mentor or specialized personnel at the school or district level? ☐

FIGURE 8.3. Classroom climate checklist.

1. Is there enough space around high-traffic areas such as pencil sharpeners, bookshelves, and the teacher's desk? ☐
2. Can students easily access their desks and chairs without bumping into others? ☐
3. Are materials and supplies strategically placed around the room to minimize traffic? ☐
4. Do students have an area to put their coats and backpacks? ☐
5. Do activity centers and gathering areas have adequate space? ☐
6. Have I accounted for daily traffic patterns and prevented trouble spots? ☐

FIGURE 8.4. Physical space checklist.

1. I have arranged the physical space in my classroom with attention to high-traffic areas, student sight lines, activity centers, small-group and whole-group instruction. ☐
2. I have critically thought about student, teacher, and school variables that affect classroom climate. ☐
3. I have introduced and reinforced positively stated rules for behavior. ☐
4. I have taught and reinforced all necessary procedures to establish routines for common classroom transitions and events. ☐
5. I consistently monitor and supervise my students to reinforce positive behavior and avert misbehavior. ☐
6. My personal space and paperwork are organized so that I can fully devote my attention to students. ☐

FIGURE 8.5. Classroom management: Teacher behavior checklist.

Chapter 4

In Chapter 4, **Low-Intensity Strategies**, we discussed a variety of low-intensity strategies for managing classroom behavior. We began with specific information on how to enhance intrinsic motivation. Then we introduced a series of low-intensity behavior management strategies, including active supervision, proximity, overlappingness and with-it-ness, pacing, praise, opportunities to respond (OTR), instructive feedback, choice and preferred activities, token economies, and the formal teaching of social skills. If you have not read Chapter 4, complete the **low-intensity strategies: knowledge, confidence, and use survey** in Figure 8.7 to evaluate and reflect on the low-intensity strategies for preventing and addressing behavioral challenges or as a preassessment to determine whether the content may be useful to you. If you have already read Chapter 4, we encourage you to complete the KCU survey to review the low-intensity strategies presented to identify your strengths and areas for potential improvement.

Chapter 5

As we described in Chapter 5, *Behavior Contracts*, a behavior contract (also known as a *contingency contract*) is a written agreement between at least two individuals in which one or both individuals agree to demonstrate certain behaviors. You may recall that we provided a step-by-step approach to developing behavior contracts. Although this is a fairly simple process, as with any task, getting started is often the most challenging part. To help facilitate writing a behavior contract, we provide a

Directions: Using the criteria provided, rate the concepts or strategies in terms of how knowledgeable you are about them, how confident you are in your ability to implement them in your classroom, and how useful each concept or strategy is for you.

Knowledge:
0—I have no knowledge of this concept or strategy.
1—I have some, but not much, knowledge of this concept or strategy.
2—I have more than average knowledge of this concept or strategy.
3—I have a substantial amount of knowledge about this concept or strategy.

Confidence:
0—I am not confident in my ability to use or implement this concept or strategy.
1—I am a little confident in my ability to use or implement this concept or strategy, but I definitely need to know more.
2—I am confident in my ability to use or implement this concept or strategy.
3—I am very confident in my ability to use or implement this concept or strategy.

Use:
0—This concept or strategy is neither useful nor relevant to my teaching.
1—This concept or strategy may be useful and/or relevant to my teaching.
2—This concept or strategy is useful and/or relevant to my teaching.
3—This concept or strategy is very useful and/or relevant to my teaching.

Concept/Strategy	**Knowledge**	**Confidence**	**Use**
1. Curriculum design	0 1 2 3	0 1 2 3	0 1 2 3
2. Zone of proximal development	0 1 2 3	0 1 2 3	0 1 2 3
3. Explicit instruction	0 1 2 3	0 1 2 3	0 1 2 3
4. Mediated scaffolding	0 1 2 3	0 1 2 3	0 1 2 3
5. Student engagement	0 1 2 3	0 1 2 3	0 1 2 3
6. Evaluating teaching practices	0 1 2 3	0 1 2 3	0 1 2 3
7. Big ideas framework	0 1 2 3	0 1 2 3	0 1 2 3
8. Strategy instruction	0 1 2 3	0 1 2 3	0 1 2 3
9. Strategic integration	0 1 2 3	0 1 2 3	0 1 2 3
10. Primed background knowledge	0 1 2 3	0 1 2 3	0 1 2 3
11. Cooperative learning	0 1 2 3	0 1 2 3	0 1 2 3
12. Planning pyramid	0 1 2 3	0 1 2 3	0 1 2 3
13. Differentiating content	0 1 2 3	0 1 2 3	0 1 2 3
14. Differentiating process	0 1 2 3	0 1 2 3	0 1 2 3
15. Differentiating product	0 1 2 3	0 1 2 3	0 1 2 3
16. Advance organizers	0 1 2 3	0 1 2 3	0 1 2 3

FIGURE 8.6. Instructional delivery self-assessment: Knowledge, confidence, and use survey.

Directions: Using the criteria provided, rate the concepts or strategies in terms of how knowledgeable you are about them, how confident you are in your ability to implement them in your classroom, and how useful each concept or strategy is for you.

Knowledge:
0—I have no knowledge of this concept or strategy.
1—I have some, but not much, knowledge of this concept or strategy.
2—I have more than average knowledge of this concept or strategy.
3—I have a substantial amount of knowledge about this concept or strategy.

Confidence:
0—I am not confident in my ability to use or implement this concept or strategy.
1—I am a little confident in my ability to use or implement this concept or strategy, but I definitely need to know more.
2—I am confident in my ability to use or implement this concept or strategy.
3—I am very confident in my ability to use or implement this concept or strategy.

Use:
0—This concept or strategy is neither useful nor relevant to my teaching.
1—This concept or strategy may be useful and/or relevant to my teaching.
2—This concept or strategy is useful and/or relevant to my teaching.
3—This concept or strategy is very useful and/or relevant to my teaching.

Concept/Strategy	Knowledge	Confidence	Useful
1. Locus of control to enhance intrinsic motivation	0 1 2 3	0 1 2 3	0 1 2 3
2. Principal of optimal challenge	0 1 2 3	0 1 2 3	0 1 2 3
3. Using curiosity to enhance intrinsic motivation	0 1 2 3	0 1 2 3	0 1 2 3
4. The use of natural and fantasy contexts to enhance intrinsic motivation	0 1 2 3	0 1 2 3	0 1 2 3
5. Active supervision	0 1 2 3	0 1 2 3	0 1 2 3
6. Precorrection	0 1 2 3	0 1 2 3	0 1 2 3
7. Proximity	0 1 2 3	0 1 2 3	0 1 2 3
8. Overlappingness	0 1 2 3	0 1 2 3	0 1 2 3
9. With-it-ness	0 1 2 3	0 1 2 3	0 1 2 3
10. Pacing	0 1 2 3	0 1 2 3	0 1 2 3
11. Appropriate use of praise	0 1 2 3	0 1 2 3	0 1 2 3
12. Opportunities to respond	0 1 2 3	0 1 2 3	0 1 2 3
13. Instructive feedback	0 1 2 3	0 1 2 3	0 1 2 3
14. Choice and preferred activities	0 1 2 3	0 1 2 3	0 1 2 3
15. Token economies	0 1 2 3	0 1 2 3	0 1 2 3
16. Formal teaching of social skills	0 1 2 3	0 1 2 3	0 1 2 3

FIGURE 8.7. Low-intensity strategies self-assessment: Knowledge, confidence, and use survey.

template for developing a contract to manage the contractual process from beginning to end (Figure 8.8). Each step is included in the template with corresponding lines to fill in the pertinent information. We hope you will find this template helpful in organizing and completing the behavior contracting process.

Just as a gentle reminder, you need to know whether the intervention is appropriate for the specified student prior to using a behavior contract. We have provided a few guiding questions for **determing student eligibility** in Figure 8.9 on page 198. If you answered "yes" to all of these questions, a behavior contract may be an effective intervention for the given student.

Once you have determined that a behavior contract is warranted and have developed the contract, it is important to make certain that the terms of the contract are carried out as intended. In short, you will need to have the structures in place to monitor treatment integrity. For many contracts, this is as simple as the monitoring form already included as part of the contract. For example, in Figure 5.6, we provide a three-party contract. On this contract, each party completes his or her portion of the monitoring form (e.g., the student writes how many pages he completed, the parent signs the form indicating that he checked in with his son, and the teacher fills in how many bonus points were awarded), which indicates that he or she fulfilled the contractual obligations. However, if this structure is not included in the contract, then we recommend that the parties involved monitor the answers to these specific questions: (1) Did the said party fulfill the obligations of the contract? (2) Was reinforcement provided for meeting the contract terms? The first question should be evaluated for each party involved (see Figure 8.10 on page 199 for a **treatment integrity checklist** that contains these questions). Of course, this will depend on the type of contract used (e.g., two-party, three-party, etc.). Additionally, for the second question, you may want to consider the timeliness of reinforcement delivery. For example, was reinforcement delivered immediately? We realize that this also may vary due to the type of behavior to be changed. Namely, consider whether the behavior must occur only once (e.g., Figures 5.1, 5.4, 5.5) or whether the behavior must occur multiple times, and, if so, whether reinforcement is delivered after each occurrence of the behavior or after a set number of occurrences (e.g., Figures 5.2, 5.3, 5.6). Further, these two questions may need to be answered either on a daily basis (for multiple occurrences of behavior) or just once (for one occurrence of the behavior).

Chapter 6

In Chapter 6, *Self-Monitoring*, we focused predominantly on providing a step-by-step approach to establishing self-monitoring interventions. To help facilitate developing a self-monitoring intervention, we provide a **self-monitoring procedural guide** that contains questions to guide the self-monitoring intervention process (Figure 8.11 on page 200). The six-step process presented in Figure 8.11 corresponds to the narrative provided in the chapter, as well as the illustrations offered.

Teacher Name:________________________________ Student Name:______________________

Step 1: Identify the target behavior.

- *Make a list of behaviors of concern*
  - o
  - o
  - o
  - o
  - o
  - o
- *From this list, select the target behavior*
  - o Target behavior: ____
  - o Examples of target behavior:__________________________________
  - o Non-examples of target behavior:______________________________

  ____
- *Data collection and A-B-C Observation*

Notes/Data:

Antecedents	Behavior	Consequence

(cont.)

FIGURE 8.8. Behavior contract: A template for developing a contract.

Step 2: Meet with stakeholders.

- *Meeting date:* ______________
- *Attendees:* ____
- *Purpose of meeting:*
    - o
    - o
    - o

Step 3: Identify student's strengths and areas of concern.

Strengths	Areas of concern
o	o
o	o
o	o
o	o
o	o

- *List specific tasks the student can perform to make him/her more successful:*
    - o
    - o
    - o
    - o
    - o

Step 4: Write behavioral objectives.

- *Who will perform the task?*______________________________________
- *What is the task?*____

  ____
- *How well does the task need to be performed?*_______________________________________
- *When does the task need to be completed?*____
    - o Behavioral Objective:

      ____

      ____

      ____

      ____

      ____

(cont.)

FIGURE 8.8. *(page 2 of 3)*

Step 5: Identify rewards and consequences.

- *What is the student willing to work for? Make a list. Consider things the student can get or get out of.*
  - o
  - o
  - o
  - o
- *Select the reward(s). Consider offering a menu.*
- *How often will the reward be delivered?* ______________________________
- *Consider a bonus clause.* ______________________________

____

Step 6: Determine the evaluation process.

- *If necessary, create a record for task completion.*
- *How long will the contract be in place?*

  ☐ Open-ended ☐ Until task is completed ☐ Other: ____________
- *Checkpoint dates:* ________, ________, ________, ________

Step 7: Sign in agreement of the contract terms.

Write up the contract. Review it. Have all parties sign on the dotted line.

FIGURE 8.8. *(page 3 of 3)*

1. Is the behavior:
   - Able to be clearly defined?
   - Readily observable?
2. Has the student been nonresponsive to other behavior management strategies (e.g., the ones discussed in Chapters 2, 3, and 4)?
3. Is the student capable of controlling the problematic behavior and performing the desired behavior?
   Note: If you answered "no," this is an acquisition deficit, and intervention efforts will need to first focus on instruction of the desired behavior (Elliott & Gresham, 1991).
4. Is the student at a developmental level that will allow him or her to understand the terms of the contract?
   Note: If you answered "no," you will need to include icons or other graphics to help delineate the terms of the contract (Cooper et al., 2007). Or you will need to try an intervention that is more developmentally appropriate.
5. Is the student willing to participate in a behavioral contract?
   Note: If the student is resistant to changing his or her behavior via a contract, you might consider a different intervention, such as self-monitoring or a functional assessment-based intervention.

FIGURE 8.9. Behavior contract: Determining student eligibility.

Student: ______________________________

Date: ____________________

	Monday	Tuesday	Wednesday	Thursday	Friday
1. Did said party fulfill the obligations of the contract?					
2. Was reinforcement provided for meeting the contract terms?					
Teacher initials					
Comments					

Questions to monitor treatment fidelity:

1. Did said party fulfill the obligations of the contract?
2. Was reinforcement provided for meeting the contract terms?

Additional considerations for monitoring fidelity:

1. Timeliness of reinforcement delivery
2. Occurrences of behavior versus occurrences of reinforcement (i.e., the number of occurrences required to obtain reinforcement)

FIGURE 8.10. Behavior contract: Treatment integrity checklist.

Step 1: Establish prerequisite conditions.

- Is the behavior able to be clearly defined, readily observable, and reasonable for the student to record?
- Is the student capable of controlling the problematic behavior and performing the desired behavior?
- Does the behavior occur at a sufficiently high frequency to allow it to be monitored?

Step 2: Identify and operationally define the behaviors of concern.

- What is the problematic behavior?
- What is the operational definition of the problem behavior (i.e., what does the behavior look like)?
- What are some examples and non-examples of the problem behavior?
- What is the appropriate behavior?
- What is the operational definition of the appropriate behavior (i.e., what does the behavior look like)?
- What are some examples and non-examples of the appropriate behavior?

Step 3: Design the self-monitoring procedures, including a monitoring form.

- How often should the student complete the self-monitoring checklist (e.g., what is the appropriate interval length to encompass times when problem behavior is likely to occur, to allow the student the opportunity to access success or reinforcement for at least one segment, and to be age appropriate and in accordance with the daily schedule)?
- Is the self-monitoring form age appropriate (e.g., appropriate reading level, with visuals for younger students)?
- Will a reinforcement contingency be used?
- What will the reinforcers be? (Be sure the reinforcer chosen is valued by the student and meets the same function previously obtained with the problem behavior.)
- What will be the criteria to earn a reinforcer?
- Are the goals realistic for this student (i.e., will the student be allowed to experience success)?

Step 4: Teach the student the self-monitoring procedures.

- What are the procedures for explicitly communicating the target behavior and operational definition to the student (e.g., discussion, modeling, role play)?
- What are some benefits to using this intervention for the student (e.g., improved behavior or grades; reinforcers; that it is not a punishment but a tool to increase self awareness)?
- What will the teacher do to enhance student success with the self-monitoring system (e.g., reminders to complete checklist at appropriate time; explicit verbal reminders of expected behavior; faded support)?

Step 5: Monitor student progress.

- What was the student's baseline level of performance before the self-monitoring intervention?
- How will the teacher record student progress (e.g., academic performance, behavioral observation)?
- Will the teacher's records be compared with the student's self-recording (e.g., matching; McLaughlin et al., 1981)?
- How will the teacher provide feedback to the student on progress (e.g., how often; by providing visual displays using graphed performance; with self-graphing)?
- Who else will this information be shared with (e.g., parents, other school staff, IEP team)?

Step 6: Consider maintenance and follow-up.

- How will the self-monitoring intervention be faded when the student has reached desired performance level (e.g., lengthening intervals, fading teacher support, having the student self-monitor for a shorter duration or during fewer activities)?
- What will be done if the problem behavior occurs after self-monitoring has been faded?

FIGURE 8.11. Self-monitoring procedural guide.

Just as with behavior contracting, you need to know whether the self-monitoring strategy is appropriate for a given student prior to developing the intervention. Therefore, before beginning a self-monitoring intervention with a student, ask yourself the **quick-check** questions provided in Figure 8.12. If you answered "yes" to all of these questions, a self-monitoring intervention or another self-management strategy may be effective with this student.

Once you have designed the intervention, we encourage you to monitor treatment integrity. To support you in this effort, we have designed a simple **treatment integrity checklist** that can be modified to fit the specific details of your self-monitoring intervention (see Figure 8.13). For the sample treatment integrity form provided, the teacher or an outside observer (e.g., behavior specialist or paraprofessional) would mark the presence (1 = *yes, it did occur as planned*) or absence (0 = *no, it did not occur as planned*) for each of the five behavioral components listed in the treatment integrity form. A percentage of daily integrity can be computed by summing the number of components that did occur (number of yes responses, e.g., 4) by the total number of points possible (total number of components, e.g., 5). Then you multiply that quantity by 100 to obtain a percentage: $\frac{4}{5} \times 100 = 80\%$ treatment integrity. Measuring treatment integrity is critical, as it allows you to draw accurate conclusions regarding intervention outcomes. For example, if you do not get the changes in student behavior that you had hoped for, it may be because the plan was not implemented as designed. Treatment integrity will give you the information you need to help interpret intervention outcomes and to ensure that people remain accountable for their responsibility in the intervention process (Lane, Kalberg, & Menzies, 2009).

1. Is the behavior:
   - Able to be clearly defined?
   - Readily observable?
   - Reasonable for the student to record?
2. Is the student capable of controlling the problematic behavior and performing the desired behavior?

   Note: If you answered "no," this may be an acquisition deficit, and intervention efforts will need to first focus on instruction of the desired behavior (Elliott & Gresham, 1991).
3. Does the behavior occur at a sufficiently high frequency to allow it to be monitored?

   Note: If you answered "no" and the behavior occurs with low frequency but is high in intensity, other behavioral interventions, such as differential reinforcement schedules or functional assessment-based interventions, may need to be employed before beginning with metacognitive strategies.

FIGURE 8.12. Self-management strategies quick check.

Student: ____

Date: ______________________

Component	Monday	Tuesday	Wednesday	Thursday	Friday
1. Student completed self-monitoring checklist.					
2. Teacher completed self-monitoring checklist.					
3. Teacher checked student response to verify accuracy.					
4. Teacher provided student with feedback regarding behavior.					
5. Teacher provided student with reinforcer if earned.					
Teacher initials					
Comments					

FIGURE 8.13. Self-monitoring: Treatment integrity checklist.

Chapter 7

In Chapter 7, *Functional Assessment-Based Interventions*, we discussed strategies for improving the problem behavior of students who require the most intensive levels of behavioral support, either because they have been exposed to multiple risk factors (e.g., harsh and inconsistent discipline or frequent changes of schools) or because they have been unresponsive to less intensive intervention efforts (e.g., behavior contracts). Before conducting a functional assessment and designing and implementing a subsequent intervention, you need to know whether the intervention is appropriate for the specified student. To help you determine this, we provide a few guiding questions for **determining student eligibility** in Figure 8.14. If you answered "yes" to the first three questions, you may want to consider a functional assessment-based intervention as a strategy for improving the student's behavior. If you answered "yes" to question 4, the IDEA (first in 1997 and again in 2004) mandates that a functional assessment be conducted for students who are currently receiving special education services.

We also provide you with a **functional assessment-based intervention** and **behavior intervention planning form** (Figure 8.15) to guide you in conducting the functional assessment process, identifying the function of the target behavior, selecting the appropriate intervention method, designing the identifying intervention, and evaluating outcomes, as developed by Umbreit and colleagues (2004;

1. Does the student's behavior impede his or her learning or the learning of others (Drasgow & Yell, 2001)? Or does the student pose a threat to him- or herself or others (Drasgow & Yell, 2001)?
2. Has the student been nonresponsive to other intervention efforts (e.g., the ones discussed in Chapters 2–6)?
3. Does the student have multiple risk factors (e.g., harsh and inconsistent parenting or high mobility) that make him or her more susceptible to school failure and/or dangerous behavior?
4. A functional behavioral assessment *must* be conducted and a behavioral intervention plan *must* be implemented when
   (a) school-based teams conduct a manifestation determination (i.e., a review of the relationship between a student's misbehavior that led to a disciplinary action and the student's disability) and conclude that the student's misbehavior that led to a school's disciplinary sanction was related to his or her disability.
   (b) a student in special education is
      (1) removed from school for more than 10 consecutive days for a disciplinary infraction *if* the student's misbehavior was a manifestation of his or her disability and
      (2) removed to a interim alternative educational placement for drug or weapons violations or the infliction of serious bodily injury, *regardless* of whether the misbehavior was a manifestation of the student's disability (Drasgow & Yell, 2001)

FIGURE 8.14. Determining whether a functional assessment-based intervention is warranted: Determining student eligibility.

Student Name: ______________________ Student ID: ______________

School: ______________________ Date of Birth: ______________

Parent(s): ______________________ Parent(s) Contact Number: ______________

Date of Assessment: ______________ Teacher: ______________

Person conducting the assessment: ______________________

Role: ☐ Behavior Specialist ☐ Teacher ☐ Intern ☐ University Student ☐ Other

Identifying the Problem: Defining Target and Replacement Behaviors

Target Behavior: ______________________

Operational Definition (observable, measurable, repeatable): ______________________

____

____

Examples: ______________________

____

Non-examples: ______________________

____

Data Recording System (e.g., event recording, permanent product): ______________

____

Replacement Behavior: ______________________

Operational Definition (observable, measurable, repeatable): ______________________

____

____

Examples: ______________________

____

Non-examples: ______________________

____

Data Recording System (e.g., event recording, permanent product): ______________

____

Rationale: ______________________

____

Baseline: ______________________

____

(cont.)

FIGURE 8.15. Functional assessment-based intervention and behavior intervention planning form. Function-Based Intervention Decision Model. From Umbreit, Ferro, Liaupsin, and Lane (2007). Copyright 2007 by Pearson Education, Inc. Reprinted by permission.

Functional Behavioral Assessment: Interviews and Direct Observations

Interviews Completed: ☐ Yes ☐ No

Interviewees: ☐ Teacher ☐ Parent ☐ Student

Rating Scales: ____

Hours of Total Direct Observation (A–B–C): ____________________,

Setting(s) of Observations: (1) ____________, (2) ____________, (3) ____________

Determining the Function of the Behavior: Using the Function Matrix

	Positive Reinforcement (Access Something)	**Negative Reinforcement (Avoid Something)**
Attention		
Tangibles/ Activities		
Sensory		

(cont.)

FIGURE 8.15. *(page 2 of 9)*

Outcome of Function Matrix: Hypothesized Function: ______________________________

____

Behavioral Objective: ____

____

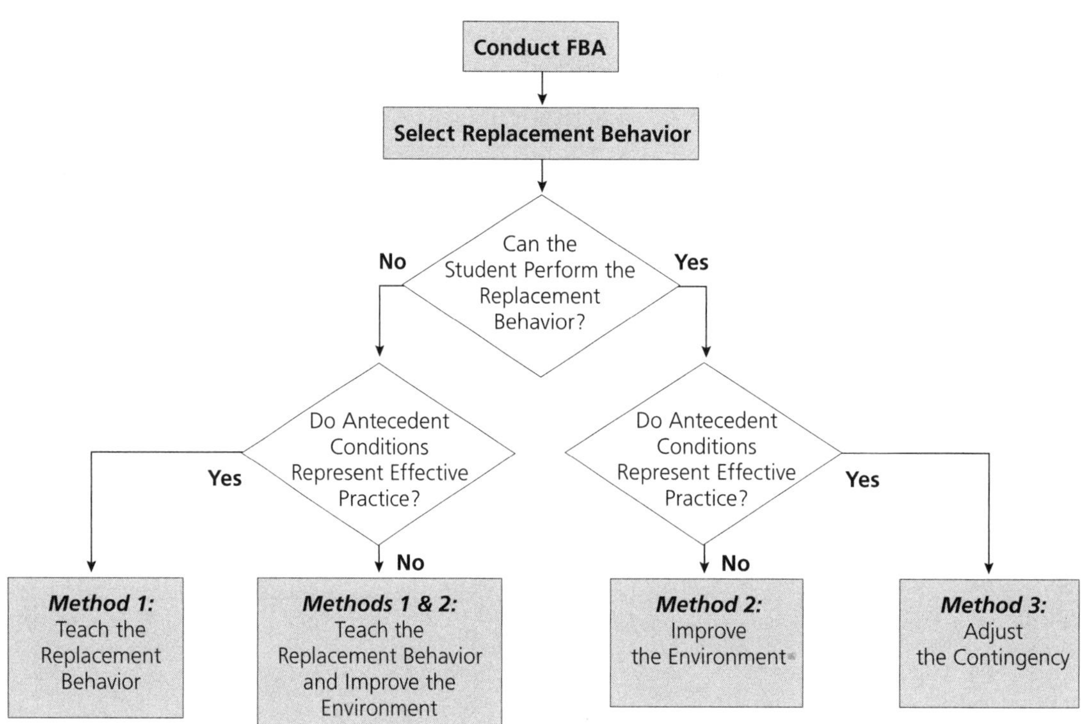

Function-Based Intervention Decision Model. From Umbreit, Ferro, Liaupsin, and Lane (2007). Copyright 2007 by Pearson Education, Inc. Reprinted by permission.

(cont.)

FIGURE 8.15. *(page 3 of 9)*

Functional Behavioral Assessment: Determining the Intervention Method

Question 1: Can the student perform the replacement behavior?

Question 2: Do antecedent conditions represent effective practice?

Method Selected:

☐ Method 1: Teach the Replacement Behavior

☐ Method 2: Improvement the Environment

☐ Method 3: Adjust the Contingencies

☐ Methods 1 and 2: Teach the Replacement Behavior and Improve the Environment

Note: After you have selected the appropriate method, draft an intervention for the selected intervention on pages 208, 209, 210, *or* 211. Do not draft *all interventions.*

Method	**Description**
Method 1: Teach the Replacement Behavior	• Adjust antecedent conditions so new behaviors are learned and aversive conditions avoided. • Provide appropriate reinforcement for the replacement behavior. • Withhold the consequence that previously reinforced the target behavior.
Method 2: Improve the Environment	• Adjust antecedent variables so the conditions that set the occasion for the target behavior are eliminated and new conditions are established in which the replacement behavior is more likely to occur. • Provide appropriate positive reinforcement for replacement behavior. • Withhold the consequence that previously reinforced the target behavior.
Method 3: Adjust the Contingencies	• Adjust the antecedent conditions to make it more likely that the replacement behavior will occur. • Provide the consequence that previously reinforced the target behavior, but only for the replacement behavior. • Withhold the consequence when the target behavior occurs (extinction).
Methods 1 and 2: Teach the Replacement Behavior and Improve the Environment	• Adjust antecedent variables so (a) new behaviors are learned and aversive conditions avoided and (b) the conditions that set the occasion for the target behavior are eliminated and new conditions are established in which the replacement behavior is more likely to occur. • Provide appropriate positive reinforcement for replacement behavior. • Withhold the consequence that previously reinforced the target behavior.

(cont.)

FIGURE 8.15. *(page 4 of 9)*

Method 1—Teach the Replacement Behavior

Adjust antecedent conditions so new behaviors are learned and aversive conditions avoided.
Provide appropriate reinforcement for the replacement behavior.
Withhold the consequence that previously reinforced the target behavior.

(cont.)

FIGURE 8.15. *(page 5 of 9)*

Method 2—Improve the Environment

Adjust antecedent variables so the conditions that set the occasion for the target behavior are eliminated and new conditions are established in which the replacement behavior is more likely to occur.
Provide appropriate positive reinforcement for replacement behavior.
Withhold the consequence that previously reinforced the target behavior.

(cont.)

FIGURE 8.15. *(page 6 of 9)*

Method 3—Adjust the Contingencies

Adjust the antecedent conditions to make it more likely that the replacement behavior will occur.
Provide the consequence that previously reinforced the target behavior, but only for the replacement behavior.
Withhold the consequence when the target behavior occurs (extinction).

(cont.)

FIGURE 8.15. *(page 7 of 9)*

Methods 1 and 2: Teach the Replacement Behavior and Improve the Environment

Adjust antecedent variables so that (a) new behaviors are learned and aversive conditions avoided and (b) the conditions that set the occasion for the target behavior are eliminated and new conditions are established in which the replacement behavior is more likely to occur.
Provide appropriate positive reinforcement for replacement behavior.
Withhold the consequence that previously reinforced the target behavior.

(cont.)

FIGURE 8.15. *(page 8 of 9)*

Data to Be Collected

Target Behavior: ______________________________

____

____

Replacement Behavior: ______________________________

____

____

Treatment Integrity: ______________________________

____

____

____

____

Social Validity: ______________________________

____

____

____

____

Fading and Generalization: ______________________________

____

____

____

____

Program Review Date: ______________________________

____

____

Personnel and Roles: ______________________________

____

____

____

____

____

Emergency Procedures: ______________________________

____

____

FIGURE 8.15. *(page 9 of 9)*

see this article for more precise information on this systematic approach to designing, implementing, and evaluating functional assessment-based interventions). Once you have completed this planning document, then you can use this information to complete the **behavior intervention: functional assessment outcomes and corresponding intervention planning form** (Figure 8.16). We hope you will find these planning forms useful in keeping organized, as well as providing you with an easy visual depiction of the process.

Additionally, we include a **treatment integrity checklist** (Figure 8.17 on page 216). This form can be used to monitor intervention implementation. It is necessary to monitor the degree to which the intervention was implemented in order to determine intervention effects. As we mentioned previously, if you do not know how well the intervention was implemented, then you cannot know whether changes in behavior were a result of the intervention or of other variables. To use this form, on the left side, list vertically the antecedent (A1, A2, A3, etc.), reinforcement (R1, R2, R3, etc.), and extinction (E1, E2, E3, etc.) components that you will be using for the intervention. Then each day record whether or not each component was in place (1 = *yes*, 0 = *no*). Not only does this checklist provide a record of implementation but it also serves as a reminder to you by making you more aware of what intervention components are in place. You can adapt this form to fit your needs. Regardless as to which type of treatment integrity form you develop, we encourage you to use one that is both easy to complete and that includes all intervention components.

In the section that follows, we provide you with information on screening and assessing student performance in behavioral and social domains to help you determine (a) how the school as a whole is responding to primary prevention efforts as discussed in Chapters 1–4 and (b) which students might benefit from more focused intervention efforts such as behavior contracting (Chapter 5), self-monitoring (Chapter 6), and functional assessment-based interventions (Chapter 7).

SCREENING AND ASSESSING: STUDENT PERFORMANCE

Academic and behavioral assessment of students who experience behavioral challenges is critical in crafting effective supports and interventions. As we have emphasized throughout this book, teachers, administrators, and other school-site personnel must remember to think about students' behavior within the context of the curriculum. There are students who will need both focused academic support *and* a behavioral or social intervention. Addressing either academics or behavior in the absence of the other leaves you with an incomplete view of the factors that may be contributing to a student's lack of success (Lane, Kalberg, & Menzies, 2009). A comprehensive approach considers the relation between a student's behavior and his or her academic performance. In the sections that follow, we discuss, first, behavioral screening tools and, second, academic screening and progress monitoring tools.

Student Name: ______________________ Student ID: ______________

School: ______________________ Date of Birth: ______________

Parent(s): ______________________ Parent(s) Contact Number: ______________

Date of Assessment: ______________ Teacher: ______________________

Person conducting the assessment: ______________________

Role: ☐ Behavior Specialist ☐ Teacher ☐ Intern ☐ University Student ☐ Other

Behavioral Definitions

Target Behavior: ______________________

Replacement Behavior: ______________________

Rationale: ______________________

____

Baseline: ______________________

____

Functional Behavioral Assessment: Interviews and Direct Observations

Interviews Completed: ☐ Yes ☐ No

Interviewees: ☐ Teacher ☐ Parent ☐ Student

Rating Scales: ______________________

Hours of Total Direct Observation (A–B–C): ______________,

Setting(s) of Observations: (1) __________, (2) __________, (3) __________

Determining the Function of the Behavior: Using the Function Matrix

	Positive Reinforcement (Access Something)	**Negative Reinforcement (Avoid Something)**
Attention		
Tangibles/ Activities		
Sensory		

(cont.)

FIGURE 8.16. Behavior intervention: Functional assessment outcomes and corresponding intervention planning form.

Outcome of Function Matrix: Hypothesized Function: ______________________________

____

Behavioral Objective: ______________________________

____

____

Functional Behavioral Assessment: Determining the Intervention Method

☐ Method 1: Teach the Replacement Behavior

☐ Method 2: Improvement Environment

☐ Method 3: Adjust the Contingencies

☐ Methods 1 and 2: Teach the Replacement Behavior and Improve the Environment

Data to Be Collected

Target Behavior: ______________________________

Replacement Behavior: ______________________________

Treatment Integrity: ______________________________

____

Social Validity: ______________________________

____

Fading and Generalization: ______________________________

____

Program Review Date: ______________________________

Personnel and Roles: ______________________________

____

____

Emergency Procedures: ______________________________

____

FIGURE 8.16. *(page 2 of 2)*

Student: ______________________________

Date: ____________

			Monday	Tuesday	Wednesday	Thursday	Friday
Antecedent	**A1**						
	A2						
	A3						
Reinforcement	**R1**						
	R2						
	R3						
Extinction	**E1**						
	E2						
		Teacher initials					
Comments							

FIGURE 8.17. Functional assessment-based intervention: Treatment integrity checklist.

Behavior Screening Tools

As we mentioned in Chapter 1, many schools are moving toward developing three-tiered models of prevention to better meet the academic, behavioral, and social needs of an increasingly diverse student body (Lane, Kalberg, & Menzies, 2009). One central component of these models is use of a data-driven process by which student performance is monitored over time to make certain determinations as to (a) how the overall school is responding and (b) identify specific students who might be better supported with secondary (Tier 2) and tertiary (Tier 3) supports (Lane, Kalberg, Bruhn, Mahoney, & Driscoll, 2008). Important consequences are associated with these objectives. For example, judgments will be made regarding how the whole school is progressing over time that are often reported in school improvement plans. Also, judgments will be made regarding which individual students will be considered for extra supports. Given the importance of consequences, it is imperative that data collected to make such determinations are reliable as well as feasible.

In terms of behavioral performance, schools have often relied on office discipline referral (ODR) data to drive the decision-making process (Sugai & Horner, 2006). Yet, although they are a readily available source of information, ODR data tend to suffer from poor reliability unless there is a system in place (e.g., School-Wide Information Systems [SWIS]; May et al., 2000) that provides clear procedural guidelines regarding which behaviors are offenses (as well as operational definitions of each offense) and the context in which an ODR is warranted. Yet, even when such systems are in place, oftentimes school-site personnel struggle with the consistency with which the overall procedures are implemented as planned (procedural fidelity), thereby limiting the utility of ODR data (Kalberg, Lane, & Menzies, 2009).

Fortunately, there are a number of validated screening tools that can be administered as part of regular school practices to (a) monitor the overall level of risk evident in a building over time (see Lane, Kalberg, et al., 2008) and (b) identify students for secondary and tertiary levels of support (Lane, 2007). Although it is beyond the scope of this chapter to provide a thorough discussion of each screening tool and how it can be used to identify students with various behavioral challenges, we encourage you to consider using one or more of the following behavior screeners: (1) Early Screening Project (ESP; Walker, Severson, & Feil, 1995); (2) Systematic Screening for Behavior Disorders (SSBD; Walker & Severson, 1992); (3) Student Risk Screening Scale (SRSS; Drummond, 1994); (4) Strengths and Difficulties Questionnaire (SDQ; Goodman, 1997); (5) Behavioral and Emotional Screening System (BESS; Kamphaus & Reynolds, 2007); and (6) Social Skills Improvement System (SSIS; Elliott & Gresham, 2007).

See Table 8.1 for information on how to obtain these measures. These tools are reliable and valid, as evidenced by high internal consistency, test–retest stability, and convergence with each other (American Educational Research Association, 1999).

TABLE 8.1. Behavior Screening Tools

Measure	Authors	Ordering information
Early Screening Project	Walker, Severson, & Feil (1995)	Available for purchase from *www.wcfd.info/docs/FORMS/ESP%20packet.doc*
Systematic Screening for Behavior Disorders	Walker & Severson (1992)	Available for purchase from Cambium Learning/ Sopris West *store.cambiumlearning.com/ProductPage.aspx?parentId=019000902&functionID=009000008*
Student Risk Screening Scale	Drummond (1994)	Free
Strengths and Difficulties Questionnaire	Goodman (1997)	Free *www.sdqinfo.com*
Behavior and Emotional Screening System	Kamphaus & Reynolds (2008)	Available for purchase from Pearson/PsychCorp *www.pearsonassessments.com/HAIWEB/Cultures/en-us/Productdetail.htm?Pid=PAaBASC2bess* *www.pearsonassessments.com/pai/ca/training/webinars/BASC-2BESSWebinar.htm*
Social Skills Improvement System	Elliott & Gresham (2007)	Available for purchase from Pearson/PsychCorp *www.pearsonassessments.com/HAIWEB/Cultures/en-us/Productdetail.htm?Pid=P14000&Mode=summary* *psychcorp.pearsonassessments.com/haiweb/cultures/en-us/productdetail.htm?pid=P14000&Community=CA_Psych_AI_Behavior*

For a full discussion of the following measures, we recommend that you see Lane, Menzies, Oakes, and Kalberg (2010). This book was designed as a guide for selecting behavior screening measures for use within the context of these three-tiered models of prevention. Specifically, this book begins with an overview of the importance of conducting systematic screenings for behavior and explains how to implement these tools within the context of three-tiered models of prevention. This book also provides specific details on how to analyze academic and behavioral data in tandem in a user-friendly manner. Each of the subsequent chapters features a validated screening tool and contains a description of the screening tool and step-by-step procedures on how to complete the screener. Next, the supporting research for each measure is synthesized to provide the reader with information on reliability and validity. In addition, each chapter offers an even-handed discussion of the strengths and challenges of preparing, administering, scoring, and interpreting findings of each screening tool. Each chapter concludes with two illustrations of how to (1) connect data from each specific tool with academic data collected within a three-tiered model of support and (2) use the information to inform instruction, including how to provide students with evidence-based secondary (Tier 2) and tertiary (Tier 3) supports. One illustration focuses on the elementary level and the second on either middle or high school levels, as appropriate. The final chapter provides information on how to select a screening tool that is psychometrically sound, socially valid, and culturally responsive to the needs and values of a given context (e.g., a rural middle school; an urban elementary school).

We hope that you will consider implementing systematic screening in your school and/or district so that you can obtain accurate information on students' behavior patterns that can be analyzed in conjunction with other data collected as part of regular school practices, particularly academic data.

Academic Screening and Progress Monitoring Tools

In addition to conducting behavior screenings, it is also important to conduct academic assessments (which are probably more familiar to most teachers relative to behavior screeners). Although many teachers are quite expert with academic assessment, the topic deserves some attention here. Specifically, we review the purpose of academic screeners, discuss the elements of curriculum-based measurement (CBM) so teachers and other instructional leaders can create formative assessments to measure student progress, and introduce data-management programs that are available to help teachers track academic growth.

As schools move to tiered models of instruction for reading (much like the tiered model of behavior support we discussed in Chapter 1), the practice of using academic screeners is growing more popular. A screener allows teachers to identify students who may need to be monitored closely to be sure they are benefiting from instruction. The screener is administered to all students in the class, a cut score is determined, and any student whose performance falls below the cut score is assessed on a frequent schedule to track individual growth. This type of repeated assessment is called *progress monitoring*. Some districts use statewide testing scores or district-created measures to identify those who may be at risk. Others use assessments created by commercial management systems, such as Edusoft, that are available for a fee. These measures serve as the screener. Then the teacher uses a more sensitive measure to monitor those identified as being at risk. For example, a second-grade teacher may decide to monitor all students who were not proficient on the statewide measure with the use of a brief, weekly assessment that provides instructional information on the students' oral reading fluency. Information from this weekly assessment will help the teacher decide which teaching strategies are working well and which need to be changed. The screener is a type of *summative* assessment, whereas the progress monitoring is a type of *formative* assessment.

Most teachers are very familiar with summative assessment, or the evaluation of a student's performance on an assignment or report card. It is summative in that it *sums up* how the student did. This is the most common type of assessment. In formative assessment, the teacher uses information about student performance as an indicator of how effective his or her *instruction* has been. In a sense, it evaluates teacher performance, not student performance. Whereas summative assessment is useful in determining a student's proficiency in a particular area and whether he or she is ready to move to the next grade level or course, formative assessment is critical in fine-tuning instruction. Progress monitoring, a type of formative assessment, provides a sensitive measure of growth that most summative assessments cannot. So the teacher or reading specialist who is using a weekly fluency measure will see within 3–4 weeks if a student is making progress or growth. It is unnecessary to monitor students who are *not* at risk, as we can assume that they will follow a typical growth trajectory. The benefit of closely monitoring those at risk is that we can intervene with them far earlier than if we waited and then used a summative assessment at the end of a grading period.

Curriculum-Based Measurement

Although many schools have implemented academic screeners and progress monitoring measures, others have not. If you are at a school that does not yet have such a system in place, CBM (Deno, 2003) procedures provide a guideline for creating effective progress monitoring measures. CBM is simply a way to make sure you are creating valid and reliable tools so that the information you take from them is useful and accurate.

CBM probes should be brief and easy to administer. They should also be *standardized*. This simply means that anyone can administer the probe because there are clear directions available for giving the assessment and because it is given the same way each time. The next step in creating high-quality progress monitoring assessments is to decide on a target skill that is representative of the content you want to the student to master. For example, in early reading, a phonemic awareness or a decoding task often serves as a progress monitoring target skill. Then you would create several equivalent probes that measure the same skill. One type of probe (or progress monitoring assessment) in the Dynamic Indicators of Basic Early Literacy Skills (DIBELS; Good, Gruba, & Kaminski, 2002) is a nonsense-word fluency exercise. Each probe has 50 items. Each item is a three-letter nonsense word for students to decode. In this way, the probes are equivalent, and there are enough probes that a different one can be administered for many weeks. Students have a specified amount of time to complete each probe, typically 1 minute. The number of items correct and incorrect is tallied. It is extremely important that the probes be equivalent, or, in other words, that they measure the same skill in the same way. If they are not, you cannot measure student progress accurately. Once you change the probe, you are changing the demands of the task and measuring something different. Finally, the results of each probe are graphed so that it is easy to see how the student is progressing. If the growth trend is sufficiently upward, then you know that your instruction is effective. If it is not, you will want to change your instructional practice.

Academic screeners and CBMs are tools designed to help teachers collect and analyze student data. Next, we introduce a few commercial data management systems that have already created measures for use in particular content areas.

Data Management Systems

Several companies offer screening and progress monitoring tools for districts and individual schools. In addition to published assessments, many of them offer web-based data management software that allows teachers to disaggregate data, create graphs, and run reports based on the assessment results. These are not typically programs that a teacher would purchase. However, there are also resources offered by IRIS Center and the National Center on Student Progress that can assist teachers, administrators, and school-site personnel in creating assessment tools, as well as learning how to use them (see Table 8.2).

Heinemann Publishers offer Fountas and Pinnell's Benchmark Assessment System. This product is for use in grades K–8 and provides assessments in reading. In addition to assessing students for instructional purposes and intervention, it includes information on selecting texts for students and grouping students for reading instruction. This is not a web-based product. See Table 8.3 for a complete list of commercial products discussed in this chapter.

Edusoft is published by Houghton Mifflin. It is a web-based assessment system that allows school districts, teachers, and parents to analyze student performance on state exams, district benchmarks, and classroom tests. It includes assessments in all core K–12 academic subjects and standards: math, English language arts, science, and social studies. The assessments are scored online, which reduces teacher time spent on progress monitoring.

AIMSweb is a web-based progress monitoring system published by Pearson. It provides both benchmark assessments (screenings) and progress monitoring assessments for frequent and continuous student assessment. Results can be reported to students, parents, teachers, and administrators using its web-based data management and reporting system. It is designed for use in a response-to-intervention model. AIMSweb has measures available in language arts, reading, and mathematics.

DIBELS is available through the University of Oregon. The measures themselves are available for free, or districts can purchase the web-based program, which offers a variety of data management tools. DIBELS assesses the areas of literacy identified by the National Reading Panel, which include phonemic awareness, the alphabetic principle, accuracy and fluency, vocabulary, and comprehension.

STAR is a web-based information program published by Renaissance Learning. It includes both screening and progress monitoring tools that can be used for

TABLE 8.2. Websites for Information on Progress Monitoring

Resource	Description	Website
IRIS Center	Offers a variety of teaching resources including several modules on how to conduct assessment.	*iris.peabody.vanderbilt.edu*
National Center on Student Progress Monitoring	Offers extensive information and resources on how to conduct progress monitoring.	*www.studentprogress.org*

TABLE 8.3. Data Management Systems for Screening and Progress Monitoring: Academic Outcomes

Publisher	Product
Heinemann	Fountas & Pinnell Benchmark Assessment System Series *www.heinemann.com/series/90.aspx*
Houghton Mifflin	Edusoft *www.edusoft.com/corporate/products.html*
Pearson	AIMSweb *www.aimsweb.com*
University of Oregon	Dynamic Indicators of Basic Early Literacy Skills (DIBELS) *dibels.uoregon.edu*
Renaissance Learning, Inc.	STAR *www.renlearn.com/STARproducts.aspx*

a variety of purposes, such as placement, diagnostic assessment, progress monitoring, growth measurement, and outcomes assessment. It has measures available in the areas of reading, early literacy, and mathematics.

Whether you use a commercial product or design your own assessment tools, the point is to carefully evaluate student outcomes both academically and behaviorally. This will ensure a comprehensive approach to supporting students in achieving a successful school experience.

Analyzing Behavior and Academic Data in Tandem

We encourage you to consider strategic methods for conducting systematic screenings of students' social, behavioral, and academic performance to identify students with individual or combined deficits. It is critical that these pieces of information be analyzed in tandem with one another as well as with other schoolwide data (e.g., attendance, unexcused absences) to determine how best to support students' multiple needs. For example, a second-grade student who is performing below benchmark on oral reading fluency as measured by Fountas and Pinnell's Benchmark Assessment System requires a Tier 2 reading intervention. However, if this same student exceeded normative criteria on the Internalizing subscale of the SSBD (Walker & Severson, 1992), then the teacher might want to increase the student's participation by (1) making certain to increase this student's OTR and (2) giving the student a certain number of pogs (small, circular pieces of cardboard or plastic that depict a logo or sports team) to be exchanged for participation, thereby removing any anxiety associated with being called on in class but still enforcing the expectation of participation (Lane, Kalberg, & Menzies, 2009).

Once these data are collected and analyzed to determine students with specific areas of need, the next step is to support these students. Although we view the strategies covered in this book as highly useful, you will likely need additional strategies to implement as part of secondary (Tier 2) and tertiary (Tier 3) supports. In the next section, we offer you suggestions for selecting and evaluating promising practices to implement systematically within the context of your comprehensive three-tiered model of prevention.

SELECTING AND EVALUATING PROMISING PRACTICES

As you consider how best to support students who are unresponsive to primary prevention efforts, we encourage you to make certain that you are identifying, implementing, and evaluating targeted supports and practices that have a sufficient knowledge base to support use in your classroom. Namely, we recommend that you move forward with practices that are evidence based or at least promising. Your time and your students' time is simply too important to waste on practices that do not have scientific merit. For example, consider an elementary school teacher who is asked to provide support to fourth-grade students who have been identified by schoolwide data as having abnormally high levels of hyperactivity as measured by the Hyperactivity subscale of the SDQ (Goodman, 1997) and who are performing below benchmark on oral reading fluency as measured by DIBELS (Kaminski & Good, 1996). One of your first tasks is to decide on a small-group, Tier 2 (secondary) reading curriculum to improve fluency. Given the students' struggles with attention, you will also need to consider which behavioral supports are necessary to help these youngsters engage in the Tier 2 reading program.

In determining which reading program and which behavioral support to implement, we recommend that you determine whether there is sufficient evidence that the practice (e.g., repeated readings) is warranted for use with your students. One way to do this is to look for studies conducted with similar populations and in similar contexts (e.g., other upper-middle-school-age students educated in inclusive rural settings). Yet just the fact that a study is published does not necessarily mean that it is a good study in terms of scientific rigor. Fortunately, guidelines have been established for determining whether a practice is indeed evidence based or promising for use. For example, Horner et al. (2005) have provided guidelines for examining studies conducted using the single-case method. One should examine the quality of an individual article (e.g., one study on repeated readings) to determine whether the given study meets specific standards and the body of literature as a whole (e.g., all studies conducted that have examined repeated readings) to determine whether the practice is actually evidence based. Gersten et al. (2005) have provided similar guidelines for evaluating studies conducted using group-design methodology. This way we can feel confident that the articles we are relying on for information are credible.

Yet as practitioners we likely will not have the time to spend days in the library stacks or conducting electronic searches to identify and subsequently evaluate the studies we have identified (although I am sure you'd like to, Abe!). But many members of the research community have already taken the time to synthesize the research for us. For example, Bryan Cook, Melody Tankersley, and Tim Landrum (2009) edited a special issue of the journal *Exceptional Children* during Steve Graham's editorship to provide practitioners and researchers with information on practices such as: self-regulated strategy instruction in writing for students at risk (Baker, Chard, Ketterlin-Geller, Apichataburtra, & Doabler, 2009); cognitive strategy instruction and mathematical problem solving (Montague & Dietz, 2009); repeated reading interventions for students with learning disabilities (Chard, Ketterlin-Geller, Baker, Doabler, & Apichatabutra, 2009); functional assessment-based interventions for middle and high school students with emotional and behavioral disorders (Lane, Kalberg, & Shepcaro, 2009); and using time delay to teach literacy to students with severe developmental disabilities (Browder, Ahlgrim-Delzell, Spooner, Mims, & Baker, 2009). Such articles and resources will be helpful for you in determining what practices to select for use at your school.

In addition, websites such as the What Works Clearinghouse site (*ies.ed.gov/ncee/wwc*) also provide results of rigorous reviews of the literature that may prove highly useful for you as you make important decisions regarding what and how to teach students requiring more intensive academic, behavioral, and social supports beyond a school's primary prevention program (Lane, Kalberg, & Menzies, 2009). The take-away message is this: *Invest your time in learning and using practices that have a sufficient knowledge base to support implementation.* Please resist the temptation to implement a practice (e.g., chanting spelling words) just because it was the way you were taught or because you were inspired at an inservice or other staff development opportunity. Ask yourself the question "Does the research support the use of this practice with students who have similar needs as those identified in my school?" Going back to our example, you might elect to implement repeated readings as the Tier 2 intervention to improve oral reading fluency (Chard et al., 2009), and you might also provide a self-monitoring intervention to help your students stay engaged in the oral reading fluency intervention (Mooney et al., 2005)–particularly given that the fact that a student is assigned to an academic intervention does not mean that all students participate equally. Both of these practices are supported by research and are likely worth the investment of your precious resources—time, money, and personnel.

SUMMARY

Now that you have had an opportunity to read this book and consider where you are in terms of readiness with respect to these various proactive and reactive approaches to supporting students' learning and behavioral performance, we wish you well. Please remember that our first choice would be for you to implement these new (and revisited) tools and strategies within the context of three-tiered models of prevention. Such models offer a structure for supporting these efforts, providing school-site teams with a data-driven method of meeting the academic, behavioral, and social needs of all students—including those with and at risk for EBD (Walker et al., 2004). If you are interested in establishing such a program, we recommend that you begin by learning more about how to design, implement, and evaluate an integrated model that is culturally responsive to the values of your school and greater community (see Lane, Kalberg, & Menzies, 2009, for a step-by-step process). This book will be equally important, and perhaps more so, to teachers and other school-site personnel who do not have the benefit of working at a school site that has a three-tiered model of support already in place. The information it offers will help you (1) prevent the development of learning and behavior problems from occurring in the first place and (2) respond more efficiently and effectively to problem behaviors that do occur so that you can move toward your original goal when you entered the teaching profession: to teach and inspire students!

We hope that you find the strategies presented in this book to be reasonable and effective. If you see us at a conference or would like to send us an e-mail, we would enjoy hearing your thoughts on the strategies you have learned and implemented in your classrooms. We wish you the best as you move forward with what we believe to be one of the most important and meaningful jobs—teaching.

References

Achenbach, T. M. (1991). *Manual for the child behavior checklist/4–18 and 1991 profile*. Burlington: University of Vermont, Department of Psychiatry.

Alderman, M. K. (1999). *Motivation for achievement: Possibilities for teaching and learning*. Mahwah, NJ: Erlbaum.

Allen, S. J., Howard, V. F., Sweeney, W. J., & McLaughlin, T. F. (1993). Use of contingency contracting to increase on-task behavior with primary students. *Psychological Reports, 72*, 905–906.

Allen, S. J., & Kramer, J. J. (1990). Modification of personal hygiene and grooming behaviors with the use of contingency contracting: A brief review and case study. *Psychology in the Schools, 27*, 244–251.

Amato-Zech, N. A., Hoff, K. E., & Doepke, K. J. (2006). Increasing on-task behavior in the classroom: Extension of self-monitoring strategies. *Psychology in the Schools, 43*, 211–221.

American Educational Research Association. (1999). *Standards for educational and psychological testing*. Washington, DC: Author.

American Psychological Association Classroom Violence Directed Against Teachers Task Force. (2009). *Understanding and preventing violence against teachers: Recommendations for a national policy, practice and research agenda*. Manuscript in preparation.

Arter, P. (2007). The Positive Alternative Learning Supports program: Collaborating to improve student success. *Teaching Exceptional Children, 40*, 38–46.

Au, K. H. (1980). Participation structures in a reading lesson with Hawaiian children: Analysis of a culturally appropriate instructional event. *Anthropology and Education Quarterly, 11*, 91–115.

Au, K. H., & Carroll, J. H. (1997). Improving literacy achievement through a constructivist approach: The KEEP demonstration classroom project. *Elementary School Journal, 97,* 203–221.

Ausubel, D. P. (2000). *The acquisition and retention of knowledge: A cognitive view.* Boston: Kluwer.

Ayllon, T. (1999). *How to use token economy and point systems* (2nd ed.). Austin, TX: Pro-Ed.

Baer, D. M., Wolf, M. M., & Risley, T. R. (1968). Some current dimensions of applied behavior analysis. *Journal of Applied Behavior Analysis, 1,* 91–97.

Baker, J. A., Clark, T. P., Maier, K. S., & Viger, S. (2008). The differential influence of instructional context on the academic engagement of students with behavior problems. *Teaching and Teacher Education, 24,* 1876–1883.

Baker, S. K., Chard, D. J., Ketterlin-Geller, L. R., Apichatabutra, C., & Doabler, C. (2009). Teaching writing to at-risk students: The quality of evidence for self-regulated strategy development. *Exceptional Children, 75,* 303–318.

Barr, R. D., & Parrett, W. H. (2008). *Saving our students, saving our schools: 50 proven strategies for helping underachieving students and improving schools* (2nd ed.). Thousand Oaks, CA: Corwin Press.

Barton-Arwood, S., Morrow, L., Lane, K. L., & Jolivette, K. (2005). Project IMPROVE: Improving teachers' ability to address students' social needs. *Education and Treatment of Children, 28,* 430–443.

Beck, I. L., McKeown, M. G., & Kucan, L. (2002). *Bringing words to life.* New York: Guilford Press.

Bergan, J. R., & Kratochwill, T. R. (1990). *Behavioral consultation and therapy.* New York: Plenum Press.

Berlyne, D. (1966). Curiosity and exploration. *Science, 153,* 25–33.

Bijou, S. W., Peterson, R. F., & Ault, M. H. (1968). A method to integrate descriptive and experimental field studies at the level of data and empirical concepts. *Journal of Applied Behavior Analysis, 1,* 175–191.

Bloom, K. C., & Shuell, T. (1981). Effects of massed and distributed practice on learning and retention of second-language vocabulary. *Journal of Educational Research, 74,* 245–248.

Boniecki, K. A., & Moore, S. (2003). Breaking the silence: Using a token economy to reinforce classroom participation. *Teaching of Psychology, 3,* 224–227.

Botvin, G. J., Mihalic, S. F., & Grotpeter, J. K. (1998). *Blueprints for violence prevention: Book 5. Life skills training.* Boulder: University of Colorado, Institute of Behavioral Science, Center for the Study and Prevention of Violence.

Brophy, J. (1986a). Classroom management as socializing students into clearly articulated roles. *Journal of Classroom Interaction, 33,* 1–4.

Brophy, J. (1986b). Classroom management techniques. *Education and Urban Society, 18,* 182–94.

Brophy, J. (1986c). Teacher influences on student achievement. *American Psychologist, 41*(10), 1069–1077.

Brophy, J., & Good, T. (1986). Teacher behavior and student achievement. In M. C. Wittrock (Ed.), *Handbook of research on teaching* (3rd ed., pp. 933–958). New York: MacMillan.

Brouwers, A., & Tomic, W. (2000). A longitudinal study of teacher burnout and perceived self-efficacy in classroom management. *Teaching and Teacher Education, 16,* 239–253.

Browder, D., Ahlgrim-Delzell, L., Spooner, F., Mims, P. J., & Baker, J. N. (2009). Using time delay to teach literacy to students with severe developmental disabilities *Exceptional Children, 75,* 343–364.

Brownell, M. T., & Walthe-Thomas, C. (2001). Stephen W. Smith: Strategies for building a positive classroom environment by preventing behavior problems. *Intervention in School and Clinic, 37,* 31–35.

Burgess, J. W., & Fordyce, W. K. (1989). Effects of preschool environments on nonverbal social behavior: Toddlers' interpersonal distances to teachers and classmates change with environmental density, classroom design, and parent–child interactions. *Journal of Child Psychology and Psychiatry, 30,* 261–276.

Burnett, P. (2001). Elementary students' preferences for teacher praise. *Journal of Classroom Interaction, 36,* 16–23.

Butler, D. L. (1998). The strategic content learning approach to promoting self-regulated learning: A report of three studies. *Journal of Educational Psychology, 90,* 682–697.

California Department of Education. (2000). *Historical–social science content standards for California public schools, kindergarten through grade twelve.* Retrieved from *www.cde.ca.gov/be/st/ss/documents/histsocscistnd.pdf.*

Cameron, J., & Pierce, W. (1994). Reinforcement, reward, and intrinsic motivation: A meta-analysis. *Review of Educational Research, 64,* 363–423.

Cameto, R., Levine, P., Wagner, M., & Marder, C. (2003). The emerging independence of youth with disabilities. In M. Wagner, L. Marder, J. Blackorby, R. Cameto, L. Newman, P. Levine, et al. (Eds.), *The achievements of youth with disabilities during secondary school* (pp. 6.1–6.22). Menlo Park, CA: SRI International.

Canter, L. (2006). *Classroom management for academic success.* Bloomington, IN: Solution Tree.

Caprara, G., Barbaranelli, C., Pastorelli, C., Bandura, A., & Zimbardo, P. (2000). Prosocial foundations of children's academic achievement. *Psychological Science, 11,* 302–305.

Carr, E. G., Levin, L., McConnachie, G., Carlson, J. I., Kemp, D. C., & Smith, C. E. (1994). *Communication-based intervention for problem behavior: A user's guide for producing positive change.* Baltimore: Brookes.

Carr, S. C., & Punzo, R. P. (1993). The effects of self-monitoring of academic accuracy and productivity on the performance of students with behavioral disorders. *Behavioral Disorders, 18,* 241–250.

Carter, E. W., Lane, K. L., Pierson, M. R., & Glaeser, B. (2006). Self-determination skills and opportunities of transition-age youth with emotional disturbances and learning disabilities. *Exceptional Children, 72,* 333–346.

Carter, E. W., Lane, K. L., Pierson, M. R., & Stang, K. K. (2008). Promoting self-determination for transition-age youth: Views of high school general and special educators. *Exceptional Children, 75,* 55–70.

Center for the Prevention and Study of Violence. (2004). Blueprints for violence prevention. Retrieved February 13, 2008, from *www.colorado.edu/cspv/blueprints.*

Chard, D. J., Ketterlin-Geller, L. R., Baker, S. K., Doabler, C., & Apichatabutra, C. (2009). Repeated reading interventions for students with learning disabilities: Status of the evidence. *Exceptional Children, 75,* 263–281.

Clarke-Edmands, S. (2004). *S.P.I.R.E.* Cambridge, MA: Educators Publishing Service.

Colvin, G. (2002). Designing classroom organization and structure. In K. L. Lane, F. M. Gresham, & T. E. O'Shaughnessy (Eds.), *Intervention for children with or at risk for emotional and behavioral disorders* (pp. 159–174). Boston: Allyn & Bacon.

Colvin, G. (2004). *Managing the cycle of serious acting out behavior.* Eugene, OR: Behavior Associates.

Colvin, G., Kame'enui, E. J., & Sugai, G. (1993). Reconceptualizing behavior management and school-wide discipline in general education. *Education and Treatment of Children, 16,* 361–381.

Colvin, G., Sugai, G., Good, R. H., & Lee, Y. (1997). Using active supervision and precorrection to improve transition behaviors in an elementary school. *School Psychology Quarterly, 12,* 344–363.

Committee for Children. (2007). *Second Steps Violence Prevention.* Seattle, WA: Author.

Conroy, M. A., Asmus, J. M., Ladwig, C. N., Sellers, J. A., & Valcante, G. (2004). The effects of proximity on the classroom behaviors of students with autism in general education settings. *Behavior Disorders, 29,* 119–129.

Conroy, M. A., Dunlap, G., Clarke, S., & Alter, P. J. (2005). A descriptive analysis of positive behavioral intervention research with young children with challenging behavior. *Topics in Early Childhood Special Education, 25,* 157–166.

Conroy, M. A., Sutherland, K. S., Snyder, A. L., & Marsh, S. (2008). Classwide interventions: Effective instruction makes a difference. *Teaching Exceptional Children, 40*(6), 24–30.

Cook, B., Tankersley, M., & Landrum, T. J. (2009). Determining evidence-based practices in special education. *Exceptional Children, 75,* 365–383.

Cook, C., Gresham, F., Kern, L., Barreras, R., Thornton, S., & Crews, S. (2008). Social skills training for secondary students with emotional and/or behavioral disorders: A review and analysis of the meta-analytic literature. *Journal of Emotional and Behavioral Disorders, 16,* 131–144.

Cook, M. N. (2005). The disruptive or ADHD child: What to do when kids won't sit still and be quiet. *Focus on Exceptional Children, 37,* 1–9.

Cooper, J. O., Heron, T. E., & Heward, W. L. (2007). *Applied behavior analysis* (2nd ed.). Upper Saddle River, NJ: Merrill/Prentice Hall.

Cosden, M., Gannon, C., & Haring, T. G. (1995). Teacher control versus student control over choice of task and reinforcement for students with severe behavior problems. *Journal of Behavioral Education, 5,* 11–27.

Council for Exceptional Children. (1987). *The academy for effective instruction: Working with mildly handicapped students.* Reston, VA: Author.

Coyne, M., Kame'enui, E., & Carnine, D. (2007). *Effective teaching strategies that accommodate diverse learners.* Upper Saddle River, NJ: Pearson Merrill Prentice Hall.

Crago, M., Eriks-Brophy, A., Pesco, D., & McAlpine, L. (1997). Culturally based miscommunication in classroom interaction. *Language, Speech, and Hearing Services in Schools, 28,* 245–254.

Creating Caring Communities. (2008). *Bully-proofing your school.* Denver, CO: Author.

Crick, N., Grotpeter, J., & Bigbee, M. (2002). Relationally and physically aggressive children's intent attributions and feelings of distress for relational and instrumental peer provocations. *Child Development, 73,* 1134–1142.

Crone, D. A., & Horner, R. H. (2003). *Building positive behavior support systems in schools: Functional behavioral assessment.* New York: Guilford Press.

Crone, D. A., Horner, R. H., & Hawken, L. S. (2004). *Responding to problem behavior in schools: The Behavior Education Program*. New York: Guilford Press.

Dardig, J. C., & Heward, W. L. (1981). *Sign here: A contracting book for children and their parents* (2nd ed.). Bridgewater, NJ: Fournies.

De La Paz, S., & Graham, S. (2002). Explicitly teaching strategies, skills, and knowledge: Writing instruction in middle school classrooms. *Journal of Educational Psychology, 94*, 687–698.

De Pry, R. L., & Sugai, G. (2002). The effect of active supervision and pre-correction on minor behavioral incidents in a sixth grade general education classroom. *Journal of Behavioral Education, 11*, 255–267.

deCharms, R. (1976). *Enhancing motivation*. New York: Irving.

deCharms, R. (1984). Motivating enhancement in educational settings. In R. Ames & C. Ames (Eds.), *Research on motivation in education: Vol. 1. Student motivation* (pp. 275–310). New York: Academic Press.

Deci, E. (1975). *Intrinsic motivation*. New York: Plenum Press.

Deci, E. L., & Ryan, R. M. (1985). *Intrinsic motivation and self-determination in human behavior*. New York: Plenum Press.

DeMartini-Scully, D., Bray, M. A., & Kehle, T. J. (2000). A packaged intervention to reduce disruptive behaviors in general education students. *Psychology in the Schools, 37*, 149–156.

Deno, S. L. (2003). Developments in curriculum-based measurement. *Journal of Special Education, 37*, 184–192.

DiPerma, J., & Elliott, S. N. (2002). Promoting academic enablers to improve student achievement: An introduction to the mini-series. *School Psychology Review, 31*, 293–297.

Dixon-Krauss, L. (1996). *Vygotsky in the classroom: Mediated literacy instruction and assessment*. White Plains, NY: Longman.

Downey, J. (2008). Recommendations for fostering educational resilience in the classroom. *Preventing School Failure, 53*, 56–64.

Downing, J. A. (2002). Individualized behavior contracts. *Intervention in School and Clinic, 37*, 168–172.

Drasgow, E., & Yell, M. L. (2001). Functional behavior assessment: Legal requirements and challenges. *School Psychology Review, 30*, 239–251.

Drummond, T. (1994). *The Student Risk Screening Scale (SRSS)*. Grants Pass, OR: Josephine County Mental Health Program.

Dunlap, G., dePerczel, M., Clarke, S., Wilson, D., Wright, S., White, R., et al. (1994). Choice making to promote adaptive behavior for students with emotional and behavioral challenges. *Journal of Applied Behavior Analysis, 27*, 505–518.

Dunlap, G., Foster-Johnson, L., Clarke, S., Kern, L., & Childs, K. (1995). Modifying activities to produce functional outcomes: Effects on the problem behaviors of students with disabilities. *Journal of the Association for Persons with Severe Handicaps, 20*, 248–258.

DuPaul, G. J., McGoey, K. E., & Yugar, J. M. (1997). Mainstreaming students with behavior disorders: The use of classroom peers as facilitators of generalization. *School Psychology Review, 26*, 634–650.

Eber, L., Sugai, G., Smith, C., & Scott, T. (2002). Wraparound and positive behavioral interventions and supports in the schools. *Journal of Emotional and Behavioral Disorders, 10*, 171–180.

Elliott, S., & Gresham, F. M. (1991). *Social skills intervention guide: Practical strategies for social skills training.* Circle Pines, MN: American Guidance.

Elliott, S. N., & Gresham, F. M. (2007). *SSIS Classwide Intervention Program.* Bloomington, MN: Pearson Assessments.

Embry, D. D. (2002). The Good Behavior Game: A best practice candidate as a universal behavioral vaccine. *Clinical Child and Family Psychology Review, 5,* 273–297.

Embry, D. D., Straatemeier, G., Lauger, K., & Richardson, C. (2003). *The PAX Good Behavior Game Schoolwide Implementation Guide.* Center City, MN: Hazeldon.

Emmer, E. T., Evertson, C. M., & Worsham, M. E. (2006). *Classroom management for secondary teachers* (6th ed.). Boston: Allyn & Bacon.

Englert, C. S. (1984). Effective direct instruction practices in special education settings. *Remedial and Special Education, 5,* 38–47.

Epstein, M., Atkins, M., Cullinan, D., Kutash, K., & Weaver, R. (2008). *Reducing behavior problems in the elementary school classroom: A practice guide* (NCEE No. 2008-012). Washington, DC: U.S. Department of Education, Institute of Education Sciences, National Center for Education Evaluation and Regional Assistance.

Ervin, R. A., DuPaul, G. J., Kern, L., & Friman, P. C. (1998). Classroom-based functional and adjunctive assessments: Proactive approaches to intervention selection for adolescents with attention-deficit/hyperactivity disorder. *Journal of Applied Behavior Analysis, 31,* 65–78.

Ervin, R. A., Kern, L., Clarke, S., DuPaul, G. J., Dunlap, G., & Friman, P. C. (2000). Evaluating assessment-based intervention strategies for students with ADHD and comorbid disorders within the natural classroom context. *Behavioral Disorders, 25,* 344–358.

Espin, C., & Yell, M. (1994). Critical indicators of effective teaching for preservice teachers: Relationships between teaching behaviors and ratings of effectiveness. *Teacher Education and Special Education, 17,* 154–169.

Evertson, C. M., & Weinstein, C. S. (2006). *Handbook of classroom management: Research, practice, and contemporary issues.* Mahwah, NJ: Erlbaum.

Feldman, K., & Denti, L. (2004). High-access instruction: Practical strategies to increase active learning in diverse classrooms. *Focus on Exceptional Children, 36,* 2–12.

Filcheck, H., McNeil, C., Greco, L., & Bernard, R. (2004). Using a whole-class token economy and coaching of teacher skills in a preschool classroom to manage disruptive behavior. *Psychology in the Schools, 41,* 351–361.

Fish, M. C., & Mendola, L. R. (1986). The effect of self-instruction training on homework completion in an elementary special education class. *School Psychology Review, 15,* 268–276.

Flood, W. A., & Wilder, D. A. (2002). Antecedent assessment and assessment-based treatment of off-task behavior in a child with attention-deficit/hyperactivity disorder (ADHD). *Education and Treatment of Children, 25,* 331–338.

Florio, S., & Schultz, J. (1979). Social competence at home and at school. *Theory into Practice, 18,* 234–243.

Foegen, A., Jiban, C., & Deno, S. (2007). Progress monitoring measures in mathematics: A review of the literature. *Journal of Special Education, 41,* 121–139.

Forehand, R. L., & McMahon, R. J. (1981). *Helping the noncompliant child: A clinician's guide to parenting.* New York: Guilford Press.

Fuchs, D., Fuchs, L. S., & Burish, P. (2000). Peer-assisted learning strategies: An evidence-based practice to promote reading achievement. *Learning Disabilities Research and Practice, 15,* 85–91.

Fuchs, D., Fuchs, L. S., Mathes, P. G., & Martinez, E. (2002). Preliminary evidence on the social standing of students with learning disabilities in PALS and No-PALS classrooms. *Learning Disabilities Research and Practice, 17,* 205–215.

Fuchs, D., Fuchs, L. S., Mathes, P. G., & Simmons, D. C. (1997). Peer-assisted learning strategies: Making classrooms more responsive to diversity. *American Educational Research Journal, 34,* 174–206.

Gable, R. A., Hester, P. H., Rock, M. L., & Hughes, K. G. (2009). Back to basics: Rules, praise, ignoring, and reprimands revisited. *Intervention in School and Clinic, 44,* 195–205.

Garrity, C. B., Jens, K., & Porter, W. W. (1997). Bully proofing your school: Creating a positive climate. *Intervention in School and Clinic, 32,* 235–343.

Gay, G. (2006). Connections between classroom management and culturally responsive teaching. In C. M. Evertson & C. S. Weinstein (Eds.), *Handbook of classroom management: Research, practice, and contemporary issues* (pp. 343–370). Mahwah, NJ: Erlbaum.

Gersten, R., Baker, S. K., Smith-Johnson, J., Dimino, J., & Peterson, A. (2006). Eyes on the prize: Teaching complex historical content to middle school students with learning disabilities. *Exceptional Children, 72,* 264–280.

Gersten, R., Fuchs, L. S., Compton, D., Coyne, M., Greenwood, C., & Innocenti, M. S. (2005). Quality indicators for group experimental and quasi-experimental research in special education. *Exceptional Children, 71,* 149–164.

Gettinger, M. (1986). Issues and trends in academic engaged times of students. *Special Services in the Schools, 2,* 1–17.

Gettinger, M., & Kohler, K. M. (2006). Process-outcome approaches to classroom management and effective teaching. In C. M. Evertson & C. S. Weinstein (Eds.), *Handbook of classroom management: Research, practice, and contemporary issues* (pp. 73–96). Mahwah, NJ: Erlbaum.

Gettinger, M., & Seibert, J. K. (2002). Contributions of study skills to academic competence. *School Psychology Review, 31,* 350–365.

Gickling, E., & Armstrong, D. (1978). Levels of instructional difficulty as related to on-task behavior, task completion, and comprehension. *Journal of Learning Disabilities, 11,* 559–566.

Ginott, H. (1971). *Teacher and child.* New York: Macmillan.

Glasser, W. (1969). *Schools without failure.* New York: Harper & Row.

Glasser, W. (1985). *Control theory in the classroom.* New York: Perennial Library.

Good, R., Gruba, J., & Kaminski, R. (2002). Best practices in using Dynamic Indicators of Basic Early Literacy Skills (DIBELS) in an outcomes-driven model. In A. Thomas & J. Grimes (Eds.), *Best practices in school psychology: IV* (Vols. 1 & 2, pp. 699–720). Washington, DC: National Association of School Psychologists.

Good, T., & Grouws, D. (1977). Teaching effects: A process–product study in fourth grade mathematics classrooms. *Journal of Teacher Education, 28,* 49–54.

Goodman, R. (1997). The Strengths and Difficulties Questionnaire: A research note. *Journal of Child Psychology and Psychiatry, 38,* 581–586.

Graham, S. (2006). Strategy instruction and the teaching of writing: A meta-analysis. In C. MacArthur, S. Graham, & J. Fitzgerald (Eds.), *Handbook of writing research* (pp. 187–207). New York: Guilford Press.

Graham, S., & Harris, K. R. (2005). *Writing better: Effective strategies for teaching students with learning difficulties*. Baltimore: Brookes.

Graham, S., Harris, K. R., & Reid, R. (1992). Developing self-regulated learners. *Focus on Exceptional Children, 24*, 1–16.

Graham, S., & Perin, D. (2007). A meta-analysis of writing instruction for adolescent students. *Journal of Educational Psychology, 3*, 445–476.

Greenberg, M. T., Kusché, C. A., Cook, E. T., & Quamma, J. P. (1995). Promoting emotional competence in school-aged children: The effects of the PATHS curriculum. *Development and Psychopathology, 7*, 117–136.

Greenberg, M. T., Kusché, C., & Mihalic, S. F. (1998). *Blueprints for Violence Prevention: Book 10. Promoting Alternative Thinking Strategies (PATHS)*. Boulder: University of Colorado, Institute of Behavioral Science, Center for the Study and Prevention of Violence.

Greenwood, C. R., Horton, B. T., & Utley, C. A. (2002). Academic engagement: Current perspectives on research and practice. *School Psychology Review, 31*, 328–349.

Gresham, F. M. (1989). Assessment of treatment integrity in school consultation and prereferral intervention. *School Psychology Review, 18*, 37–50.

Gresham, F. M. (2002a). Responsiveness to intervention: An alternative approach to learning disabilities. In R. Bradley, L. Danielson, & D. Hallahan (Eds.), *Identification of learning disabilities: Research to practice*. Mahwah, NJ: Erlbaum.

Gresham, F. M. (2002b). Best practices in social skills training. In A. Thomas & J. Grimes (Eds.), *Best practices in school psychology: IV* (Vols. 1 & 2, pp. 1029–1040). Bethesda, MD: National Association of School Psychologists.

Gresham, F. M. (2002c). Social skills assessment and instruction for students with emotional and behavioral disorders. In K. L. Lane, F. M. Gresham, & T. E. O'Shaughnessy (Eds.), *Interventions for children with or at risk for emotional and behavioral disorders* (pp. 242–258). Boston: Allyn & Bacon.

Gresham, F. M. (2004). Current status and future directions of school-based behavioral interventions. *School Psychology Review, 33*, 326–343.

Gresham, F. M., & Elliott, S. N. (1990). *Social Skills Rating System (SRSS)*. Circle Pines, MN: American Guidance Service.

Gresham, F. M., Sugai, G., Horner, R., Quinn, M., & McInerney, M. (1998). *Classroom and schoolwide practices that support students' social competence: A synthesis of research*. Washington, DC: Office of Special Education Programs.

Griffin, K. W., Botvin, G. J., Nichols, T. R., & Doyle, M. M. (2003). Effectiveness of a universal drug abuse prevention approach for youth at high risk for substance use initiation. *Preventive Medicine, 36*, 1–7.

Guess, D., Benson, H. A., & Siegel-Causey, E. (1985). Concepts and issues related to choice making and autonomy among persons with severe disabilities. *Journal of the Association for Persons with Severe Handicaps, 10*, 79–86.

Gunter, P. L., Hummel, J. H., & Venn, M. L. (1998). Are effective academic instructional practices used to teach students with behavior disorders? *Beyond Behavior, 9*, 5–11.

Gunter, P. L., Miller, K. A., & Venn, M. L. (2003). A case study of the effects of self-graphing reading performance data for a girl identified with emotional/behavioral disorders. *Preventing School Failure, 48*, 28–31.

Hall, R. V., Lund, D., & Jackson, D. (1968). Effects of teacher attention on study behavior. *Journal of Applied Behavior Analysis, 1*, 1–12.

Halle, J. W. (1995). Innovations in choice-making research: An editorial introduction. *Journal of the Association for Persons with Severe Handicaps, 20,* 173–174.

Hariman, M., & Toth, M. (1994). *Inspiring active learning: A complete handbook for today's teachers* (2nd ed.). Alexandria, VA: ASCD.

Harris, K. R., & Graham, S. (1996a). *Making the writing process work: Strategies for composition and self-regulation* (2nd ed.). Cambridge, MA.: Brookline Books.

Harris, K. R., & Graham, S. (1996b). Constructivism and students with special needs: Issues in the classroom. *Learning Disabilities Research and Practice, 11,* 134–137.

Harris, K. R. Graham, S., Mason, L. H., & Friedlander, B. (2008). *Powerful writing strategies for all students.* Baltimore: Brookes.

Harris, L. (1991). *The Metropolitan Life Survey of the American Teacher, 1991: The first year: New teachers' expectations and ideals.* New York: Metropolitan Life Insurance.

Hartley, J., & Davies, I. (1976). Preinstructional strategies: The role of pretests, behavioral objectives, overviews, and advanced organizers. *Review of Educational Research, 46,* 239–265.

Hersh, R., & Walker, H. M. (1983). Great expectations: Making schools effective for all children. *Policy Studies Review, 2,* 147–188.

Hess, A. M., Rosenberg, M. S., & Levy, G. K. (1990). Reducing truancy in students with mild handicaps. *Remedial and Special Education, 11,* 14–19.

Hoover, J. J., & Patton, J. R. (2005). *Curriculum adaptations.* Austin, TX: Pro-Ed.

Horner, R. H., Carr, E. G., Halle, J., McGee, G., Odom, S., & Wolery, M. (2005). The use of single-subject research to identify evidence-based practice in special education. *Exceptional Children, 71,* 165–179.

Horner, R. H., & Sugai, G. (2000). School-wide behavior support: An emerging initiative. *Journal of Positive Behavior Interventions, 2,* 231.

Houchins, D. E. (2002). Self-determination knowledge instruction and incarcerated students. *Emotional and Behavioural Difficulties, 7,* 132–151.

Hunt, J. M. (1965). Intrinsic motivation and its role in psychological development. In D. Levine (Ed.), *Nebraska Symposium on Motivation* (Vol. 13, pp.189–282). Lincoln: University of Nebraska Press.

Hunter, M. (1976). *Prescription for improved instruction.* El Segundo, CA: TIP.

Hutchinson, S., Murdock, J., & Williamson, R. (2000). Self-recording plus encouragement equals improved behavior. *Teaching Exceptional Children, 32,* 54–58.

Individuals with Disabilities Education Act Amendments of 1997, Publication Law No. 105-17, §20, 111 Stat. 37 (1997).

Individuals with Disabilities Education Improvement Act of 2004, 20 U.S.C. 1400 *et seq.* (2004).

Ingersoll, R., & Smith, T. (2003). The wrong solution to the teacher shortage. *Educational Leadership, 60*(8), 30.

Iwata, B. A., Dorsey, M. F., Slifer, K. J., Bauman, K., & Richman, G. S. (1982). Toward a functional analysis of self-injury. *Analysis and Intervention in Developmental Disabilities, 2,* 3–20.

Jameson, J., McDonnell, J., Johnson, J., Riesen, T., & Polychronis, S. (2007). A comparison of one-to-one embedded instruction in the general education classroom and one-to-one massed practice instruction in the special education classroom. *Education and Treatment of Children, 30,* 23–44

Jitendra, A. (2002). Teaching students math problem solving through graphic representations. *Teaching Exceptional Children, 34,* 34–38.

Johnson, D., & Johnson, R. (1999). Making cooperative learning work. *Theory into Practice, 38,* 67–73.

Johnson, G. M. (1998). Principles of instruction for at-risk learners. *Preventing School Failure, 4,* 167–174.

Jolivette, K., Stichter, J., & McCormick, K. (2002). Making choices—improving behavior—engaging in learning. *Teaching Exceptional Children, 34,* 24–29.

Kagan, J. (1972). Motives and development. *Journal of Personality and Social Psychology, 22,* 51–66.

Kalberg, J. R., Lane, K. L., & Menzies, H. M. (2010). *Using systematic screening procedures to identify students who are nonresponsive to primary prevention efforts: Integrating academic and behavioral measures.* Manuscript submitted for publication.

Kaminski, R. A., & Good, R. H., III. (1996). Toward a technology for assessing basic early literacy skills. *School Psychology Review, 25*(2), 215–227.

Kamphaus, R. W., & Reynolds, C. R. (2008). *Behavioral and Emotional Screening System.* Bloomington, MN: Pearson.

Kauffman, J., & Landrum, T. (2009). Politics, civil rights, and disproportional identification of students with emotional and behavioral disorders. *Exceptionality, 17,* 177.

Kauffman, J. M., & Brigham, F. J. (2009). *Working with troubled children.* Verona, WI: Full Court.

Kazdin, A. E. (1977). Assessing the clinical or applied importance of behavior change through social validation. *Behavior Modification, 1,* 427–452.

Kazdin, A. E. (1987). Treatment of antisocial behavior in children: Current status and future directions. *Psychological Bulletin, 102,* 187–203.

Kelley, M. L., & Stokes, T. F. (1982). Contingency contracting with disadvantaged youths: Improving classroom performance. *Journal of Applied Behavior Analysis, 15,* 447–454.

Kern, L. Bambara, L., & Fogt, J. (2002). Class-wide curricular modification to improve the behavior of students with emotional or behavioral disorders. *Behavioral Disorders, 27,* 317–326.

Kern, L., Delaney, B., Clarke, S., Dunlap, G., & Childs, K. (2001). Improving the classroom behavior of students with emotional and behavioral disorders using individualized curricular modifications. *Journal of Emotional and Behavioral Disorders, 9,* 239–247.

Kern, L., Hilt, A. M., & Gresham, F. (2004). An evaluation of the functional behavioral assessment process used with students with or at risk for emotional and behavioral disorders. *Education and Treatment of Children, 27,* 440–452.

Kern, L., Mantegna, M. E., Vorndran, C. M., Bailin, D., & Hilt, A. (2001). Choice of task sequence to reduce problem behaviors. *Journal of Positive Interventions, 3,* 3–10.

Kern, L., & Manz, P. (2004). A look at current validity issues of school-wide behavior support. *Behavioral Disorders, 30,* 47–59.

Kern, L., Vorndran, C. M., Hild, A., Ringdahl, J. E., Adehan, B., & Dunlap, G. (1998). Choice as an intervention to improve behavior: A review of the literature. *Journal of Behavioral Education, 8,* 151–169.

Kerr, M. M., & Nelson, C. M. (2010). *Strategies for addressing behavior problems in the classroom* (6th ed.). Upper Saddle River, NJ: Pearson Merrill Prentice Hall.

Kerr, M. M., & Zigmond, N. (1986). What do high school teachers want? A study of expectations and standards. *Education and Treatment of Children, 9,* 239–249.

Kidd, T. A., & Saudargas, R. A. (1988). Positive and negative consequences in contingency contracts: Their relative effectiveness on arithmetic performance. *Education and Treatment of Children, 11,* 118–126.

Kim, A.-H., Vaughn, S., Wanzek, J., & Wei, S. (2004). Graphic organizers and their effects on the reading comprehension of students with LD: A synthesis of research. *Journal of Learning Disabilities, 37,* 105–118.

Kinder, D., & Carnine, D. (1991). Direct instruction: What it is and what it is becoming. *Journal of Behavioral Education, 1,* 193–213.

Kirschenbaum, D. S., & Flanery, R. C. (1984). Toward a psychology of behavioral contracting. *Clinical Psychology Review, 4,* 597–618.

Klem, A. M., & Connell, J. P. (2004). Relationships matter: Linking teacher support to student engagement and achievement. *Journal of School Health, 74,* 262–273.

Knapczyk, D. (2004). *Teaching self-discipline: A self-monitoring program.* Verona, WI: Attainment.

Kounin, J. (1977). *Discipline and group management in classrooms.* New York: Holt, Rinehart, & Winston.

Kounin, J. S., Friesen, W. V., & Norton, A. E. (1966). Managing emotionally disturbed children in regular classrooms. *Journal of Educational Psychology, 57,* 1–13.

Kounin, J. S., & Obradovic, S. (1968). Managing emotionally disturbed children in regular classrooms: A replication and extension. *Journal of Special Education, 2,* 129–135.

Landrum, T., & Kauffman, J. (2006). Behavioral approaches to classroom management. In C. M. Evertson & C. S. Weinstein (Eds.), *Handbook of classroom management: Research, practice, and contemporary issues* (pp. 47–71). Mahwah, NJ: Erlbaum.

Landrum, T., J., Tankersley, M., & Kauffman, J. M. (2003). What is special about special education for students with emotional or behavioral disorders? *Journal of Special Education, 37,* 148–156.

Lane, K. (2007). Identifying and supporting students at risk for emotional and behavioral disorders within multi-level models: Data-driven approaches to conducting secondary interventions with an academic emphasis. *Education and Treatment of Children, 30*(4), 135–164.

Lane, K., Wehby, J., Menzies, H., Doukas, G., Munton, S., & Gregg, R. (2003). Social skills instruction for students at risk for antisocial behavior: The effects of small-group instruction. *Behavioral Disorders, 28,* 229–248.

Lane, K. L., & Beebe-Frankenberger, M. E. (2004). *School-based interventions: The tools you need to succeed.* Boston: Allyn & Bacon.

Lane, K. L., Bruhn, A. L., Crnobori, M. L., & Sewell, A. L. (2009). Designing functional assessment-based interventions using a systematic approach: A promising practice for supporting challenging behavior. In T. E. Scruggs & M. A. Mastropieri (Eds.), *Policy and practice: Advances in learning and behavioral disabilities* (Vol. 22, (pp. 341–370). Bingley, UK: Emerald.

Lane, K. L., Eisner, S. L., Kretzer, J. M., Bruhn, A. L., Crnobori, M. E., Funke, L. M., et al. (2009). Outcomes of functional assessment-based interventions for students with and at risk for emotional and behavioral disorders in a job-share setting. *Education and Treatment of Children, 32,* 573–604.

Lane, K. L., Harris, K., Graham, S., Weisenbach, J., Brindle, M., & Morphy, P. (2008). The effects of self-regulated strategy development on the writing performance of second-grade students with behavioral and writing difficulties. *Journal of Special Education, 41*, 234–253.

Lane, K. L., Kalberg, J. R., Bruhn, A. L., Mahoney, M. E., & Driscoll, S. A. (2008). Primary prevention programs at the elementary level: Issues of treatment integrity, systematic screening, and reinforcement. *Education and Treatment of Children, 31*, 465–494.

Lane, K. L., Kalberg, J. R., & Menzies, H. M. (2009). *Developing schoolwide programs to prevent and manage problem behaviors: A step-by-step approach.* New York: Guilford Press.

Lane, K. L., Kalberg, J. R., & Shepcaro, J. C. (2009). An examination of the evidence base for function-based interventions for students with emotional and/or behavioral disorders attending middle and high schools. *Exceptional Children, 75*, 321–341.

Lane, K. L., Menzies, H. M., Oakes, W. P., & Kalberg, J. R. (2010). *Systematic screenings of behavior to support instruction: From preschool to high school.* Manuscript in preparation.

Lane, K. L., Pierson, M., & Givner, C. C. (2003). Teacher expectations of student behavior: Which skills do elementary and secondary teachers deem necessary for success in the classroom? *Education and Treatment of Children, 26*, 413–430.

Lane, K. L., Pierson, M., Stang, K., & Carter, E. W. (2010). Teacher expectations of students' classroom behavior: Do expectations vary as a function of school risk? *Remedial and Special Education, 31*, 163–174.

Lane, K. L., Robertson, E. J., & Graham-Bailey, M. A. L. (2006). An examination of schoolwide interventions with primary level efforts conducted in secondary schools: Methodological considerations. In T. E. Scruggs & M. A. Mastropieri (Eds.), *Applications of research methodology: Advances in learning and behavioral disabilities* (Vol. 19, pp. 157–199). Oxford, UK: Elsevier.

Lane, K. L., Rogers, L. A., Parks, R. J., Weisenbach, J. L., Mau, A. C., Merwin, M. T., et al. (2007). Function-based interventions for students nonresponsive to primary and secondary prevention efforts: Illustrations at the elementary and middle school levels. *Journal of Emotional and Behavioral Disorders, 15*, 169–183.

Lane, K. L., Smither, R., Huseman, R., Guffey, J., & Fox, J. (2007). A function-based intervention to decrease disruptive behavior and increase academic engagement. *Journal of Early and Intensive Behavioral Intervention*, 3(4)–4(1), 348–364.

Lane, K. L., & Wehby, J. (2002). Addressing antisocial behavior in the schools: A call for action. *Academic Exchange Quarterly, 6*, 4–9.

Lane, K. L., Wehby, J. H., & Cooley, C. (2006). Teacher expectations of student's classroom behavior across the grade span: Which social skills are necessary for success? *Exceptional Children, 72*, 153–167.

Lane, K. L., Weisenbach, J. L., Little, M. A., Phillips, A., & Wehby, J. (2006). Illustrations of function-based interventions implemented by general education teachers: Building capacity at the school site. *Education and Treatment of Children, 29*, 549–671.

Lane, K. L., Weisenbach, J. L., Phillips, A., & Wehby, J. (2007). Designing, implementing, and evaluating function-based interventions using a systematic, feasible approach. *Behavioral Disorders, 32*, 122–139.

Lassman, K. A., Jolivette, K., & Wehby, J. H. (1999). "My teacher said I did good work today!": Using collaborative behavioral contracting. *Teaching Exceptional Children, 31*, 12–18.

Lepper, M. (1988). Motivational considerations in the study of instruction. *Cognition and Instruction, 5,* 289–309.

Levendoski, L. S., & Cartledge, G. (2000). Self-monitoring for elementary school children with serious emotional disturbances: Classroom applications for increased academic responding. *Behavioral Disorders, 25,* 211–224.

Lewis, T. J., & Sugai, G. (1999). Effective behavior support: A systems approach to proactive schoolwide management. *Focus on Exceptional Children, 31,* 1–24.

Liaupsin, C. J., Umbreit, J., Ferro, J. B., Urso, A., & Upreti, G. (2006). Improving academic engagement through systematic, function-based intervention. *Education and Treatment of Children, 29,* 573–591.

Lindamood, P. C., & Lindamood, P. D. (1998). *Lindamood Phoneme Sequencing Program for Reading, Spelling, and Speech (LiPS).* Austin, TX: Lindamood-Bell Learning Processes.

Little, M. A., Lane, K. L., Harris, K., Graham, S., Brindle, M., & Sandmel, K. (2010). Self-regulated strategies development for persuasive writing in tandem with schoolwide positive behavioral support: Effects for second-grade students with behavioral and writing difficulties. *Behavior Disorders.*

Lloyd, J. W., Bateman, D. F., Landrum, T. J., & Hallahan, D. P. (1989). Self-recording of attention versus productivity. *Journal of Applied Behavior Analysis, 22,* 315–323.

Lockavitch, J. F. (2000). *Failure free reading.* Concord, NC: Failure Free Reading.

MacArthur, C., Schwartz, S., Graham, S., Molloy, D., & Harris, K. R. (1996). Integration of strategy instruction into a whole-language classroom: A case study. *Learning Disabilities Research and Practice, 11,* 168–176.

Mace, F. C., Belfiore, P. J., & Hutchinson, J. M. (2001). Operant theory and research on self-regulation. In B. J. Zimmerman & D. H. Schunk (Eds.), *Self-regulated learning and academic achievement: Theoretical perspectives* (2nd ed., pp. 39–65). Mahwah, NJ: Erlbaum.

Maggin, D. M. (2008). A *model of teacher–student interactions in classrooms serving students with behavioral problems.* Unpublished manuscript, Center for Behavioral Education and Research, University of Connecticut, Storrs.

Malott, R. W., & Garcia, M. E. (1987). A goal-directed model approach for the design of human performance systems. *Journal of Organizational Behavior Management, 9,* 125–159.

Martin, A. J., Linfoot, K., & Stephenson, J. (1999). How teachers respond to concerns about misbehavior in their classroom. *Psychology in the Schools, 36,* 347–358.

Marzano, R. J., Marzano, J. S., & Pickering, D. J. (2003). *Classroom management that works: Research-based strategies for every teacher.* Alexandria, VA.: Association for Supervision and Curriculum Development.

Matson, J., & Boisjoli, J. (2009). The token economy for children with intellectual disability and/or autism: A review. *Research in Developmental Disabilities: A Multidisciplinary Journal, 30,* 240–248.

Mattison, R. E., Hooper, S. R., & Glassberg, L. A. (2002). Three-year course of learning disorders in special education students classified as behavioral disorder. *Journal of the American Academy of Child and Adolescent Psychiatry, 41,* 1454–1461.

Maxwell, L. E. (1989). Multiple effects of home and daycare crowding. *Environment and Behavior, 28,* 494–511.

May, S., Ard, W., III, Todd, A. W., Horner, R. H., Glasgow, A., Sugai, G., et al. (2000). *School-*

Wide Information System (SWIS). Eugen: University of Oregon, Educational and Community Supports.

McDougall, D., & Brady, M. P. (1995). Using audio-cued self-monitoring for students severe behavior disorders. *Journal of Educational Research, 88*, 309–317.

McIntosh, K., Herman, K., & Sanford, A. (2004). Teaching transitions: Techniques for promoting success between lessons. *Teaching Exceptional Children, 37*, 32–38.

McLaughlin, T. F. (1984). A comparison of self-recording and self-recording plus consequences for on-task and assignment completion. *Contemporary Educational Psychology, 9*, 185–192.

McLaughlin, T. F., Burgess, N., & Sackville-West, L. (1981). Effects of self-recording and self-recording + matching on academic performance. *Child Behavior Therapy, 3*, 17–27.

McLaughlin, T. F., & Truhlicka, M. (1983). Effects on academic performance of self-recording and self-recording and matching with behaviorally disordered students: A replication. *Behavioral Engineering, 8*, 69–74.

McLaughlin, T. F., & Williams, R. L. (1988). The token economy in the classroom. In J. C. Witt, S. N. Elliott, & F. M. Gresham (Eds.), *Handbook of behavior therapy in education* (pp. 469–487). New York: Plenum.

McMahon, S. D., & Washburn, J. J. (2003). Violence prevention: An evaluation of program effects with urban African-American students. *Journal of Primary Prevention, 24*, 43–62.

Meichenbaum, D. H., & Goodman, J. (1971). Training impulsive children to talk to themselves: A means of developing self-control. *Journal of Abnormal Psychology, 77*, 115–126.

Menzies, H., Lane, K. L., & Lee, J. M. (2009). Self-monitoring strategies for use in the classroom: A promising practice to support productive behavior for students with emotional or behavioral disorders. *Beyond Behavior, 18*, 27–35.

Meyer, A., & Farrell, A. (1998). Social skills training to promote resilience in urban sixth grade students: One product of an action research strategy to prevent youth violence in high-risk environments. *Education and Treatment of Children, 21*, 461–488.

Miller, D. L., & Kelley, M. L. (1994). The use of goal setting and contingency contracting for improving children's homework performance. *Journal of Applied Behavior Analysis, 27*, 73–84.

Miller, M., Lane, K., & Wehby, J. (2005). Social skills instruction for students with high-incidence disabilities: A school-based intervention to address acquisition deficits. *Preventing School Failure, 49*, 27–39.

Miller, M., Miller, S. R., Wheeler, J., & Selinger, J. (1989). Can a single-classroom treatment approach change academic performance and behavioral characteristics in severely behaviorally disordered adolescents? An experimental inquiry. *Behavioral Disorders, 14*, 215–225.

Miller, S. P. (2008). *Validated practices for teaching students with diverse needs and abilities*. Boston: Allyn & Bacon.

Miltenberger, R. G. (2007). *Behavior modification: Principles and procedures* (4th ed.). Belmont, CA: Wadsworth Thomson Learning.

Molina, J., & Molina, M. (1997). *PeaceBuilders*. Long Beach, CA: Author.

Montague, M., & Dietz, S. (2009). Evaluating the evidence base for cognitive strategy instruction and mathematical problem solving. *Exceptional Children, 75*, 285–302.

Mooney, P., Ryan, J. B., Uhing, B. M., Reid, R., & Epstein, M. H. (2005). A review of self-management interventions targeting academic outcomes for students with emotional and behavioral disorders. *Journal of Behavioral Education, 14,* 203–221.

Morrow, L. M., Reutzel, D. R., & Casey, H. (2006). Organization and management of language arts teaching: Classroom environments, grouping practices, and exemplary instruction. In C. M. Evertson & C. S. Weinstein (Eds.), *Handbook of classroom management: Research, practice, and contemporary issues* (pp. 559–582). Mahwah, NJ: Erlbaum.

Mruzek, D. W., Cohen, C., & Smith, T. (2007). Contingency contracting with students with autism spectrum disorders in a public school setting. *Journal of Developmental and Physical Disabilities, 19,* 103–114.

Murphy, J. J. (1987). Use of behavioral contracting to increase school attendance. *Techniques, 3*(4), 306–311.

Murphy, J. J. (1988). Contingency contracting in schools: A review. *Education and Treatment of Children, 11,* 257–269.

National Council of Teachers of English. (1996). *Standards for the English language arts.* Newark, DE: International Reading Association.

National Council of Teachers of Mathematics. (2000). *Principles and standards for school mathematics.* Reston, VA: Author.

Nelson, J. R., Benner, G. J., Lane, K., & Smith, B. W. (2004). An investigation of the academic achievement of K–12 students with emotional and behavioral disorders in public school settings. *Exceptional Children, 71,* 59–73.

Nelson, J. R., Benner, G. J., & Mooney, P. (2008). *Instructional practices for students with behavioral disorders: Strategies for reading, writing, and math.* New York: Guilford Press.

Nelson, J. R., Smith, D. J., Young, R. K., & Dodd, J. M. (1991). A review of self-management outcome research conducted with students who exhibit behavioral disorders. *Behavioral Disorders, 16,* 169–179.

Newman, F. (1991). Student engagement in academic work: Expanding the perspective on secondary school effectiveness. In J. R. Bliss & W. A. Firestone (Eds.), *Rethinking effective schools: Research and practice* (pp. 58–76). Englewood Cliffs, NJ: Prentice-Hall.

Newstrom, J., McLaughlin, T. F., & Sweeney, W. J. (1999). The effects of contingency contracting to improve the mechanics of written language with a middle school student with behavior disorders. *Child and Family Behavior Therapy, 21*(1), 39–48.

Olweus, D. (1991). Bully/victim problems among schoolchildren: Basic facts and effects of a school-based intervention program. In D. J. Pepler & K. H. Rubin (Eds.), *The development and treatment of childhood aggression* (pp. 411–448). Hillsdale, NJ: Erlbaum.

O'Neill, R. E., Horner, R. H., Albin, R. W., Sprague, J. R., Storey, K., & Newton, J. S. (1997). *Functional assessment and program development for problem behavior: A practical handbook.* Pacific Grove, CA: Brooks/Cole

Ormrod, J. A. (2000). *Educational psychology: Developing learners* (3rd ed.) Upper Saddle River, NJ: Merrill/Prentice Hall.

Osborne, S. S., Kosiewicz, M. M., Crumley, E. B., & Lee, C. (1987). Distractible students use self-monitoring. *Teaching Exceptional Children, 19,* 66–69.

Paine, S. C., Radicchi, J. Rosellini, L. C., Deutchman, L., & Darch, C. B. (1983). *Structuring your classroom for academic success.* Champaign, IL: Research Press.

Parish, T., & Mahoney, S. (2006). Classrooms: How to turn them from battlegrounds to connecting places. *Education, 126,* 437–440.

Partin, T. (2009). *The value of teacher attention as a reinforcer for problem behavior: Implications for future research*. Unpublished manuscript.

Pelco, L. E., & Reed-Victor, E. (2007). Self-regulation and learning-related social skills: Intervention ideas for elementary school students. *Preventing School Failure, 51*, 36–42.

Pemberton, J., & Borrego, J. (2007). Increasing acceptance of behavioral child management techniques: What do parents say? *Child and Family Behavior Therapy, 29*, 27–45.

Pentz, M. A., Mihalic, S. F., & Grotpeter, J. K. (1998). *Blueprints for violence prevention: Book 1. The Midwestern Prevention Project*. Boulder: University of Colorado, Institute of Behavioral Science, Center for the Study and Prevention of Violence.

Pianta, R. C. (1994). Patterns of relationships between children and kindergarten teachers. *Journal of School Psychology, 32*, 15–31.

Pianta, R. C. (2006). Classroom management and relationships between children and teachers: Implications for research and practice. (pp. 685–710). In C. M. Evertson & C. S. Weinstein (Eds.), *Handbook of classroom management: Research, practice, and contemporary issues* (pp. 685–710). Mahwah, NJ: Erlbaum.

Pianta, R. C., La Paro, K. M., & Hamre, B. K. (2008). *Classroom Assessment Scoring System: Manual K–3*. Baltimore: Brookes.

Pintrich, P. R., & Schunk, D. H. (2002). *Motivation in education: Theory, research, and applications* (2nd ed.). Upper Saddle River, NJ: Pearson.

Pressley, M., Johnson, C. J., Symons, S., McGoldrick, J. A., & Kurita, J. A. (1989). Strategies that improve children's memory and comprehension of text. *Elementary School Journal, 90*, 3–32.

Pressley, M., & McCormick, C. B. (1995). *Advanced educational psychology: For educators, researchers, and policymakers*. New York: Harper Collins College.

Quinn, M. M., Gable, R. A., Fox, J., Rutherford, R. B., Jr., Van Acker, R., & Conroy, M. (2001). Putting quality functional assessment into practice in schools: A research agenda on behalf of E/BD students. *Education and Treatment of Children, 24*, 261–275.

Quinn, M. M., Kavale, K., Mathur, S., Rutherford, R., & Forness, S. (1999). A meta-analysis of social skill interventions for students with emotional or behavioral disorders. *Journal of Emotional and Behavioral Disorders, 7*, 54–64.

Ramirez, M., III, & Castaneda, A. (1974). *Cultural democracy, biocognitive development and education*. New York: Academic.

Redmon, W. K., & Farris, H. E. (1985). Improving the academic productivity of high school students through behavioral contracting: A model project. *Journal of Instructional Psychology, 12*, 46–58.

Reid, J. B., & Patterson, G. R. (1991). Early prevention and intervention with conduct problems: A social interactional model for the integration of research and practice. In G. Stoner, M. R. Shinn, & H. M. Walker (Eds.), *Interventions for achievement and behavior problems* (pp. 715–739). Bethesda, MD: National Association of Social Psychologists.

Reid, R., Gonzalez, J. E., Nordness, A. T., Trout, A., & Epstein, M. H. (2004). A meta-analysis of the academic status of students with emotional/behavioral disturbance. *Journal of Special Education, 38*, 130–143.

Reinke, W., Lewis-Palmer, T., & Merrell, K. (2008). The classroom check-up: A classwide teacher consultation model for increasing praise and decreasing disruptive behavior. *School Psychology Review, 37*, 315–332.

Reis, S., & Renzulli, J. (1992). Using curriculum compacting to challenge the above average. *Educational Leadership, 50*, 51–57.

Renshaw, T. L., Christensen, L., Marchant, M., & Anderson, T. (2008). Training elementary school general educators to implement function-based support. *Education and Treatment of Children, 31*, 495–521.

Rock, M. L. (2005). Use of strategic self-monitoring to enhance academic engagement, productivity, and accuracy of students with and without exceptionalities. *Journal of Positive Behavior Interventions, 7*, 3–17.

Rosenshine, B., & Stevens, R. (1986). Teaching functions. In M. C. Wittrock (Ed.), *Handbook of research on reading* (3rd ed., pp. 376–391). New York: Macmillan.

Rowe, M. B. (1986). Wait time: Slowing down may be a way of speeding up! *Journal of Teacher Education, 37*, 43–50.

Ruth, W. J. (1996). Goal setting and behavior contracting for students with emotional and behavioral difficulties: Analysis of daily, weekly, and total goal attainment. *Psychology in the Schools, 33*, 153–158.

Ryan, A. L., Halsey, H. N., & Matthews, W. J. (2003). Using functional assessment to promote desirable student behavior in schools. *Teaching Exceptional Children, 35*, 8–15.

Sandmel, K., Brindle, M., Harris, K., Lane, K., Graham, S., Nackel, J., et al. (2009). Making it work: Differentiating tier two self-regulated strategies development in writing in tandem with schoolwide positive behavioral support. *Teaching on Exceptional Children, 42*, 22–33.

Santangelo, T., Harris, K. R., & Graham, S. (2008). Using self-regulated strategy development to support students who have "Trubol Giting Thangs Into Werds." *Remedial and Special Education, 29*, 78–89.

Sasso, G. M., Conroy, M. A., Stichter, J. P., & Fox, J. J. (2001). Slowing down the bandwagon: The misapplication of functional assessment for students with emotional or behavioral disorders. *Behavioral Disorders, 26*, 282–296.

Sasso, G. M., Reimers, T. M., Cooper, L. J., & Wacker, D. P. (1992). Use of descriptive and experimental analyses to identify the functional properties of aberrant behavior in school settings. *Journal of Applied Behavior Analysis, 25*, 809–821.

Schumm, J. S., & Vaughn, S. (1995). General education teacher planning: What can students with learning disabilities expect? *Exceptional Children, 61*, 335–353.

Schumm, J. S., Vaughn, S., & Leavell, A. G. (1994). Planning pyramid: A framework for planning for diverse student needs during content area instruction. *Reading Teacher, 47*, 608–615.

Schunk, D. (1985). Self-efficacy and classroom learning. *Psychology in the Schools, 22*, 208–223.

Schunk, D. H. (2001). *Self-regulation through goal setting*. Greensboro, NC: ERIC Clearinghouse on Counseling and Student Services.

Seabaugh, G. O., & Schumaker, J. B. (1994). The effects of self-regulation training on the academic productivity of secondary students with learning problems. *Journal of Behavioral Education, 4*, 109–133.

Seligman, M. (1975). *Helplessness: On depression, development, and death*. San Francisco, CA: Freeman.

Sharan, S., Kussell, P., Hertz-Lazarowitz, R., Bejarano, Y., Ravivi, S., & Sharan, Y. (1984).

Cooperative learning in the classroom; Research in desegregated schools. Hillsdale, NJ: Erlbaum.

Shogren, A., Fagella-Luby, M., Bae, S. J., & Wehmeyer, M. L. (2004). The effect of choice-making as an intervention for problem behavior: A meta-analysis. *Journal of Positive Behavior Interventions, 6,* 228–237.

Shores, R. E., Jack, S. L., Gunter, P. L., Ellis, D. N., DeBriere, T. J., & Wehby, J. H. (1993). Classroom interactions of children with behavior disorders. *Journal of Emotional and Behavioral Disorders, 1,* 27–39.

Siegle, D., & McCoach, D. (2005). Making a difference: Motivating gifted students who are not achieving. *Teaching Exceptional Children, 38,* 22–27.

Silver, R. B., Measelle, J. R., Armstrong, J. M., & Essex, M. J. (2005). Trajectories of classroom externalizing behavior: Contributions of child characteristics, family characteristics, and the teacher–child relationship during the school transition. *Journal of School Psychology, 43,* 39–60.

Simek, T., O'Brien, P., & Figlerski, L. (1994). Contracting and chaining to improve the performance of a college golf team. *Perceptual and Motor Skills, 78,* 1099–1105.

Simmons, D., & Kame'enui, E. (1996). A focus on curriculum design: When children fail. *Focus on Exceptional Children, 28,* 1–16.

Simonsen, B., Fairbanks, S., Briesch, A., Myers, D., & Sugai, G. (2008). Evidence-based practices in classroom management: Considerations for research to practice. *Education and Treatment of Children, 31,* 351–380.

Skinner, B. F. (1953). *Science and human behavior.* New York: Macmillan.

Skinner, B. F. (1969). *Contingencies of reinforcement: A theoretical analysis.* Englewood Cliffs, NJ: Prentice Hall.

Skinner, E., & Belmont, M. (1993). Motivation in the classroom: Reciprocal effects of teacher behavior and student engagement. *Journal of Educational Psychology, 85,* 571. Retrieved from *search.ebscohost.com.mimas.calstatela.edu.*

Slavin, R. E. (1986). *Using student team learning* (3rd ed.). Baltimore: Johns Hopkins University, Center for Research on Elementary and Middle Schools.

Slavin, R. E. (1995). *Cooperative learning* (2nd ed.). Boston: Allyn & Bacon.

Slavin, R. E., & Karweit, N. L. (1985). Effects of whole-class, ability-grouped, and individualized instruction on mathematics achievement. *American Educational Research Journal, 22,* 351–367.

Smith, D. J., Nelson, J. R., Young, K. R., & West, R. P. (1992). The effect of a self-management procedure on the classroom and academic behavior of students with mild handicaps. *School Psychology Review, 21,* 59–72.

Smith, R., & Lambert, M. (2008). Assuming the best. *Educational Leadership, 66*(1), 16–20.

Smith, S. E. (1994). Parent-initiated contracts: An intervention for school-related behaviors. *Elementary School Guidance and Counseling, 28,* 182–187.

Stahr, B., Cushing, D., Lane, K. L., & Fox, J. (2006). Efficacy of a function-based intervention to decrease off-task behavior exhibited by a student with attention-deficit/hyperactivity disorder. *Journal of Positive Behavior Interventions, 8,* 201–211.

Stevens, R. J., Madden, N. A., Slavin, R. E., & Farnish, A. M. (1987). Cooperative integrated reading and composition: Two field experiments. *Reading Research Quarterly, 22,* 433–454.

Stichter, J., Conroy, M., & Kauffman, J. (2008). *An introduction to students with high-incidence disabilities*. Upper Saddle River, NJ: Pearson Merrill Prentice Hall.

Stipek, D. J. (1993). *Motivation to learn: From theory to practice* (2nd ed.). Boston: Allyn & Bacon.

Sugai, G., Horner, R., & Gresham, S. (2002). Behaviorally effective school environments. In M. R. Shinn, H. M. Walker, & G. Stoner (Eds.), *Interventions for academic and behavior problems: II. Preventive and remedial approaches*. Washington, DC: National Association of School Psychologists.

Sugai, G., & Horner, R. H. (2002). Introduction to the special series on positive behavior support in schools. *Journal of Emotional and Behavioral Disorders, 10*, 130.

Sugai, G., & Horner, R. H. (2006). A promising approach for expanding and sustaining school-wide positive behavior support. *School Psychology Review, 35*, 245–260.

Sulzer-Azaroff, B., & Mayer, G. R. (1994). *Achieving educational excellence: Behavior analysis for achieving classroom and schoolwide behavior change*. San Marcos, CA: Western Image.

Sun, W., Skara, S., Sun, P., Dent, C. W., & Sussman, S. (2006). Project Towards No Drug Abuse: Long-term substance use outcomes evaluation. *Preventive Medicine, 42*, 188–192.

Sussman, S., Rohrbach, L., & Mihalic, S. (2004). *Blueprints for Violence Prevention: Book 12. Project Towards No Drug Abuse*. Boulder: University of Colorado, Institute of Behavioral Science, Center for the Study and Prevention of Violence.

Sutherland, K., Wehby, J., & Copeland, S. (2000). Effect on varying rates of behavior-specific praise on the on-task behavior of students with EBD. *Journal of Emotional and Behavioral Disorders, 8*, 2–8.

Sutherland, K. S., Alder, N., & Gunter, P. L. (2003). The effect of varying rates of opportunities to respond on academic requests to the classroom behavior of students with EBD. *Journal of Emotional and Behavioral Disorders, 11*, 239–248.

Sutherland, K. S., & Wehby, J. H. (2001). Exploring the relationship between increased opportunities to respond to academic requests and the academic and behavioral outcomes of students with EBD. *Remedial and Special Education, 22*, 113–122.

Sutherland, K. S., Wehby, J. H., & Yoder, P. J. (2002). Examination of the relationship between teacher praise and opportunities for students with EBD to respond to academic requests. *Journal of Emotional and Behavioral Disorders, 10*, 5–13.

Sutherland, K. S., & Wright, S. A. (in press). Students with disabilities and academic engagement: Classroom-based interventions.

Thomas, J. R., Lee, A. M., McGee, L., & Silverman, S. (1987). Effects of individual and group contingencies on disruptive playground behavior. *Journal of Research and Development in Education, 20*, 66–76.

Tomlinson, C. A. (2005). *How to differentiate instruction in mixed-ability classrooms*. Upper Saddle River, NJ: Pearson Education.

Tomlinson, C. A., & McTighe, J. (2005). *Integrating differentiated instruction: Understanding by design*. Alexandria, VA: Association for Supervision and Curriculum Development.

Tracy, B., Reid, R., & Graham, S. (2009). Teaching young students strategies for planning and drafting stories: The impact of self-regulated strategy development. *Journal of Educational Research, 102*, 323–331.

Trice, A. D. (1990). Adolescents' locus of control and compliance with contingency contracting and counseling interventions. *Psychological Reports, 67*, 233–234.

Turton, A. M., Umbreit, J., Liaupsin, C. J., & Bartley, J. (2007). Function-based intervention for an adolescent with emotional and behavioral disorders in Bermuda: Moving across culture. *Behavioral Disorders, 33*, 23–32.

Uberti, H., Scruggs, T., & Mastropieri, M. (2003). Keywords make the difference! Mnemonic instruction in inclusive classrooms. *Teaching Exceptional Children, 35*, 56–61.

Umbreit, J., Ferro, J. B., Liaupsin, C. J., & Lane, K. L. (2007). *Functional behavioral assessment and function-based intervention: An effective, practical approach.* Upper Saddle River, NJ: Pearson Education.

Umbreit, J., Lane, K. L., & Dejud, C. (2004). Improving classroom behavior by modifying task difficulty: The effects of increasing the difficulty of too-easy tasks. *Journal of Positive Behavior Interventions, 6*, 13–20.

Urdan, T., & Schoenfelder, E. (2006). Classroom effects on student motivation: Goal structures, social relationships, and competence beliefs. *Journal of School Psychology, 44*, 331–349.

Valenzuela, A. (1999). *Subtractive schooling: U. S.–Mexican youth and the politics of caring.* Albany: State University of New York Press.

Vanderbilt, A. (2005). Designed for teachers: How to implement self-monitoring in the classroom. *Beyond Behavior, 15*, 21–24.

Vazsonyi, A. T., Bellison, L. M., & Flannery, D. J. (2004). Evaluation of a school-based, universal violence prevention program: Low-, medium-, and high-risk children. *Youth Violence and Juvenile Justice, 2*, 185–206.

Vygotsky, L. S. (1978). *Mind in society: The development of higher psychological processes.* Cambridge, MA: Harvard University Press.

Wagner, M., & Davis, M. (2006). How are we preparing students with emotional disturbances for the transition to young adulthood? Findings from the National Longitudinal Transition Study—2. *Journal of Emotional and Behavioral Disorders, 14*, 86–98.

Walker, H., Irvin, L., Noell, J., & Singer, G. (1992). A construct score approach to the assessment of social competence: Rationale, technological considerations, and anticipated outcomes. *Behavior Modification, 16*, 448–474.

Walker, H., Ramsey, E., & Gresham, F. (2004). *Antisocial behavior in school: Evidence-based practices.* Belmont, CA: Thomson/Wadsworth.

Walker, H. M., Colvin, G., & Ramsey, E. (1994). *Antisocial behavior in school: Strategies and best practices.* Pacific Grove, CA: Brooks/Cole.

Walker, H. M., Horner, R. H., Sugai, G., Bullis, M., Sprague, J. R., Bricker, D., et al. (1996). Integrated approaches to preventing antisocial behavior patterns among school-age children and youth. *Journal of Emotional and Behavioral Disorders, 4*, 193–256.

Walker, H. M., & Severson, H. (1992). *Systematic Screening for Behavior Disorders: User's guide and technical manual.* Longmont, CO: Sopris West.

Walker, H. M., & Severson, H. H. (2002). Developmental prevention of at-risk outcomes for vulnerable antisocial children and youth. In K. L. Lane, F. M. Gresham, & T. E. O'Shaughnessy (Eds.), *Interventions for children with or at risk for emotional and behavioral disorders* (pp. 177–194). Boston: Allyn & Bacon.

Walker, H. M., Severson, H. H., & Feil, E. (1995). *The Early Screening Project: A proven child-find process.* Longmont, CO: Sopris West.

Wayman, M., Wallace, T., Wiley, H., Ticha, R., & Espin, C. (2007). Literature synthesis on curriculum-based measurement in reading. *Journal of Special Education, 41*, 85–120.

Wehmeyer, M. L., & Field, S. L. (2007). *Self-determination: Instructional and assessment strategies*. Thousand Oaks, CA: Corwin Press.

Weiner, B. (1985). An attributional theory of achievement motivation and emotion. *Psychological Review, 92*, 548–573.

Weinstein, C., Curran, M., & Tomlinson-Clarke, S. (2003). Culturally responsive classroom management: Awareness into action. *Theory into Practice, 42*, 269–279.

Werts, M., Wolery, M., Holcombe, A., & Gast, D. (1995). Instructive feedback: Review of parameters and effects. *Journal of Behavioral Education, 5*, 55–75.

White, R. (1959). Motivation reconsidered: The concept of competence. *Psychological Review, 66*, 297–333.

White-Blackburn, G., Semb, S., & Semb, G. (1977). The effects of a good-behavior contract on the classroom behaviors of sixth-grade students. *Journal of Applied Behavior Analysis, 10*, 312.

Wilkinson, L. A. (2003). Using behavioral consultation to reduce challenging behavior in the classroom. *Preventing School Failure, 47*, 100–105.

Williams, R. L., Long, J. D., & Yoakley, R. W. (1972). The utility of behavior contracts and behavior proclamations with advantaged senior high school students. *Journal of School Psychology, 10*, 329–338.

Wilson, B. A. (2000). *Wilson reading system*. Oxford, MA: Wilson Language Training.

Wolf, M. M. (1978). Social validity: The case for subjective measurement: How applied behavior analysis is finding its heart. *Journal of Applied Behavior Analysis, 11*, 203–214.

Wong, H., & Wong, R. (1998). *The first days of school*. Mountain View, CA: Harry Wong.

Wood, B. K., Umbreit, J., Liaupsin, C. J., & Gresham, F. M. (2007). A treatment integrity analysis of function-based intervention. *Education and Treatment of Children, 30*, 105–120.

Zimmer, P., Whitmore, H., & Eller, B. F. (1981). A comparison of instructional techniques to improve academic grades of low-achieving rural Appalachian elementary students. *Journal of Instructional Psychology, 8*, 146–153.

Index

C

D

E

F

N

O

P

Q

R

S

T

U

W

Z